THE GROWTH AND DECADENCE
OF CONSTITUTIONAL GOVERNMENT

THE GROWTH AND DECADENCE OF
CONSTITUTIONAL GOVERNMENT

BY

J. ALLEN SMITH, LL.B., Ph.D.

LATE PROFESSOR OF POLITICAL SCIENCE
UNIVERSITY OF WASHINGTON

AUTHOR OF "THE SPIRIT OF AMERICAN GOVERNMENT"
"THE MULTIPLE MONEY STANDARD"

INTRODUCTION BY THE LATE
PROFESSOR VERNON LOUIS PARRINGTON

NEW YORK
HENRY HOLT AND COMPANY

ACKNOWLEDGMENT

In preparing the manuscript of this book for publication I have had the invaluable help and advice of the late Professor Vernon Louis Parrington of the University of Washington. I desire to acknowledge my great indebtedness to him and to Professor Edward McMahon of the University of Washington and to Professor Peter Odegard of Williams College.

ELFREDA ALLEN SMITH

CONTENTS

INTRODUCTION

The late Professor J. Allen Smith, the results of whose last studies in American government appear in the present volume, was one of the intellectual leaders of the Progressive movement that so creatively influenced the political thought of the past generation. His earlier writings were an influential contribution to the great uprising of liberalism that between the years 1903 and 1917 sought to adjust the cumbersome machinery of government to the changing needs of a democratic people. His political philosophy, with its strong Jeffersonian sympathies, was shaped by the democratic awakening that issued from the crude exploitations and sordid machine politics of the Gilded Age; and he was fortunate in writing at a time when the liberal thought of America was becoming conscious of the gross contradictions between our traditional ideals and a Tory political practice. His notable study, *The Spirit of American Government,* published at a moment when liberal thought was beginning to clarify, was singularly opportune. It made wide appeal and it did more perhaps than any other single study to explain the constitutional sources of the democratic shortcomings and suggest the logical remedies.

The significance of that work is to be found in the realism of its method and the historical validity of its findings. At the time of its appearance the rising liberalism was in a realistic mood. The blowsy romanticisms that earlier had befuddled the American mind were pretty much dissipated.

The argument of events had long been sobering and chasten-
ing the slack frontier faith in our manifest destiny. The
long agrarian revolt that culminated in the campaign of 1896,
and the Muckraking movement that got under way in 1903,
had destroyed the comfortable illusion that democracy in
America was a going concern that needed no oversight, and
groups of volunteer political thinkers in every part of the
country were considering ways and means of returning the
great experiment to the path it had wandered from. It was
a time of wide and serious interest in the theory and practice
of politics. Historical scholarship — particularly the school
of Turner with its discovery of the influence of the frontier
on American psychology and institutions — was beginning
to resurvey the American scene in a spirit of critical inquiry
that was to throw a flood of light on our origins. The Age
of Innocence was past, and a mood of honest realism was
putting away the naïve myths that passed for history and
substituting homely authentic fact. With the growing recognition of the intimate relations between economics and politics, America was on the threshold of intellectual maturity.

In this inevitable *rapprochement* of scholarship and
reality, academic political scientists were slow to join. It
was repugnant to their conservative temper. The more
vigorous amongst them — capable men like Professor John
W. Burgess — were still engaged in erecting speculative
systems, deifying the abstract political state, exalting the
doctrines of sovereignty, laying snares for democracy in
the shape of a Teutonic cult of power impersonal as fate.
They had turned away from our Jeffersonian past and were
outrunning the forces of an encompassing consolidation.
From such thinkers, even less than from the academic
apologists of the existing order, the democratic liberalism
of the times could receive no help. They were partisan ad-

vocates of the very forces the new liberalism was seeking
to curb. In his early recognition of this fact Professor
Smith stood almost alone amongst our academic political
scientists. He was one of the first to subject the new theory
of sovereignty to critical analysis and demonstrate its undemocratic tendencies. All his liberal instincts protested
against such attempts to erect fresh tyrannies in the form
of a superpolitical state, above the subject-citizen, irrespon-
sive to the popular will, useful only to the masters who
controlled it. He wanted rather to travel in the opposite
direction, to complete the democratic programme that had
been left unfulfilled by the Jacksonian revolution. To
accomplish that purpose new democratic machinery must
be provided. The Jacksonian movement had been a frontier
uprising against the rule of eighteenth-century aristocracy.
It had been animated by a spirit of rude leveling, of *laissez-
faire* individualism, and having established the principle of
manhood suffrage it was content to leave democracy to its
own devices. From such slackness had issued all the evils
of the Gilded Age plutocracy that discovered in Jacksonian
individualism a heaven-sent opportunity. A lawless and
unregulated individualism was destroying democracy. Government was becoming the mouthpiece and agent of property
interests. Something had gone wrong with the democratic
plans and it was time for the friends of democracy to take
stock of the situation.

In its consideration of the causes of so great a mis-
carriage, the liberalism of the early years of the century
came finally to question the system of government laid
down in the fundamental law. Considered historically perhaps the chief contribution of the Progressive movement
to American political thought was its discovery of the essentially undemocratic nature of the federal constitution.

That so obvious a fact escaped attention so long was due to political causes easily understood. For a century the Constitution had been a symbol of national unity, a strong cohesive force amidst the anarchisms of expansion, a counter influence to the disintegrations implied in local interests and sectional jealousies. To strengthen its influence as a common bond was a useful and necessary tendency, quickening the national consciousness in every commonwealth. To criticise it soon came to be reckoned disloyal, and as the interpretation of its terms fell increasingly into the hands of lawyers, who were eloquent in praise of its excellence, it was invested with reverence and the pride of patriotism by the rank and file of the American people.

In all the abundant commentary that grew up around it — except for a small group of left-wing Abolitionists who scandalously rejected the entire instrument — no question as to the democratic spirit of the Constitution was raised, no doubts as to its sufficiency as a fundamental democratic law were suggested. The aristocratic spirit of its makers was ignored and the bitter class divisions that accompanied its adoption were forgotten. But with the liberal revolt against the custodianship of government by financial and industrial interests came a new critical interest in the terms of the Constitution. Discovering when it attempted to regulate business that its hands were tied by judicial decrees, the democracy began to question the reason for the bonds that constrained its will. Distrust of the judicial exercise of sovereign powers spread widely with the setting aside of successive legislative enactments, and it became acute when the Supreme Court declared unconstitutional the Federal Income Tax Law. From that moment the question of the desirability of an eighteenth-century Constitution that by its complexity unduly impeded the functioning of the majority will was thrust into the foreground of political debate. It was the struggle of 1789 over again.

The new school of criticism was historical rather than legalistic. It went back to the origins of the Constitution. It inquired into the political theories and class interests of the men who framed the instrument; it analysed the reasons for the several articles as well as the effect of them; it gathered materials from many sources to throw light on the deliberations of the Convention. From such realistic historical investigation it discovered — so it believed — the vital issue of the political struggles of the " critical period " — the question of majority or minority control of the new venture in republicanism. The Constitution took its special form in response to the demands of financial and landed interests for adequate protection against democratic control with its populistic measures. In the difficult days following the Peace of Paris, agrarian majorities in such states as Rhode Island and New Hampshire had enacted legislation favorable to the poorer classes. The business interests had taken alarm at the prospect of a future government more friendly to poverty than to wealth, and they were quietly casting about for ways and means of taking control out of the hands of the agrarian democracy. The solution of the problem was obvious. It lay in substituting for the democratic Articles of Confederation — which the aristocratic party organized all its forces to cry down — an instrument more adapted to their needs. Hence the complexity of the Constitution as it came from the Convention — a complexity that was of the essence of their plan. Hence the elaborate system of checks and balances that limited the powers of the majority will and reduced the democracy, as Franklin observed, to the plight of the two-headed snake, which coming to a twig on the way to water debated so long over the better path that it died of thirst. Studied thus in the light of *Elliot's Debates*, set against the bitter class struggles that came to a dramatic issue in Shays' Rebellion, the conservative temper of the Constitution explains itself. It was a deliberate and well-considered protective measure designed by able men who represented the aristocracy and wealth of America; a class instrument directed against the democracy that took form in the reactionary interval between two radical democratic periods, the earlier American Revolution and the later French. To assume that it is a democratic document is to misread history and misinterpret fact.

Established thus in the historical method the new criticism quickly passed through two phases, the political and the economic. The first was concerned with an examination of the Constitution in the light of the class alignments of its makers — the clash between aristocracy and democracy from 1783 to 1789; and the second, in the light of their economic affiliations — the clash between the greater landed and financial interests and the agrarian interests. The two in reality were one, but as the economic interpretation of history grew in favor stronger emphasis came to be thrown on the latter. Of the earlier phase Professor Smith's *The Spirit of American Government* (1907) was the authoritative embodiment; and of the later Charles A. Beard's *An Economic Interpretation of the Constitution* (1913), and *The Economic Origins of Jeffersonian Democracy* (1915). These searching studies sum up the democratic case against the Constitution at it was formulated by the liberalism of pre-war days, and they go far to explain the temper of the Progressive movement in its labors to democratize the instrument through the direct primary, the initiative, the referendum, the recall, and the like.

The Spirit of American Government was published at a moment when the public mind was peculiarly receptive to its liberal interpretation, and its influence in shaping the programme of the Progressive party was immediate and stimulating. It provided the leaders of the La Follette "Insurgent group" with an interpretation of American constitutional history congenial to their temper; it gave them a convincing explanation of the reasons for the failure of democracy in American political practice; and it was drawn upon freely in Congressional debates. The theme of the book is an expositional of the checks and balance theory of government, the reasons why so cumbersome a system was adopted and the impossibility of effective democratic government under it. To the liberalism of 1907, however, the most suggestive contribution was the demonstration from the speeches and writings of the time that the system was devised deliberately for undemocratic ends. Since then the dramatic story of this struggle between rival economies has been retold many times, but in 1907 it was new and strange and it came home to the liberal mind with startling significance. From the appearance of Professor Smith's work must be dated a changed attitude towards the Constitution. The note of indiscriminate praise has given place to rational commentary. Amongst competent students today the undemocratic nature and intent of the fundamental law is accepted as a commonplace. There are no longer grounds for difference of opinion in the matter. But with the decline of liberalism since the war the defenders of the existing order have chosen to set up the logical defense that the Constitution is wisely undemocratic, for under a democratic instrument good government would be impossible. We have come back at last to the frank honesty of 1789 when gentlemen did not conceal their low opinion of the ways of the majority.

Professor Smith refused to be discouraged by the conservative reaction that was in full swing while he was preparing his studies for the press, and in the volume now appearing he has carried further his exposition of the gentle art of thwarting the majority will by legal and constitutional means. A democrat grown old in the cause, a confirmed and unrepentant liberal, he was too strongly saturated with Jeffersonian ideals to approve the ways of our triumphant plutocracy. The present volume, the manuscript of which has been revised by his daughter, Miss Elfreda Allen Smith, who served as his secretary in the preparation of the work, unfortunately will not find so well-informed or liberal a public as welcomed his earlier study, and its popular influence no doubt will be less. That it will make its way ultimately to wide influence one may at least hope. . . . . .

I have written these few meagre pages of comment on the life-work of a courageous and self-sacrificing scholar with a deep sense of personal loss. For nearly twenty years Professor Smith was my colleague and friend, and our intellectual interests and political sympathies travelled congenially the same paths. A vigorous and stimulating teacher, he trained large numbers of young men, some of them of unusual ability, who have carried his liberal spirit to widely scattered academic posts. That so outspoken a critic of the Constitution should have suffered ungenerous attack was, no doubt, to be expected. The hornets are quick with their stings if the nest of privilege is disturbed. The high price exacted of him for his courage and sincerity, his friends are well aware of, yet none ever heard him complain or recriminate. It was part of the price the scholar must pay for his intellectual integrity and he paid it ungrudgingly.

Vernon Louis Parrington [1]

The University of Washington
Seattle

[1] Died June 16, 1929, at Winchcombe, Gloucestershire, England.

THE GROWTH AND DECADENCE
OF CONSTITUTIONAL GOVERNMENT

Chapter I

INFLUENCE OF THEOLOGICAL SPECULATION ON THE EARLY CONSTITUTIONAL MOVEMENT

Modern constitutional government had its origin in the struggle to limit irresponsible power. Before the American Revolution, political authority was everywhere largely monarchic or aristocratic. The people generally had little or no direct influence upon governmental policies. The problem which then confronted political reformers was not the establishment of democratic government with the people as the recognized source of authority in the state, but rather the provision of adequate checks upon the exercise of irresponsible power.

England was the only great country in the eighteenth century in which substantial progress had been made in limiting irresponsible authority. It was not, however, democratic as that term is now understood. The distinguishing feature of its governmental organization was a distribution and balancing of political powers, which, by requiring the concurrence of king, lords, and commons, was supposed to limit the exercise of political authority. At that time, when the state was everywhere unrepresentative of the people generally, the main object of liberal thinkers was to provide a form of governmental organization which would more or less effectively check and restrain those who exercised political power. Only in so far as this had been accomplished was a state supposed to have a constitutional form of government. This limitation of political authority was, in the

3

opinion of eighteenth century thinkers, the essential feature of constitutional government. Accustomed to regard governmental authority as irresponsible, as it very largely was at that time even in England, they accepted it as a necessary evil and believed that it should be hedged about with safeguards which would make it less dangerous to the people.

The idea of sovereignty as the supreme unlimited power of the state had no place in liberal thought prior to the nineteenth century. To understand the eighteenth century viewpoint, one must bear in mind the character of the political struggle which produced the modern state. In the Middle Ages the contest was between church and king, each contending for what was in effect unlimited and politically irresponsible power. In this struggle for power between king and church, each laid claim to it by divine right. The assumption that authority had a divine origin implied that it was unlimited by any human agency; and that the king or other agent through whom it was exercised was restrained only by his accountability to God, the ultimate source of all legitimate power. The outcome of this struggle was the modern national state, in which practically supreme power was in the hands of a king claiming authority by divine right. Had the church succeeded in establishing its spiritual overlordship, the authority of the king would have been subordinated to a Christian super-state, invested, for all practical purposes, with sovereign power.

The danger of a sovereign church was averted through the creation of a lesser evil, the sovereign kingship. But in the state, no less than in the church, the ultimate source of authority was assumed to be theocratic. Temporal as well as spiritual power was conceived to have its basis and justification in a divinely established social order. In theory, the power of the king was subject to such limitation as was implied in his obligation to rule in accordance with divine law. But this check on his power was supposititious rather than real. As the embodiment of the authority of the state, and as a putative divine agent, he was, in fact, the judge of his own powers and subject to no limiting authority except such moral restraint as organized society imposed largely through the church. And this check on the power of the king, slight as it was in appearance, vanished completely, and even became the means of extending and securing his authority, in proportion as he acquired a directing influence in the church. There was at that time no clear distinction between politics and religion. Conservative political thought was essentially theological. The conception of the state was merely a miniature of the Christian conception of the universe; the sovereignty of God was its distinguishing feature. Theological doctrine and religious belief supplied the justification for absolute monarchy. In the state no more than in the church was authority conceived to emanate from the people themselves. The assumption that God was the ultimate source of political power meant, in its practical application, the sovereignty of the king.

Unlimited power can be viewed with complacency only when it is conceived as divine. The attempt to justify absolute monarchy as a divinely ordained institution, encountered the opposition of those who saw in it an effort to secure general acquiescence in the exercise of unlimited authority, under the pretense of divine sanction. Resistance to the absolute power of the king assumed various forms. The authority of the temporal ruler might be legally unlimited; but it could not entirely protect itself against the growth of a body of religious and political doctrines which tended to undermine the belief that supported it. No state church, as a bulwark of royal power, could wholly protect that power against insidious attacks which assumed the form of religious speculation.

What was true in the case of theological doctrines was also true in the field of political thought. Unlimited power inevitably led to the formulation and diffusion of ideas designed to weaken and eventually destroy the popular support without which a system of absolutism could not be maintained. The claim of absolute power was met by an opposing theory of the limitation of authority. It must be recognized that there were assumed to be checks, even on the king who ruled by divine right. To a people accustomed to think of God as ultimate ruler, divine right as a justification of kingship implied the limitation of royal authority. The king, as a divine agent, was assumed to be accountable to a higher will. Thus, even in the theory of absolute monarchy, all human authority, as such, was conceived to be limited. Only the power of the Supreme Being was absolute and unlimited. Theoretically, there was no sovereign authority except that of God. All power exercised in human society was assumed to be subject to the limitations imposed by the Divine Will. The Christian view of the world recognized the sovereignty of God; and by necessary implication all human authority, including that of the king, was strictly subordinate. The orthodox defense of monarchy thus had as its starting point or major premise the assumed divine limitation of monarchic authority. All instruments and agents through which power was exercised in human society were conceived to be subject to the restraints implied in ultimate divine control. Only when authority was traced to its original source, the Divine Will, was it conceived to be unlimited. Monarchy, when viewed as a part of the Christian conception of the world, involved belief in the existence of restraints on the exercise of political power.

There was always the assumption of a divine or natural order to which the king or other earthly authority should conform. In the orthodox Christian view, this took the form of a personal God to whom the king was accountable for the exercise of authority. This conception kept alive the idea of, and belief in, the limitation of political power; although, in its practical application to the state, its immediate result was to make the king actually supreme.

In the long run, however, society will not be content with a theory which attempts to satisfy the generally recognized need for limitation of authority, without adequate provision for enforcing it. With the growth of political intelligence, faith in the efficacy of divine control disappeared. Political and religious ideas became less confused and interblended. Governmental arrangements came to be regarded more and more as essentially human agencies; and, as such, subject to human control. The conception of the state as a divinely controlled institution gradually gave place to the idea that the source of political authority is in society itself. This change in viewpoint was reflected in a corresponding development of ideas and agencies, designed to provide the means by which power could be effectively limited. As is always the case when any great transformation in thought is taking place, old conceptions had to be modified and adapted to the new outlook. This development can be easily traced in the history of political doctrines, which are in a sense mere intellectual tools, employed often to defend and justify the established order or, by discrediting existing arrangements, to bring about political reforms.

The basic conception of the old political order was not the divine right of kings, but the sovereignty of God. The assumed divine right of the temporal ruler was not an essential part of this doctrine. Divine sovereignty, as envisaged in the Christian theory of the world, was simply a conception of God as the ultimate source of authority. Direct human intermediaries, such as pope or king, were purely adventitious features of this belief. They were mere accretions added to the doctrine of divine sovereignty in the course of political and theological controversy. As such, they could be discarded without weakening or destroying the belief in God as ultimate ruler. One might question the right of any individual to exercise power as a divinely appointed agent, and at the same time believe in God as the creator and final source of all authority.

The attack on monarchy, both religious and secular, assumed the form of an attempt to discredit the claim that pope or king was a divinely commissioned agent. The movement to overthrow absolutism in church and state was in no sense a denial of the ultimate sovereignty of God, but a repudiation of the extraneous doctrine of divine agency, which had been made the bulwark of absolute and irresponsible authority. It challenged the right of either priest or king to act as the exclusive and final interpreter of the Divine Will. It sought to limit power by creating socialized and unofficial agencies which would function as interpreters of divine law. It made an appeal to the collective intelligence and conscience of men, through the dissemination of ideas which laid the foundation for a socialized interpretation of the Divine Will. The development of such agencies, by divesting the monarch of his most important prerogative, would in the end effectively limit his power. With the interpretation of divine law no longer a prerogative of the king, the Christian doctrine of the sovereignty of God served the purpose of limiting his authority.

The movement to socialize the interpretation of divine law brought into existence a body of doctrines which have had an important influence on the trend of modern constitutional development. All of these had their origin directly or indirectly in the Christian conception of the ultimate sovereignty of God. Chief among them may be mentioned, as the original and basic idea, the belief in a fundamental divine or natural law. Around this conception have grown up various derivative ideas or doctrines which constitute the intellectual and moral basis of the modern constitutional movement. The Christian view of the universe, though essentially monarchical, did not necessarily imply a monarchically organized church and state. Belief in the sovereignty of God, though employed in defense of the claims of pope and king, supplied a precarious justification for monarchical authority. The conception of a Divine Will, which found expression in the Scriptures and in the law of nature, involved logically the idea that all human authority was limited. To make this limitation effective, it was necessary to deprive the ruler of his prerogative as official interpreter of divine law.

The Protestant Reformation was the outcome of the movement to limit monarchic power in the church, as constitutional government was a check upon that power in the state. The trend of religious and political thought was toward decentralization and diffusion of the power to interpret divine or natural law. This was accomplished in part by bringing into existence other governmental organs whose authority was not derived from the monarch, and which could, therefore, serve as checks on monarchic power. It was, however, largely through the growth of political ideas favoring the diffusion of power, that restraints were imposed on the exercise of irresponsible authority. Around the belief in divine or natural law, developed a group of doctrines which served the purpose of making the conception of natural law a more or less effective restraint on arbitrary power.

The specious claim of divine right, advanced in support of monarchic power, was opposed by the assertion of the divine right of the people to control the state. This was the significance of the social contract theory, which made the people rather than the king the legitimate source of authority. Acceptance of this theory involved the belief that the people themselves were the final authority for the interpretation of natural law. There would thus be created outside of the government a public opinion which would restrain those who exercised political power. The doctrine that the people were the original source of political authority was reinforced by such subsidiary doctrines as those of natural rights and the right of revolution. The former marked off a field within which natural law did not permit interference by the state, while the latter supplied the means of enforcing this limitation. Moreover, the emphasis which Christianity placed on the individual, and the doctrine that all men are equal before God, likewise tended to undermine the foundation of irresponsible power. The prestige of governmental authority declined in proportion as a body of opinion crystallized around these ideas and utilized them as standards by which official conduct was to be judged. The foundation was thus laid for the development of an organization outside of the state itself, which would interpret, and in the last resort enforce, the limitation which natural law imposed on governmental authority.

In the earlier stages of the modern constitutional movement, the great outstanding fact was the recognized need for a check on irresponsible power. This was to be accomplished by dividing and distributing governmental powers, and by creating an organized opinion which would serve as

a restraining influence on the government as a whole.
Supreme unlimited power had no place in the political
thought of the early constitutionalists.   All human authority
was conceived to be limited.   The theory of individual
liberty, the doctrine of natural rights, and the basic conception of society as controlled by principles rooted in the ultimate sovereignty of God, precluded the idea that any human
authority could be unlimited.   The essence of constitutional
government was the system of restraints with which it sur-
rounded the exercise of political power.

Chapter II

LIMITATION OF POLITICAL POWER IN THE
PERIOD IMMEDIATELY FOLLOWING THE
AMERICAN REVOLUTION

The American Revolution may be regarded as one of the important incidents in the struggle against irresponsible political authority. It was, in fact, the culminating point in the modern movement to limit the power of the state. It brought together, organized, and made definite and concrete application of the liberal political ideas of the seventeenth and eighteenth centuries. It emphasized, as had never been emphasized before, the inalienable right of the people to interpret the limitations on governmental authority implied in the theories of natural law, natural rights, and individual liberty, and to enforce them, if other means failed, by resort to the right of revolution.

It assumed the existence of a law of nature of which the people themselves were the final interpreters. All governmental authority was regarded as conditioned and limited by certain fundamental principles of human nature and social organization. These basic principles constituted a fundamental law to which statutes, policies, and the general conduct of the state should conform. It is in this conception of a law of nature, as guaranteeing certain rights to the individual and limiting governmental authority, that we find the principle which largely determined the character of the early constitutional development of the United States. Indeed, it may be said that the American Revolution was fought by our forefathers in defense of the rights claimed under the law of nature; and that, in setting up governments of their own, the safeguarding of these rights against governmental encroachment was their chief concern.

The elimination of monarchy and aristocracy removed what had been the chief menace to liberty, but it brought society face to face with a new danger. The long struggle against hereditary power had finally resulted, in the political practice of America, in the transfer of all political authority to governmental organs more or less directly representing the voters. Irresponsible power had been limited through the development of the check and balance type of governmental organization, and finally, as a result of the American Revolution, political authority had come to rest wholly upon a popular basis.

Throughout the long struggle to establish and maintain a constitutional form of governmental organization, the limitation of authority was the end which had been kept constantly in view. The chief reason for emphasizing the necessity of limiting power was to be found in the fact that it was largely irresponsible; but the viewpoint which had been evolved in the constitutional struggle of the seventeenth and eighteenth centuries reflected, in the conception of natural law, natural rights, and individual liberty, a distrust of unlimited authority of any sort. Liberal thinkers, who denied the sovereignty of the king, were unwilling to concede unlimited power even to a democratic state. The social compact theory, as a basis of political organization, was interpreted in the light of the belief in a fundamental law of nature to which all governmental arrangements, even those set up by the people themselves, should conform. Quite naturally then, with the disappearance of monarchy and aristocracy, the emphasis, which up to this time had been placed on irresponsible power as the greatest menace to liberty, was now transferred to the power of the people as organized in the democratic state. The social contract theory, as generally accepted, did not imply that political power was unlimited. It was possible to regard the people as the sole source of political authority, and at the same time to think of that authority as subject to certain definite limitations imposed upon it by the nature and purpose of human society.

The conception of the state which prevailed in the Revolutionary period was very largely that which we find in the political writings of John Locke. His defense of the social compact was not a defense of unlimited power. Such authority as the state had was derived, in his view, from the people; but the state was not entitled to claim supreme power. Sovereignty in the sense of unlimited power could have no place in the philosophy of the free state.

This view is reflected in the Declaration of Independence and in the early state constitutions. In American political thought of this period, governmental authority was definitely subordinated. The people were conceived to be the ultimate and only legitimate source of power in society. But the conception was still somewhat vague. Power, even though supposed to rest wholly upon a popular basis, was, nevertheless, thought of as limited. The limitation of governmental power rested in part on a legal basis, through the participation of the voters in the actual organization of the state. But it was not only governmental authority that was legally limited. The constitutional arrangements which the Revolution brought into existence suggested a pronounced distrust of what may be called the power of the people. Legal restrictions on popular power have been, from the beginning, fundamental features of the American government. Under the suffrage qualifications of the time, the majority of adult male citizens were denied the right to vote. It was only in this restricted sense that the people were thought of as constituting a political organization, the ultimate source of authority. Moreover, the political power of the voters was definitely limited through officeholding qualifications, which narrowed further the range of popular choice. Such restrictions, it was thought, would limit both popular and governmental authority.

There is another kind of constitutional provision in which the theory that political power is limited finds definite expression. The Declaration of Independence was not a constitution as that term is generally understood. It contained no plan of governmental organization; but it did formulate the fundamental principles which were supposed to inhere in the nature of political society and to which constitutions and governmental policies should conform. It laid claim to certain " unalienable rights," to which men were entitled under the " laws of nature." It proclaimed the doctrine that governmental authority was subordinate to this higher law, and made the people the final interpreters of the restraints on governmental authority, which were to be enforced, if necessary, by resort to the right of revolution.

The political thought of the Revolutionary period was conspicuously individualistic. Its distinguishing trait was distrust of governmental authority. Throughout the long struggle for constitutional government, the dominant purpose had been the protection of the individual against unwarranted interference at the hands of the state. The natural law political philosophy, so widely accepted in the seventeenth and eighteenth centuries, derived its popularity from the fact that it provided a justification for the view that the authority of the state was limited. It assumed that the state, as exemplified in governmental organization and constitutional arrangements, was not unlimited, but that it was subject to the restraints imposed by the unwritten or natural constitution of human society, upon which the theory of individual liberty was based. The individual had certain fundamental or natural rights which were not derived from the state, of which it could not be regarded as the final judge, and which it might at times be tempted to abridge. The inherent conflict between the authority of the state and the liberty of the individual implied of necessity the doctrine that political power was limited. Nor was the need of limitation confined to the undemocratic state. Natural law, which supplied the justification for limiting the power of monarchy and aristocracy, was a theory that applied to the democratic state as well. Political authority, irrespective of its source, was conceived to be limited by the inalienable rights to which the individual was entitled under the law of nature.

This view is distinctly reflected in the development of our constitutional system. The theory of natural law, natural rights, and individual liberty not only served to justify the Revolution, but also constituted the philosophic foundation of the American political system. This is clearly indicated in our early political documents. The distinguishing feature of the Declaration of Independence and of the state documents of this period is the emphasis on natural law and natural rights. Of the eleven states which adopted constitutions during the Revolutionary period, six [1] included in their constitutions a more or less elaborate statement of individual rights. New York quoted the Declaration of Independence in full as an introduction to its own constitution. New Jersey, in the preamble of its constitution, proclaimed the

[1] Md., Mass., N. H., N. C., Penn., and Va.

right of revolution; and in the South Carolina Constitution of 1776, two-fifths of the document was devoted to an enumeration of the crimes of Great Britain and a defense of the Revolution. The Georgia Constitution of 1777 justified resistance to " oppressive measures," and asserted the right of revolution in defense " of rights and privileges, they [the people] are entitled to by the laws of nature and reason." The Constitution of Delaware was the only one adopted during this period which contained no defense of the Revolution.

The natural rights of the individual, existing independently of the state and limiting its authority, were regarded as having a higher sanction than could be conferred by mere constitutional enactment. They were derived from the law of nature itself, to which all governmental arrangements should conform. This conception of a higher law limiting all authority in human society had been the guiding principle of the modern movement in both church and state. It was the foundation of the belief that institutional control should be limited, and the justification for the emphasis on the freedom of the individual in political, economic, and religious thought.

Up to the time of the American Revolution, liberty had been a purely negative conception. It existed only where, and to the extent that, governmental power had been restrained. It meant freedom from interference at the hands of the state. This was the only kind of liberty possible while the state continued to rest in part upon a monarchic and aristocratic basis. But with the Revolution there came into existence for the first time a modern state which derived all its authority from the people. Popular control of the state was regarded less as an end in itself, than as a safeguard against the abuse of governmental authority;

individual liberty was supposed to be made more secure through the establishment of political liberty. The political rights of the citizen in a democratic state were supposed to afford him in some measure the means of protecting his liberty as an individual.

Political liberty, or collective control of the state, was a natural right. It was, however, restricted by, and subordinate to, the natural rights of individuals as such, which not even the democratic state could justly override. The American political system, based as it was on eighteenth century political philosophy, recognized the people as the only source of legitimate authority in the state; but at the same time sought to limit popular control to the end of protecting individual liberty against governmental interference.

Political liberty was not regarded as in itself an adequate protection and guaranty of individual rights. The social contract theory of the state, as interpreted in connection with the doctrine of natural rights, necessarily implied the limitation of political authority regardless of its source. The doctrine of divine right, whether advanced to support the power of the king or of the popular majority, had no place in eighteenth century thought. It was not the aim of the Revolutionary leaders to set up a government endowed with unlimited power. The individualistic philosophy of the time was inherently opposed to the establishment of such a state. Government was admitted to be necessary, but at best it was a necessary evil. To make individual liberty reasonably secure, the authority of the state, it was thought, must be definitely limited.

Our political system, having its origin in armed resistance to what was regarded as an arbitrary and unwarranted exercise of political power, was based on the theory that the authority of the state should be carefully restricted by a written constitution. But the constitution was itself subject to a higher law — the source of those fundamental rights of the individual, for the protection of which it was necessary to limit political power. The limitation of authority was secured, in part, through checks and balances within the governmental organization itself. The graduated office-holding qualifications, inherited from pre-Revolutionary days, made the official class a check on the voters while the government, as distinguished from the people, or rather that part of the people having the right to vote, was subject to the restraint implied in frequent elections. A further limitation of authority within the governmental organization itself was effected through a distribution of political power, based on the check and balance plan of the state, although this method of limiting authority had much less importance in the beginning than it assumed later.[2]

It is evident that the political philosophy of the American Revolutionary period repudiated the idea that the state, as represented by the electorate and the governmental organization, possessed unlimited power. It definitely recognized the need of unofficial and extra-legal channels through which influence, pressure, or even, if necessary, force could be exerted to the end of keeping the government within the limits fixed by the written constitution and by that higher law of nature from which the rights of the individual, as against the state, were derived. The social contract theory, with its implication of governmental dependence on the people, was accepted as a matter of course. But in working out the details of its application, the founders of our government proceeded on the assumption that all authority,

[2] See the author's *The Spirit of American Government*, Chs. II to VI inclusive.

even that of the people, must be hedged about with limitations imposed to safeguard individual liberty.

The term, people, was more or less loosely used to designate the final source of authority in society. In the strictly political sense, it included only those who had the right to vote. The political power of this limited electorate was checked through the governmental organization and also by the individual rights of the great body of non-voters. The dependence of the government on the voting class, though accepted in principle, was not regarded as implying that the voters, as such, were the final and only source of power. They were, it is true, the only means by which public opinion could be brought to bear in an orderly and legally established way upon governmental affairs. But the voters did not represent the people as a whole; only in a restricted sense could they be regarded as expressing that larger public opinion which no government could afford to ignore. Consistent with the political thought of the period, the founders of our government sought to temper authority within the governmental organization itself by means of checks on both voters and public officials. But in addition to this, and more important as an indication of their general attitude toward the state, they recognized the people in the broadest sense of the term as an extra-legal limitation on political power.

The rights of individuals were defined with some care in the written constitutions, which were designed to protect all people, whether voters or non-voters, against abuse of authority. But the fathers as clear thinking, practical men had no illusion as to the nature of constitutional guaranties. They recognized that rights must be enforced in the last resort by those for whose protection they exist. Back of and outside the formal legal organization of the state, with its restrictive voting, and still more restrictive officeholding qualifications, were the great majority of free citizens, who, though disfranchised, were not without rights or the means of defending them. Because of their numbers, they constituted the main strength of the state in time of national peril. Without any share in the usual and normal exercise of political power through the ballot, they were, however, included in the eighteenth century conception of the people as the ultimate source of authority in society. The power of the people was thought of less as a guiding, directing, initiating force, than as a negative, restraining influence. The aim of the fathers was government " with the consent of the governed," rather than government by the governed. This is indicated in the threefold classification of citizens. Political initiative, in the true sense of the term, was confined to the relatively small class possessing the qualifications requisite for the more important public offices. The elective principle upon which the governmental system was based made officeholders dependent on the support of the voters; and thus ensured, through frequent elections, a more or less effective, though negative, control by the electorate. But in the political philosophy of the Revolutionary movement, the consent of the governed meant more than the consent of the qualified voters. All citizens, whether included in the formal legal organization of the state, or excluded, were conceived to have rights as individuals and means of defending those rights against encroachment at the hands of the state itself. Since the great majority of the citizens had no part in the selection and rejection of public officials, their rights were unprotected in the formal organization of the state. But though excluded from the state as legally organized, the majority were recognized as having rights which they could defend and enforce, even against the state itself. The assertion in the Declaration of Independence and in the various state constitutions that " governments derive their just powers from the consent of the governed," can not be fairly interpreted as excluding the great body of disfranchised citizens. They were excluded, it is true, in so far as consent or dissent found expression in the regular and frequently recurring choice of public officials. The government was not conceived to rest, however, solely on the consent of the voting minority.

The guiding purpose of the modern constitutional movement, which had been the limitation of political power, was not essentially changed by the American Revolution. Political authority, though having a new basis, was still regarded as a menace to individual liberty, unless subjected to restraints imposed for the protection of individual rights. Government with the consent of the governed implied not merely the formally expressed consent of the enfranchised minority, but also the passive approval of the disfranchised majority. It was clearly recognized in the political philosophy of the Revolutionary period, that the state as legally organized was ultimately accountable to the great body of both voting and non-voting citizens. Moreover, the social compact theory of the state, which supplied the justification for the Revolutionary movement, required that some provision be made for the expression of popular disapproval of governmental policies. This is the significance of the so-called right of revolution, which was so much emphasized in our early political literature and in the constitutional documents contemporary with it. Since the social contract theory of the state was accepted as the philosophical foundation of our political organization, " the consent of the governed," which in the usual legal sense meant the consent of the qualified voters, was interpreted to include all citizens for the purposes of ultimate control — a potential source of popu-

lar power designed to be seldom if ever used, though always in reserve as a safeguard against governmental injustice. In this way, the principle of ultimate popular control
was recognized, without making the state directly and
immediately dependent on the will of the majority of the
people.

The distinction made, in the practical application of
eighteenth century theory, between voters as a legal check
on the government, and the great mass of non-voters as an
extra-legal and ultimate check, may be regarded as in the
nature of a conservative compromise. The social contract
theory of the state emphasized the principle of popular consent. Consistently applied, it would have involved a widely
extended suffrage. Not only the social contract idea of the
state, but the doctrine of natural rights, the theory of individual liberty, and the idea of equality were all incompatible with any policy which would make the state independent of the consent of the majority. Indeed, the system
of checks and balances, as applied to the organization of a
democratic state, logically included some form of majority
consent as one of the restraints on governmental power.
But since the majority did not have the legal right to vote,
their influence could not be exerted through the regular
agencies of control. But although outside of the governmental organization and having no voice within the state itself,
they were, nevertheless, recognized as an extra-legal check on
its authority. They had the right to criticize governmental
policies, a right implied in the guaranties of freedom of
speech, press, and assembly, which were embodied in the
various bills or declarations of rights. In this way they could
express their dissent, which, though without legal effect, was,
nevertheless, designed to operate as a wholesome moral restraint on political authority. Through the exercise of this

right, a very real pressure might be brought to bear in opposition to governmental policies.

The founders of our government saw clearly that political stability could not be secured by suppressing this elementary right. Freedom of speech, press, and assembly was in the nature of a safety valve. It was especially important where the majority were denied the right of suffrage, since it would serve to indicate the strength and intensity of popular opposition and would thus permit the necessary concession to public opinion, before hostility to governmental measures gathered explosive force. Through the exercise of this right, public opinion would tend to operate as an effective restraint. It was, of course, highly improbable that it would ever become necessary, under any government which respected this right, to invoke the ultimate right of revolution. But though never actually exercised, recognition of it as a right could not fail to remind public officials that the people themselves were the final interpreters of the limitations on governmental authority.

The right of a people to abolish a government which has become oppressive is, in the nature of the case, incompatible with a strong, highly centralized state. To make the right of revolution a real check on political power, the means of governmental coercion must be kept at the lowest point consistent with the satisfactory exercise of the legitimate functions of the state. Thus, in the eighteenth century, a standing army was regarded by Americans as a menace to individual liberty, in that it supplied the means of coercion and relieved the government of the necessity of tempering its policies by conciliation and compromise. To a people actually engaged in establishing their independence by war, the occasional need of an army for the purposes of national de-

fense was clear. But a strong military establishment in time
of peace was looked upon as a constant source of danger.
This view is reflected in various provisions which were incorporated in the political documents of the Revolutionary
period, and which were designed to ensure the subordination
of military to civil authority. Thus we find in the Virginia
Bill of Rights (1776), " that standing armies, in time of
peace, should be avoided, as dangerous to liberty," and in
the Pennsylvania Declaration of Rights (1776), " that as
standing armies in the time of peace are dangerous to liberty,
they ought not to be kept up."

No bill of rights was included in the Constitution of the
United States as originally framed and adopted. As this
omission was regarded as a serious defect, the ratifying conventions in the various states proposed amendments which
constituted a bill of individual rights. There was considerable dissatisfaction with the Constitution on the ground that
it did not adequately safeguard the people against the danger
of military power. New Hampshire proposed " that no
standing army shall be kept in time of peace, unless with
the consent of three-fourths of the members of each branch
of Congress." Virginia, New York, and North Carolina proposed that no standing army should be kept in time of peace,
without the consent of two-thirds of the members of both
houses of Congress. Delaware suggested a constitutional
amendment making a two-thirds majority in Congress necessary for the purpose of declaring war; and Rhode Island
proposed that compulsory service in the army should be
made unconstitutional, except in case of actual invasion. Of
similar import was the demand from various states for a
constitutional amendment recognizing the right of the people
to keep and bear arms. This right was guaranteed in the

Second Amendment to the Constitution of the United States. The fear that a strong central government might become oppressive was more or less general at that time. For this reason, constitutional provisions which tended to limit the coercive power of the state were regarded as necessary for the protection of individual liberty.

CHAPTER III

THE STRUGGLE FOR A DEMOCRATIC SUFFRAGE

Prominence was given in the public documents of the American Revolution to the social contract theory, the doctrine of natural rights, the idea of equality, and other conceptions more or less closely identified with the belief in political democracy. This tended to give to the Revolution the appearance of a genuinely popular movement, and thus aided materially in developing and crystallizing public opinion in support of the war for independence.

To proclaim that " all men are created equal " and that they are " endowed by their Creator with certain unalienable rights " which governments " deriving their just powers from the consent of the governed " are instituted to protect, may not be a positive and unequivocal statement of belief in the justice and desirability of a widely extended suffrage; but inferentially, at any rate, it constituted a solemn indictment of the then existing restrictions on the right to vote.

This Revolutionary enthusiasm for the rights of man, which found expression in the official pronouncements of representative bodies, did not commit the political leaders of that time, by any direct and specific statement, to the policy of democratizing the suffrage. It was no doubt clearly seen, however, that the doctrine of natural rights, which served the practical end of justifying the Revolution, could also be used effectively by those who wished to abolish property qualifications for voting and officeholding. That this

27

was recognized is evidenced by certain qualifying statements, obviously designed to safeguard property qualifications against an attack based on the theory that suffrage is a
natural right.   Thus the Virginia Bill of Rights, adopted
June 12, 1776, after declaring " that all men are by nature
equally free and independent " and " that all power is vested
in, and consequently derived from, the people," adds the
saving clause " that all men, having sufficient evidence of
permanent common interest with, and attachment to, the
community, have the right of suffrage."   Provisions identical in substance were incorporated in the Bills of Rights
in Pennsylvania, Maryland, New Hampshire, and Vermont.
The effort to reconcile the theory of natural rights with a
restricted suffrage probably had little effect on the outcome
of the suffrage controversy.   Nevertheless, it was half a century after this outburst of revolutionary enthusiasm for democracy in the abstract, before the movement to democratize
the suffrage was well under way.

Neither at the beginning of the Revolution, nor later when
the Constitution was framed and adopted, was the extension
of the suffrage included in the list of proposed reforms.   According to the viewpoint of the official and ruling class, government existed primarily for the protection of property and
property rights.   This was well expressed by John Adams
at the beginning of the American Revolution:

" The same reasoning which will induce you to admit all
men who have no property, to vote, with those who have,
. . . will prove that you ought to admit women and children;
for, generally speaking, women and children have as good
judgments, and as independent minds, as those men who are
wholly destitute of property; these last being to all intents
and purposes as much dependent upon others, who will
please to feed, clothe, and employ them, as women are upon

their husbands, or children on their parents. . . . Depend upon it, Sir, it is dangerous to open so fruitful a source of controversy and altercation as would be opened by attempting to alter the qualifications of voters; . . . women will demand a vote; . . . and every man who has not a farthing, will demand an equal voice with any other. . . . It tends to confound and destroy all distinctions, and prostrate all ranks to one common level." [1]

Forty-one years later,[2] in a letter to James Madison, he said:

" The questions concerning universal suffrage, and those concerning the necessary limitations of the power of suffrage, are among the most difficult. It is hard to say that every man has not an equal right; but, admit this equal right and equal power, and an immediate revolution would ensue. In all the nations of Europe, the number of persons, who have not a penny, is double those who have a groat; admit all these to an equality of power, and you would soon see how the groats would be divided. . . . There is in these United States a majority of persons, who have no property, over those who have any." [3]

Adams expressed the ruling class conviction of the time, that government is, and ought to be, founded on property, and that only those who have sufficient property to ensure their support of the established order can with safety be allowed to vote. In the earlier statement of his reasons for opposing manhood suffrage, he based his objection on the ground that the propertyless laboring man is dependent on his employer, and consequently is not a free moral agent in casting his vote. On this assumption, the enfranchisement of the laboring class would not in reality place political

---

[1] Letter to James Sullivan, May 26, 1776; *Works,* vol. IX, pp. 377–78.
[2] June 17, 1817.
[3] *Works,* vol. X, pp. 267–68.

power in their hands, but would merely increase the number of votes controlled by their employers, and thus have the effect of making government more oligarchical in character than it was before property qualifications were abolished. This argument was frequently used by the opponents of manhood suffrage, and was designed, no doubt, to influence the attitude of that large class of small landowning agricultural voters, who would not regard with favor any measure which would be likely to result in a substantial increase in the political influence of the wealthy employing class of the large cities. This particular reason for opposing the extension of the suffrage seems to have been a favorite argument of those who accepted the notion, then more or less prevalent among the ruling class, that political rights should be the exclusive privilege of landowners. Indeed, the idea that government should be controlled by landowners survived in many of the original states until well into the nineteenth century. After the Revolution there were ten states in which there was a freehold qualification for voters, though in five of these there was an alternative personal property qualification.[4] The control of the state government by the landholding interests was still further safeguarded by means of substantial property qualifications for public office. The viewpoint of the ruling class at the time the Constitution of the United States was framed is reflected in the act of Congress providing for the government of the Northwest Territory.[5] Under the provisions of this act, the governor was required to have a freehold estate of one thousand acres in the territory; the secretary of the territory and the territorial judges, estates of at least five hundred acres each. A freehold of two hundred acres was necessary for member-

---

[4] Kirk Porter, *Suffrage in the United States,* p. 13.
[5] An Ordinance for the government of the territory of the United States northwest of the river Ohio (July 13, 1787).

ship in the general assembly, and no one could vote who did not own fifty acres of land in the district.

By 1821 the suffrage question was receiving serious attention in the state of New York. In the constitutional convention of that year, the committee on the elective franchise reported in favor of giving the suffrage to every adult male citizen who contributed toward the support of the government by payment of taxes on real or personal property, by service in the state militia, or by work on the highways, provided he had resided within the state for a period of six months. This proposal was debated at length, being strenuously opposed by the conservative members of the body. In the course of the debate various amendments were offered, the object of which was to defeat the proposed extension or to nullify its effects. Two of the most active opponents of a liberal suffrage policy were Chief Justice Spencer and Chancellor Kent of the supreme court. Both believed that the proposal to extend the suffrage was revolutionary, and that it would destroy the security which property owners had up to that time enjoyed and in the end bring chaos and ruin upon the nation. Chief Justice Spencer thought the time not far distant when the agricultural interest would be in a minority. " And what," he asked, " is there to protect the landed interests of the state, the cultivators of the soil, if the wide and broad proposition on your table be adopted? " He predicted " that the landed interests of the state will be at the mercy of the other combined interests; and thus all the public burthens may be thrown on the landed property of the state." " Is it desirable," he asked, " that we should remove the safeguards of property, and destroy the incentive to acquire it, by rendering it insecure? " After attributing to the beneficence and liberality of property " all the embellishments and the comforts and blessings of life," he warned the

members of the convention to take care, " whilst we nominally give the right of voting to a particular description of
our citizens, that we do not in reality give it to their employers." [6] On another occasion in the convention, he said:
" Let me ask to whom this right will be extended? It will
principally be . . . to those who work in your factories,
and are employed by wealthy individuals, in the capacity of
labourers. Now, I hold . . . that it will be one of the most
aristocratic acts that was ever witnessed in this community — under the pretence of giving the right to them,
we in fact give it to those who employ, clothe, and feed
them." [7]

Chancellor Kent expressed the fear " that our posterity
will have reason to deplore in sackcloth and ashes, the delu-
sion of the day." [8] He contended that the landed interest of
the state should retain the exclusive control of the senate, as
a guaranty of protection to the owners of the soil. In reply
to those who like Chancellor Kent desired special protection
for property, David Buel, Jr., said:

" One ground of the argument of gentlemen who support
the amendment [to retain the freehold qualifications for
senatorial voters] is, that the extension of the right of
suffrage will give an undue influence to the rich over the
persons who depend upon them for employment; but if the
rich control the votes of the poor, the result cannot be un-
favourable to the security of property. . . .

" I contend, that by the true principle of our government, property, as such, is not the basis of representation.
Our community is an association of persons — of human
beings — not a partnership founded on property. . . .
Property is only one of the incidental rights of the person

6 N. Y. Const. Conv., 1821 *Debates,* p. 218.
7 *Ibid.,* pp. 196–97.
8 *Ibid.,* p. 220.

who possesses it; . . . it must be made secure; but it does not follow, that it must therefore be represented specifically in any branch of the government. It ought, indeed, to have an influence — and it ever will have, when properly enjoyed. So ought talents to have an influence . . . but you surely would not set up men of talents as a separate order, and give them exclusive privileges.

" The truth is, that both wealth and talents will ever have a great influence; and without the aid of exclusive privileges, you will always find the influence of both wealth and talents predominant in our halls of legislation." [9]

The effort to make men instead of property the basis of the state government was only partially successful. Several important changes were made in the suffrage plan submitted by the committee on the elective franchise which were designed to make the qualifications of voters less objectionable to the property holder. The residence requirement recommended by the committee, of six months in the state, was raised to one year, and a local residence requirement of six months in the town or county was added. The suffrage was given to adult male citizens who had paid taxes on real or personal property, or performed military service in the state militia within the year preceding the election. Adult male citizens who had not paid taxes on real or personal property, or had not served in the state militia, but who had been assessed and had performed labor on highways were allowed to vote, subject to a state residence requirement of three years and a local residence requirement of one year. No colored man was allowed to vote unless he had been for three years a citizen of the state, and owned, and had paid taxes on, a freehold estate of the value of $250.00.

The representatives of the landholding interest in the con-

[9] N. Y. Const. Conv., 1821, *Debates,* pp. 243–44.

vention were unsuccessful in their effort to deprive non-freehold voters of a voice in the selection of the members of the upper house; but they did succeed in limiting the influence of this class of voters by retaining the freehold qualification for membership in that house.

The varying and conflicting opinions concerning the suffrage which were expressed in the New York constitutional convention of 1821, may be regarded as fairly indicative of ruling class sentiment at that time. There was an increasing number who favored the view that government was an institution established and maintained for the benefit of all citizens, and that to guarantee an equitable diffusion of the benefits derived therefrom, it was necessary to abolish the special constitutional protection given to property owners through property qualifications for voting and for holding public office. But only a small minority of the members of this convention, it seems, favored the abolition of all property qualifications.[10] Martin Van Buren, afterwards President of the United States, declared that he did not believe that there were twenty members who, were " the bare naked question of universal suffrage put to them, would vote in its favour." [11]

Broadly speaking, there are but two theories of the suffrage; one may be called the aristocratic and the other the democratic. The aristocratic theory, which found expression in our state constitutions during the first half century of our history as a nation, held that voting was a privilege to be conferred upon such of the adult citizens as were fit to exercise it. The advocates of this theory made use of it for the purpose of justifying the then existing restrictions on the right to vote. They did not really believe in the doctrine of

---

[10] There were 126 members in the constitutional convention.
[11] N. Y. Const. Conv., 1821, *Debates*, p. 277.

equality or the theory of natural rights, nor did they accept Aristotle's definition of a citizen as one who shares in governing and being governed. A citizen, as such, was at the most, they thought, only a potential voter. Mere citizenship did not confer upon the individual, nor entitle him to claim, any active civic rights. The right to vote and to be elected to office did not belong to him as a citizen, but accrued to him incidentally as the owner of property. In order to justify this contention, it was necessary to make the assumption that participation in the political life of the state was but a privilege, which those in control might confer or withhold. The conservative believed then, as he does now, that men in their civic activities are very largely guided by what they consider to be their material interests. This stands out conspicuously in all the debates and other literature in opposition to the extension of the suffrage.

It has almost always been assumed, as a self-evident proposition, by the advocates of a restricted suffrage, that the poor, if granted the privilege of voting, would use the power thus given them to bring about a redistribution of wealth. It does not seem to have occurred to them that, if this contention has any merit, it could also be claimed with as much reason that under a property holding suffrage the material interests of property owners will be advanced at the expense of the classes who have little or no property. We are all too prone to assume that our particular interest is the best and most trustworthy indication of what is for the public good. It is, therefore, not difficult for any class to believe that its interests are representative of the general interests, and that legislation advantageous to it is also beneficial to the state as a whole. Without imputing, then, any consciously selfish motive to those in control, we may accept as true Professor Dicey's statement, " that from the inspection of the laws of a country it is often possible to conjecture, and this without much hesitation, what is the class which holds, or has held, predominant power at a given time." [12]

The ruling class believed in the right of the politically fit to control the state. The test of fitness, however, was not personal worth, character, or intelligence. These qualities might make one respected and trusted as a man; but they furnished no assurance that political power, if placed in his hands, would be wisely and conservatively used. James Monroe in 1831, after he had been for eight years President of the United States, wrote: " The danger is, if the right of suffrage is extended to the whole population, without any qualification, as to property, that as the difference of interest begins to operate, as it will soon do, that the mass of poor, which will be by far the most numerous, will elect persons who will be instruments in the hands of leaders who will overthrow the government. . . ." [13]

To the political liberal, citizenship implied the right to participate in the civic life of the community. To deny the individual the ballot was to deprive him of that which constituted the essence of citizenship in a democracy.

Those who believed in democracy repudiated the idea that government should be controlled by the property holding class. Citizenship, they maintained, implied the right to vote, which was a personal right of the citizen and not contingent on the ownership of a specified amount of property. Like any other right of the individual, it was subject to reasonable regulation for the common good. It was, however, a right, and not, as the conservative claimed, a mere privilege. It could and should be withheld from such as were clearly not fit to exercise it. But in determining the question of fitness,

[12] *Law and Public Opinion in England,* p. 12.
[13] Letter to John Quincy Adams; *Works,* vol. VII, p. 224.

the state should not be guided by any external test such as
the ownership of property. The grounds upon which exclusion from the suffrage could be justified were personal and
such as clearly made one incapable of a wise use of political
power. Thus naturally followed the exclusion of criminals,
paupers, minors, and even women, who in the early days of
democracy were classed with the politically unfit.

With the growth of democracy, the old or aristocratic
view of the suffrage has been largely, though not entirely,
abandoned. The idea that government exists primarily
for the protection of property still survives in the thinking
of the well-to-do classes; and, while property qualifications
have in large measure disappeared, the influence of those
who favor suffrage restrictions has been more or less effective. Even without property qualifications many adult male
citizens are practically disfranchised. The chief substitute
for the old property holding or taxpaying qualifications for
voters is the more stringent requirement concerning residence.
This is illustrated in the New York Constitution of 1821,
which abolished the freehold qualification for the suffrage.
The extent and character of the increase made in the residence requirement at that time clearly indicate an intention
to make it serve the purpose of minimizing the effect of the
non-property holding vote. While a residence requirement
of one year in the state was added to the local residence
requirement of six months for such voters as paid taxes or
performed military service in the state militia, for all other
voters, a residence of three years in the state and one in the
locality was required, together with a highway tax to be paid
in labor or its equivalent. For colored voters, a freehold
qualification was retained.

No doubt the chief purpose of these more stringent residence requirements was to limit the wage earning vote,

as may be most clearly seen in the case of the southern states. North Carolina, in the Constitution of 1876, increased the period of residence for voters from one to two years in the state, and from thirty days to six months in the county, and added a supplementary residence qualification of four months in the precinct or election district. Virginia, before 1850, required a residence of one year in the county, city, town, or borough. The Constitution of 1850, which removed property qualifications for voters, retained the local residence requirement of one year and added a state residence requirement of two years. After the Civil War this was reduced to one year in the state and three months in the locality. The movement to restrict the Negro vote, which culminated in the Constitution of 1902, restored the residence requirement of two years in the state and one in the locality. This increase in the residence requirement is an essential part of the suffrage restrictions contained in the more recently adopted constitutions of the southern states.[14]

The Rhode Island Constitution of 1842 distinguished between two classes of voters, those who paid taxes on a freehold of a specified value and for whom a residence of one year in the state was prescribed, and those who paid taxes to the amount of at least one dollar on an estate. For the latter class of voters, a residence of two years in the state was required. When the property qualification for the

---

[14] The Alabama Constitution of 1901 raised the residence requirement in the state from one to two years, in the county from three months to one year, and in the precinct from thirty days to three months. Louisiana in 1898 increased the qualifying period of residence for voters from one to two years in the state, from six months to one year in the parish, and from thirty days to six months in the precinct. In 1895, South Carolina extended the period of residence necessary for voting from one to two years in the state, from sixty days to one year in the county, and added a residence requirement of four months in the precinct. The Mississippi Constitution of 1890 raised the residence requirement in the state from six months to two years, and from one month in the county to one year in the election district.

suffrage was removed in 1888, the two years residence requirement was extended to all voters.

The effect as well as the evident purpose of these residence requirements is to diminish the influence of those who would have been excluded under the old property holding qualifications for voting. It is the tenant farmer and the wage earner who are most likely to be disfranchised by these restrictions. Even moderate residence requirements, under present-day conditions, disfranchise many members of the wage earning class.

Educational qualifications for voters may also be regarded as a partial substitute for property holding and taxpaying restrictions. They are, for the most part, a recent development, having little practical importance outside of the southern states, where they are utilized to limit the influence of the Negro vote. Until the adoption of the Fourteenth Amendment after the Civil War, the states could disfranchise the Negro, or, as in the New York Constitution of 1821, provide special and more restrictive qualifications for colored voters. The suffrage provisions in the recently adopted constitutions of the southern states, with the exception of the residence qualifications, which exclude many of the poorer class whether white or black, may be regarded as an attempt to accomplish by indirection a disfranchisement that is racial in purpose and effect. The restrictions upon the right to vote, such as the property owning, taxpaying, and literacy tests found in these constitutions, when viewed in connection with other provisions which have the effect of exempting white voters from their operation, are as clearly designed to limit the colored vote as were the direct and express provisions of this sort in some of the earlier state constitutions.

What the framers of the later constitutions did was to

revive the old property holding and taxpaying qualifications, supplemented by an alternative educational test, and to make them apply in practice exclusively to colored voters. These provisions are an expression of the conviction that the political supremacy of the white voters must be maintained. The Fourteenth Amendment made it impossible for the southern states to retain the form of manhood suffrage without incurring the danger of political control at the hands of those elected by the colored vote. The expedients resorted to for the purpose of guarding against this possibility would probably have been adopted in any northern state confronted by similar conditions.

In many states where the right to vote for elective officials is not limited by property or taxpaying restrictions, these restrictions, nevertheless, apply to the more important matter of a vote on a proposal to incur public indebtedness for some specific purpose. In this way, the control over policies is kept very largely in the hands of the property owning class, though less obviously than was the case under the early state constitutions. The difference between total disfranchisement of non-property holders and the limitation of their influence by means of constitutional provisions of this sort, is only one of degree. Under the latter system we really have two classes of voters: those who, as property owners and taxpayers, have the unrestricted right of suffrage; and those who neither own property nor pay direct taxes and whose influence as voters is rigidly limited by constitutional provisions. Restrictions of this kind may be regarded as a compromise forced upon the advocates of manhood suffrage by those who were seeking to perpetuate the influence of property.

The demand for manhood suffrage as a political right paved the way for the woman suffrage movement. The mere fact that men had monopolized political power could not be accepted as a sufficient reason for denying women the right to vote. In an age when time-honored institutions and practices were being examined and criticized in the light of reason, it was inevitable that, with the extension of the suffrage to men, a further extension of the right to women should be demanded. Indeed, even under the theory which supported the system of property qualifications, there could be no logical defense of the practice which withheld from property owning, taxpaying women the right to vote.[15] But the question of woman suffrage did not secure any recognition until the agitation for manhood suffrage had succeeded in breaking down the more obvious and direct barriers erected in the earlier state constitutions against popular control.

The rather close connection between the general movement for the extension of the suffrage to men and the woman suffrage agitation is indicated by the fact that the first woman suffrage convention in the United States was called in 1848. The movement, however, made but little progress until after the Civil War. In 1869 women were granted the suffrage in the territory of Wyoming. The question of equal political rights for women was beginning to receive serious consideration in the early seventies. The Prohibition platform of 1872 demanded equal rights for women, and the Greenback platform of 1884 favored a woman suffrage amendment to the Constitution of the United States. Generally speaking, the woman suffrage movement has had the

---

[15] Women voted in New Jersey from 1790 to 1807. In the latter year the legislature enacted a law restricting the suffrage to white male citizens, although the Constitution of 1776, then in force, gave the right to vote to " all inhabitants . . . of full age " who could meet the property and residence requirements. The question of woman suffrage did not, however, receive serious consideration at that time, even at the hands of those most active in defending suffrage as a political right.

support of the more radical minor parties for the last fifty years. In 1912 the Progressive party proclaimed its belief that " no people can justly claim to be a true democracy which denies people rights on account of sex," and in 1916 both the Democratic and the Republican parties included in their national platforms declarations favoring the extension of the suffrage to women by the states. Fifteen states had enfranchised women when the woman suffrage amendment to the Federal Constitution was adopted in 1920. Moreover, progress toward woman suffrage had been made in many other states by granting women the right to vote in school elections or on other local questions.

Women are citizens, and citizenship, to be real and effective, must confer the right to vote. One can hardly appeal to democracy in defense of manhood suffrage, without seeing that a further extension of the suffrage to women could be justified on the same grounds. From the viewpoint of democracy, suffrage is an essential right of the normal adult citizen, necessary in order that he may be guaranteed adequate protection under the laws of the state. Governmental policies are the resultant of the various interests which find expression in the votes of the people. A disfranchised class is deprived of the only means by which its interests can be adequately protected. A class thus divested of political rights is invariably discriminated against. We need not assume that this discrimination is in any sense conscious or intentional. It may be due to the more or less obvious fact that no group or class of persons having group or class interests peculiar to themselves are, or can be, adequately represented unless they have a voice in the making of the laws by which they are governed. The history of legislation shows that women as a class are no exception to this rule. Man-made laws, even in the most democratic communities, have failed to give women adequate protection where their interests conflict with those of men. The growth of democracy has brought about a much closer approximation to equality in the civil rights of men and women; but equal protection of women, where their interests as a class conflict with those of men, can be guaranteed only by an intelligent exercise of political rights by women themselves. " Men, as well as women," says John Stuart Mill, " do not need political rights in order that they may govern, but in order that they may not be misgoverned." [16]

The democratic theory of the suffrage, which would grant the right to vote to every normal adult citizen, is regarded by those who oppose democracy as an unjustifiable attempt to establish an artificial political equality. Men, they say, are not equal in physical strength, intelligence, or moral character. Why should not this natural inequality be recognized in the organization of the state, by such restrictions on the suffrage as will keep political power in the hands of the fit? Those who emphasize inequality as an argument against democracy, however, always include themselves among the fit. The democrat might reply to them in the language of that advocate of monarchy, Thomas Hobbes, who, after affirming that men are, all things considered, substantially equal, says: " From this equality of ability, ariseth equality of hope in the attaining of our Ends." [17] His argument is to the effect that whether men are equal or unequal, no man is willing to admit his own inferiority, nor will he be satisfied under institutions and laws which discriminate against him. Since every man thinks himself the equal of other men, it is necessary for the peace and safety of the state to treat all men as equals.

[16] *Representative Government,* ch. VIII.
[17] *Leviathan,* ch. XIII.

The conservative not only assumes the existence of marked inequality, but believes that such inequality is highly desirable. According to his system of political philosophy, only those whom nature has designated as the fit should be endowed with political rights. He fails, however, to recognize the important fact that any class or group of classes that may happen to be in control of the state will always seek to justify their political privileges and to retain the material advantages derived therefrom. Moreover, the inequality that now exists is, as Hobbes says, very largely the product of unjust laws. Democracy could not, it is true, remove inequalities for which nature is responsible, but it is unalterably opposed to any policy which would make inequality more pronounced. A widely extended suffrage is necessary to safeguard society against an artificial, state-created inequality. One may be a firm believer in political democracy, without believing that men are equal in ability or worth. The conservative who conceives of democracy as a plan to establish and maintain an artificial equality is setting up a man of straw.

A democratic state with a widely extended suffrage is designed as a means of establishing and maintaining equality of political opportunity. It seeks to give to each man, not equal influence, but equal opportunity to exert such influence upon the state and its policies as is implied in the right to vote. The fact that each man may have one vote, and only one, does not make men politically equal, nor is it intended to do so. Qualities of mind and character which command confidence and respect will always give to their possessor an influence over the votes of others. True leaders, men of superior intelligence and worth, who have faith in democracy and are recognized as representing its aims and aspirations, may have far greater influence in a democratic society than would be possible under a restricted suffrage. In giving each individual the right to vote, a democratic system of government merely abolishes the political privileges which have made it possible in the past for the favored classes to control the state without due regard to the wishes or interests of the disfranchised elements in the population. With the extension of the suffrage, this power has, to some extent at least, disappeared. Classes formerly disregarded, since they had no means of registering an effective protest, must now be placated in order to secure their political support. The extension of the suffrage abolished the form, if not the substance, of the political monopoly of the ruling class. It left the members of this class, however, in possession of whatever influence was due to their wealth, intelligence, or social prestige.

Closely connected with the influence of the dominant class was the method of voting. To enfranchise the wage earning population without at the same time ensuring a secret ballot was to give, in large measure, the form without the substance of political power. This fact the wealthier classes were quick to recognize. Long before the suffrage was extended, indeed, conservatives appreciated the advantages of the *viva voce* form of voting. Their point of view is well expressed by Montesquieu: " The people's suffrages ought doubtless to be public; and this should be considered as a fundamental law of democracy. The lower class ought to be directed by those of higher rank, and restrained within bounds by the gravity of eminent personages. Hence, by rendering the suffrages secret in the Roman republic, all was lost." [18]

The wealthy class clearly saw that its political influence might be endangered if secret voting should be established. A system of secret voting would deprive the rich of the op-

[18] *The Spirit of Laws*, vol. I, bk. II, ch. 2.

portunity to use economic pressure for the purpose of controlling the votes of those dependent upon them. Landlords would have less influence over tenants; creditors, over debtors; and employers, over employees. Dependent voters, who under a system of public voting could be counted on to be amenable to advice and influence, would no longer be subject to these wholesome restraints. Even under a system which limited the suffrage to property owners and taxpayers, the well-to-do regarded the political influence of the rank and file of voters with more or less apprehension, which was reflected in the high property qualifications for the important offices under the early American state constitutions.

"In any political election," says John Stuart Mill, "even by universal suffrage (and still more obviously in the case of a restricted suffrage), the voter is under an absolute moral obligation to consider the interest of the public, not his private advantage, and give his vote, to the best of his judgment, exactly as he would be bound to do if he were the sole voter, and the election depended upon him alone. This being admitted, it is at least a *prima facie* consequence that the duty of voting, like any other public duty, should be performed under the eye and criticism of the public. . . . Undoubtedly neither this nor any other maxim of political morality is absolutely inviolable. . . .

"It may, unquestionably, be the fact that if we attempt, by publicity, to make the voter responsible to the public for his vote, he will practically be made responsible for it to some powerful individual, whose interest is more opposed to the general interest of the community than that of the voter himself would be if, by the shield of secrecy, he were released from responsibility altogether." [19]

[19] *Representative Government,* ch. X.

As a rule, secrecy in voting has accompanied or followed, and not preceded the extension of the suffrage. It was opposed by the same classes that defended property qualifications and for the same reason — the desire to keep political control in the hands of the well-to-do. A widely extended suffrage without the secret ballot was, after all, less of an evil than it had seemed. The proposal, however, to make voting secret was clearly a plan designed to make it possible for members of the dependent classes to cast independent votes. A long period of agitation and discussion was required before the secret ballot in an effective form was finally and generally established. It was not until a full half century after the suffrage was extended in the American states that laws adequately safeguarding the secrecy of the ballot were generally adopted.[20]

Even now, the fight for secrecy has not been entirely won. Under the election laws of some states, voters in primary elections must declare their party affiliations and receive a ballot on which are printed only the names of those from whom their party candidates are to be selected. This type of primary election prevents some voters, perhaps many, who would vote with a radical minor party, from voting with their party in the primary. The penalty for taking part in the selection of candidates for whom they expect to vote in the final election may keep many voters from the polls, or perhaps make it seem expedient to vote in the primary with a party which they do not intend to support. Among those who vote the Socialist ticket, for example, are many who would be made to feel the effectiveness of such discrimination as is often made use of to discourage radical voting by those economically dependent.

[20] The secret ballot for all parliamentary elections was adopted by England in 1872.

The opponents of the secret ballot professed to be the defenders of a high type of political morality. Those who are fit to vote, they contended, do not need nor desire secrecy; inasmuch as voters exercise a power conferred upon them by the state, the public have the right to know how it is used; only harm would be the result of the secret ballot; fraud and deception would be encouraged.

It is difficult, for one reviewing this controversy from the standpoint of the present time, to credit the opponents of the secret ballot with a high order of political intelligence and not impute to them a certain amount of insincerity. Fraud in elections was often perpetrated under the old system of public voting. The fact that this method of voting encouraged fraud and intimidation was one of the most telling arguments for the secret ballot. Political corruption has not entirely disappeared with the introduction of secret voting; but the direct purchase of votes is no longer good business, since those who supply the funds for this purpose can have no assurance that the votes paid for will be delivered.[21]

In England at the beginning of the World War, there was much dissatisfaction with the antiquated suffrage laws which permitted plural voting and excluded women from parliamentary elections. The plural voting system gave an undue share of political influence to the landowning class, since a landowner could vote in all districts in which he owned sufficient property to qualify him for the exercise of this right. This feature of the English suffrage laws made it possible for a minority of conservative voters to cast a majority of the votes and to control a majority of the members elected to the House of Commons. Naturally enough, the efforts

---

[21] Probably the most convincing and masterly statement of the argument for the secret ballot is to be found in the two speeches of George Grote, the historian, in volumes 17 and 28 of the *English Parliamentary Debates*.

of the Liberal party to abolish plural voting encountered determined opposition in the House of Lords.

The adoption of needed suffrage reforms was made possible by the abolition in 1911 of the veto power of the House of Lords. A comprehensive bill, systematizing and simplifying the qualifications of voters, was introduced in the House of Commons May 15, 1917. The enactment of this law increased the number of voters by extending the suffrage to about six million women. No woman can vote, however, until she has reached the age of thirty years, a discrimination against women which would seem to indicate that the members of the House were reluctantly recognizing the principle of woman suffrage. Plural suffrage was not entirely abolished, but no one may now have more than two votes.

Belgium has had a system of plural voting since 1893. To every male citizen who has attained the age of twenty-five years, is given one vote. An additional vote is conferred upon those who are heads of families and pay as householders a tax of not less than five francs, or who own land or securities of a specified value. Two additional votes are given to such as are presumed to have high educational qualifications. These include graduates of higher schools, members of the professional classes, and such as have held public office. Those who had more than one vote in 1908-9 were 40 per cent of the total number of voters and were entitled to cast 62 per cent of all the votes.

Prussia, until the reforms instituted as a result of the World War, had a system of voting which distributed political power in the state according to the amount of taxes paid. The very wealthy class, which was numerically but an insignificant minority of the population, had one-third of the representation. The larger taxpayers among the remaining population constituted another political class having one-third of the total representation. The third class, which included an overwhelming majority of the people and which with manhood suffrage would have elected practically all officials, was allowed to choose but one-third of the representatives. In this way, the public interest in state and local government was effectively subordinated to the interest of the wealthy classes.

Various devices were resorted to for the purpose of restricting still further the influence of the third class of voters. They voted less frequently than the other two classes; property qualifications were required for a certain proportion of their representatives; and the absence of the secret ballot made it possible for the small minority included in the first two classes to augment their own political predominance through economic pressure.

On account of the size of Prussia and its peculiar relation to the German Empire, the spirit and character of the Prussian state government largely determined that of the Empire. Imperial elections, at which were chosen the members of the lower house of the Parliament of the Empire, were conducted on the basis of manhood suffrage and the secret ballot. This afforded some opportunity, it is true, for the expression of national public opinion. But on account of the subordinate place of this body in the general scheme of government for the Empire, it lacked the positive power which would have made it an adequate organ of public opinion. Moreover, the Reichstag was not a body which really represented the public opinion of the Empire inasmuch as the conservative rural districts were grossly over-represented.

The German system of government as it existed until 1919, in so far as it was elective, may be described as avowedly plutocratic. It would be difficult to contrive a scheme of voting that would more effectively ensure the political supremacy of the wealthy class. But although there was no adequate popular check on the power of this class, the hereditary element was a restraining influence. Moreover, the very fact that the ascendancy of wealth in the elective part of the government was legalized and generally recognized had a moderating effect. A wealthy class thus clothed with political authority, and recognized by the public as morally accountable for the use made of its privilege, is less of a menace than it would be if its control were less directly and obviously exercised and if in consequence it were less influenced by a sense of responsibility.

The suffrage may mean much or little. Its significance depends partly on the form of government and partly on the intelligence of the citizens. It may give to the people the appearance without much of the substance of political power. Where the state is of the check and balance type, the voters have less influence than under a governmental system in which the directly elected branch is supreme. Democracy, even in the negative sense of the term, would allow the people to exercise, either directly or through representatives chosen by them, a veto on all acts and policies of the government.

A government may, however, be thoroughly democratic in form without being democratic in its practical operation. According to the democratic theory of the state, public opinion should be a controlling influence. But the state as we think it ought to be is an altogether different thing from the state as it actually is. We have not yet reached the stage in political development where the people generally have sufficient civic intelligence to enable them to play the important and responsible part which is assigned to them in the theory of democracy. The extension of the suffrage to the masses does not mean effective popular control, even where the en-

tire structure of the state has been democratized, unless the
people have acquired an active and intelligent interest in
the political and economic problems with which the government has to deal.

The idea that public opinion should be a determining political force is in fact a very recent development. Even in
the Declaration of Independence, which formulated the most
advanced political thought of the time, there is little to indicate that the people were expected to have more than a
passive part in public affairs. Democracy in the active sense
of the term is, even in this twentieth century, scarcely more
than an ideal.

The growth of popular government by transforming subjects into citizens is supposed to have changed fundamentally their relation to the state. But this transition from
subject to citizen, from passive submission to active participation, calls for a more radical change in the political outlook of the average individual than it is possible to bring
about in a comparatively short period of time. Many of
those upon whom the modern democratic movement has
attempted to confer political power have not been able to
adapt themselves readily and promptly to changes in political institutions which require them to abandon the ideas
and habits that have become more or less fixed through centuries of experience. Consequently, a new system of government is always more like the old one in its actual operation and in its spirit and results than the differences in form
would indicate.

The mere fact that a man votes does not prove that he is
a good or useful citizen; his duty to the state is discharged
only by voting wisely and with due regard to the larger social
interests, to which his interests as an individual may at times
be somewhat opposed. This ideal is impossible of realization,

however, no matter what the form of government may be, unless the people have political convictions that are the result of civic intelligence. An unintelligent vote will always be a menace to popular government in that it tends to perpetuate, under the forms of democracy, all the evils which prevailed under the old political system of class rule with its restricted suffrage and its subordination of the general interests of society to the interests of the ruling few. The vote of the unintelligent citizen is likely to be counted against, rather than for, democracy.

Unless one can vote intelligently, it is his duty to leave the determination of public policies to such as measure up to the standard of civic intelligence which democracy has a right to expect of its citizens. It is not the number of votes cast but their quality that determines the success of democratic government. If a man lacks sufficient interest in public questions to vote when important matters are up for actual determination, it is obvious that he does not feel keenly enough his responsibility for the outcome to make his participation desirable from the viewpoint of the public interest. The citizen who understands what citizenship means in a democracy, who knows the extent to which individual success and well-being depend upon wise laws well administered, will no more think of ignoring his civic obligations than of neglecting his private business. No artificial devices are needed to ensure a full vote on the part of such as are fittest to share in democratic government.

There are some who believe that voting should be made compulsory. But this is, to say the least, a debatable question, whether we believe in a restricted or a widely extended suffrage. If we favor restricting the right to vote, our object is the exclusion of the unfit. But while no standard of fitness that could be adopted would exclude all of the unfit, they largely disfranchise themselves where voting is not compulsory. The view that suffrage is a right which may justly be claimed by every normal adult citizen furnishes as little justification for the policy of compulsion as does the theory that voting is a privilege. Compulsion is not needed for those who have an active interest in the outcome of the election, nor is the welfare of the state likely to be advanced by the votes of those whose chief motive in appearing at the polls is the desire to escape a legally imposed penalty.

Compulsory voting is not a recent innovation, nor should it be regarded as essentially democratic either in origin or purpose. It existed in some of the American colonies before the Revolution, along with a greatly restricted suffrage. Virginia had compulsory voting throughout the colonial period; Maryland had it in the beginning and revived it in 1715; Delaware also had compulsory voting.[22] The Constitution of Georgia (1777) imposed a penalty of not more than five pounds for failure to vote without reasonable excuse. Under the Belgian Constitution of 1893, compulsory voting is combined with a form of plural suffrage, while in some of the Swiss cantons it exists in connection with manhood suffrage.

Compulsory voting is an attempt to transform, through the imposition of penalties, the passive element of the citizenry into an active element. A policy of this sort fails to recognize the fact that there is no satisfactory substitute for an alert civic interest on the part of those who vote. It would be far better for the state if those who are not keenly alive to their civic responsibilities would stay away from the polls, than that they should vote under any form of compulsion. Indeed, democracy has far more to fear from, than to gain by, a vote cast for the purpose of securing some im-

---

[22] See Bishop, *History of Elections in the American Colonies.*

mediate personal advantage or avoiding some personal penalty. A vote cast under any form of compulsion, whether that compulsion comes from the state itself or from some powerful private interest, is a vote not for, but against, democracy. A free ballot is the foundation of free government, and means the right to vote without being influenced by any form of coercion, either political or economic. The chief danger to democracy to-day lies not so much in its large non-voting citizenry as in the large proportion of actual voters who do not have sufficient information concerning the questions presented to enable them to vote wisely, or who, through pressure of some private or partisan interest, cast votes which do not represent their independent political choice. How to safeguard the ballot so as to ensure intelligent and independent voting is a problem for which democracy must find a solution.

It is no doubt highly desirable that all normal adult citizens should have the right to vote. Democracy in the true sense of the term can not exist where any considerable part of the population is outside the pale of political rights. Equality of opportunity is a principle which must be recognized in the organization of the state, or democracy will exist only in name. The right to vote and, through the vote, to share in determining the policy of the state is the indispensable guaranty of equality of economic opportunity, which it is the duty of every free government to establish and maintain.

The right to vote, properly viewed, is an opportunity extended by the state to the citizen, and he should be free to take advantage of it or ignore it. Sound public policy points not in the direction of compelling citizens to vote, but rather in the direction of making the exercise of this right purely voluntary by removing every influence which now militates against free choice. We can readily see that a man who must be paid to go to the polls is not likely to advance the welfare of the community when he votes; nor is that man actuated by a much higher motive, whose main interest in politics depends upon some concession, favor, or office at the hands of the party to which he is giving his support.

We should discourage by legislation when possible, and by every other practicable means, all efforts to influence the outcome of elections by bringing to bear upon the individual voter either the threat of individual punishment or the promise of individual reward. To allow intimidation or coercion, direct or indirect, or the promise of some personal favor or advantage, to be a factor in determining whether or not votes are cast and how they are cast, is to place such votes at the disposal of those interests against which it behooves democracy to be on its guard.

We should not be oblivious of the fact that the right to vote is of value to citizens only to the extent that it gives them the power to control the government. If the constitutional system be such as to tie the hands of the majority, as is the case in this country, the natural and inevitable result is, by limiting the influence of the vote, to discourage political activity on the part of citizens. An election must be the means of determining legislation, or intelligent citizens are likely to feel that suffrage is the empty form of a political right without its substance. A system of government which makes it possible for a small minority to prevent the enactment and enforcement of laws which a large majority may have endorsed at the polls naturally operates to discourage political interest and activity on the part of citizens.

CHAPTER IV

SOME INDIRECT RESULTS OF THE
EXTENSION OF THE SUFFRAGE

The attempt to justify the American Revolution was based very largely on certain fundamental democratic ideas. But as soon as independence was an accomplished fact and the American colonies were bound together more securely by the adoption of the Constitution of the United States, the earlier Revolutionary propaganda, which emphasized human rights and democratic organization, largely subsided. The desire for political reconstruction along new and better lines, so much in evidence in the literature of the Revolutionary period, gave place to the desire to create an effective public opinion that would unify the country as a whole and ensure its support of the newly established federal government.

This seemingly difficult task was thoroughly accomplished. Our political institutions were all but deified. The critical attitude, so essential for the normal development of our civic life, practically disappeared. Political problems were no longer discussed in textbooks and in the accepted literature of the day with reference to fundamental principles. The basic questions were supposed to have been settled, once for all time, when the main features of our political structure were embodied in the authoritative form of constitutional law. There was created an attitude of mind that was satisfied with political discussion which took for granted the essential soundness of the constitutional groundwork of our political society, and was concerned almost exclusively with questions of constitutional interpretation and such subordinate matters of legislation and public policy as were adjudged to fall within the competence of governmental agencies.

Perhaps the most potent cause for this trend of political discussion away from the fundamentals of governmental organization and toward its more superficial aspects was the predominant influence of lawyers in the public life of the country throughout the early decades of our history. This diverted discussion of public questions into legal channels and made established constitutional rules the accepted criteria to which all matters of policy should conform. To transcend the limits thus fixed in the fundamental law, was to attack the very foundation of the state itself. Only a bold and reckless innovator would attempt this in the face of general acquiescence in the assumed soundness of the basic principles of our political structure.

This legalistic viewpoint, which has been a distinguishing characteristic of our political leaders, has made discussion of public questions turn very largely on the matter of constitutionality. The limitations which this situation imposed upon political debate favored the constitutional lawyer and discouraged constructive statesmanship. The larger aspects of social justice and political expediency were subordinated to a legal conception which practically ruled out of order all discussion except such as pertained to laws and policies within the field left open to legislation by existing constitutional law as authoritatively interpreted by the courts.

In this respect America is in striking contrast to England, the country from which we inherited our legal and political institutions. Under the English conception of fundamental law, nothing can be unconstitutional which Parliament, supposedly representing the intelligence and conscience of the nation, may deem necessary. This permits discussion of all public questions on their merits, instead of confining debate, as in this country, largely to the one point of constitutionality. Since the word unconstitutional has no place in the political dictionary of Great Britain, attention, there, is focused on the wisdom and justice of a proposal. In this country, however, it is necessary to make out a case for the constitutionality of any proposed legislation before we can hope to secure for it serious political consideration. The strongest argument against any radical measure is the purely legal one, that if the proposed law were placed upon the statute books it would be declared unconstitutional by the courts. This gives to the conservative members of legislative bodies a very real tactical advantage, which they can and do use effectively in opposing reform legislation. The possibility of judicial annulment of legislation is thus a convenient and ever ready pretext for opposition which could not be successfully made on any other grounds.

The responsibility for this situation can not, however, be attributed wholly to the influence of lawyers, since they have had the coöperation and support of the older and more conservative school of writers on political science. The latter have almost without exception made their discussion of American institutions and problems hinge on the legal theory of the Constitution, which has supplied the norm by which not only laws and policies but even the literature of politics has been evaluated. No writer could hope to win recognition in this field who did not pay homage to our constitutional system by making it the criterion by which controverted questions were to be finally decided. Any attempt to go back of the Constitution itself, and to examine the fundamental facts and principles of organization at the basis of the state, has encountered the opposition of that formidable group of interests whose main purpose is to prevent such changes in governmental organization as would make the will of the majority a more potent influence in legislation.

The legal theory of the constitutional system has been the starting point for practically every systematic treatise on American government and even for elementary books on civics designed for students in the public schools. The effect of this has been to popularize the purely legal conception of constitutional law, and thus to separate in large measure current political thinking from those basic ideas that supply the standards by which not only ordinary legislation but even constitutions should be judged. This accounts for the purely formal and, for the most part, barren character of our later contribution to the literature of political science. The mental attitude implied in the acceptance of constitutions as authoritative declarations concerning the fundamentals of political organization tends to remove all matters thus dealt with out of the realm of political controversy. It has made it possible for a political literature, conservative in origin and purpose, to ignore much that should be freely and fully discussed. The respectable conservative, who is satisfied with things as they are, is inclined to view any discussion which raises the question of the wisdom or justice of existing constitutional law, in much the same way that the constitutional lawyer regards the effort to secure the enactment of unconstitutional laws.

To start with the assumption that our constitutions were based upon the idea of popular sovereignty is a convenient political fiction which has enabled writers to evade the discussion of such vitally important questions as the extension of the suffrage and the apportionment of representation. To ignore these is, in fact, to ignore the very foundation upon which the government of the state rests. The qualifications for voting and for holding office, and the plan of apportioning representation in the legislative body, may be such as to place control of the state government in the hands of the minority. Questions such as these are supremely important from the viewpoint of political democracy. The removal of property qualifications during the first half of the nineteenth century was, in the opinion of both radicals and conservatives, one of the most important, if not the most important, fact in the political history of the United States. The radical hoped and the conservative feared that it would eventually lead to the political supremacy of the majority.

The conservatives who opposed the extension of the suffrage as a dangerous political experiment now directed their attention to the problem of minimizing its effects. One means of accomplishing this was by controlling the apportionment of representation. The advocates of political democracy saw clearly enough that the extension of the suffrage would not put political power in the hands of the majority until representation in both houses was based upon population. But as this democratic principle was recognized in state constitutions only to a limited extent, the conservative minority was, in many cases, in actual control of one or both branches of the legislature.

In a new country, such as the United States at the time of the adoption of the Constitution, with a population predominantly rural, and with what appeared to be a practically unlimited supply of agricultural land, the extension of the suffrage involved no immediate peril to the stability of government in either state or nation. The ease with which property in land could be acquired, and the restrictions on representation of mere population, furnished a reasonable assurance that for some time to come both the state and the national government would continue to reflect the viewpoint and interests of the taxpaying property holder. It was only in the cities that the existence of a numerous body of propertyless laboring men made the extension of the suffrage, in the opinion of the more conservative classes, a dangerous experiment. It was feared that the large wage earning class, having little or no property and paying little or no direct taxes, would seek to use its newly acquired political power for its own advantage, and thus place additional burdens upon those who, before the extension of the suffrage, had controlled municipal policies.

In the New York constitutional convention of 1821, the opponents of manhood suffrage repeatedly called attention to the danger of enfranchising the laboring population of the cities. " The city of New-York," said Judge Van Ness, " now contains a population of 123,000. . . . It is rapidly increasing. . . . The time is not distant, when those that have nothing, will form a majority in cities and large villages, and constitute a large portion of the population, even in the country. . . . By an irreversible decree of Providence, it is pronounced, ' the poor ye have always with you ' — people who have no interest in your institutions — no fixedness of habitation — no property to defend. And is it not in human nature to envy superiority, in whatever it may consist; and to wish to dispossess, and obtain that which is envied? " [1]

Chancellor Kent of the supreme court, one of the most uncompromising advocates of a restricted suffrage, said: " The growth of the city of New-York is enough to startle and awaken those who are pursuing the *ignis fatuus* of universal suffrage. . . . New-York is destined to become the future London of America; and in less than a century, that

[1] N. Y. Const. Conv., 1821, *Debates*, pp. 268–69.

city, with the operation of universal suffrage, and under skillful direction, will govern this state." [2]

The effect of the Constitution of 1821, according to Abraham Van Vechten, was to increase more than threefold the number of senatorial voters in the city of New York. " What their increase will be in the course of ten or twenty years," he said, " who can tell? Then, who will undertake to say that real property will remain constitutionally secure, for twenty years to come, under the operation of the proposed extension of the right of suffrage? " [3]

Albert Gallatin in a letter to Lafayette, dated May 12, 1833, expressed what was no doubt the generally accepted viewpoint of the well-to-do class at that time: " The reason [for the increase in local expenditures] appears to me obvious enough; government is in the hands of the people at large. . . . They receive an immediate benefit from the money expended amongst themselves. . . . They in fact pay little or no portion of the direct tax. . . . Those who contribute to such payment ought alone to have the privilege of being electors." [4] On another occasion he expressed the opinion, based on American experience, that the dangers of universal suffrage are most in evidence in the cities.[5]

The extension of the suffrage brought about a realignment of the political forces within the state. Even before the suffrage was extended, the political influence of cities was regarded with some apprehension. Those who owned the wealth and controlled the rapidly growing commerce of the cities had material interests that were more or less distinct from, and in some respects opposed to, the interests of the landowning, agricultural population. The extension of the

[2] N. Y. Const. Conv., 1821, *Debates*, p. 221.
[3] *Ibid.*, p. 228.
[4] *Works*, vol. II, p. 473.
[5] Letter to Louis Pictet, Oct. 23, 1842; *Works*, vol. II, p. 601.

suffrage did nót remove the cause of this conflict of interests; but it created a new political force which threatened the supremacy of the commercial class in city government and of landowners in the government of the state. The result was what we may call a defensive alliance between the landowning, agricultural population of the state and the former ruling class in the cities, the purpose of which was to minimize the political influence of the labor vote.

What the well-to-do class most feared was the effect of a democratic suffrage on taxation and expenditure. The masses within the larger cities, contributing little in the way of direct taxes and receiving much benefit from public expenditure, would, they thought, be too much inclined to favor high municipal taxes. Naturally, those who were opposed to municipal democracy appealed to the state for protection against the newly enfranchised masses. A degree of municipal self-government that would have been regarded as insufficient before the suffrage was extended now came to be looked upon by the wealthier portion of the city population as a source of real danger. Their attitude from this time on was one of distrust of, and opposition to, local self-government as applied to urban communities. State control of municipal affairs, if not in itself desirable, was at least less dangerous than a local control in which a non-taxpaying class had a leading part.[6] That the desire to counteract in some measure the influence of this new municipal electorate upon local policies had much to do with the increase of state interference in municipal affairs is clearly seen in contemporary discussions. This fact, however, has been entirely ignored by American writers on municipal government.

Up to the time the suffrage was extended, but little atten-

[6] See the author's *The Spirit of American Government*, published in 1907; pp. 285–87.

tion had been given to the question of the apportionment of representation. The system which prevailed in the United States was a compromise in which territory and population were recognized in varying degrees. In such states as Connecticut and Rhode Island apportionment was very largely based on the conservative principle of territorial representation, while in other states the emphasis was on the theory that representation should be in proportion to population.

Conservative opinion in the eighteenth century did not regard apportionment of representation as a political problem of especial importance. The idea, then generally accepted by the ruling class, that government existed primarily for the protection of property, assumed that economic interests rather than population should be the basis of representation. From the viewpoint of those who then controlled governmental policies, it was supremely important that legislators should adequately represent the property holding interests. So long as this view continued to be reflected in property qualifications for voting and for holding public office, it could not be expected that there would be much interest in theories of apportionment. The democratic theory that representation should be apportioned according to population, though entirely consistent with the social contract idea of the state, was in fact irreconcilable with property qualifications for voters. It was not until after the suffrage had been extended that the method of apportioning representation assumed real importance.

Before property qualifications for voters were abolished, the method of apportioning representation in a number of states augmented the influence of rural districts at the expense of the cities. These inequalities in representation did much to counteract the effect of a democratic suffrage. It was very soon recognized, however, that if the legislature was to be representative of the public opinion of the state, the members of that body would have to be apportioned according to population. As long as political power was distributed without regard to population, or, as was the case in many instances, so apportioned as to subordinate the influence of the majority, public opinion found little opportunity for effective political expression. The over-representation of the more conservative rural districts was the practical equivalent of a plural voting system designed to limit the political influence of the more radical urban communities.

Those who had opposed the extension of the suffrage were naturally enough arrayed against the proposal to apportion representation according to population. The struggle which has been on from that day to this in state legislatures and constitutional conventions over the question of the distribution of representation, is in reality the old suffrage question in a new form. State government can not be a very effective instrument in the hands of democracy until representation is so apportioned as to make the legislature a fairly accurate reflection of the public opinion of the state.

There are seventeen states [7] whose constitutions provide that the members of both houses are to be apportioned according to population.[8] In the remaining thirty-one states there are constitutional provisions which discriminate against the more populous counties or the distinctly urban districts. A common form of discrimination is the requirement that each county shall have at least one representative in the lower house. This may be very effective where the constitution limits the number of members and where the power

[7] Calif., Colo., Ill., Ind., Ky., Mass., Mich., Minn., Neb., Nev., N. M., N. D., Ore., S. D., Tenn., Wash., and Wis.
[8] Ewan Clague, *The Theory and Practice of Representation in the United States,* a thesis submitted for the M. A. degree in Political Science, University of Washington, 1921.

of the legislature to create new counties may be freely exercised.

An examination of the state constitutions shows that some form of discrimination against the larger cities is the rule rather than the exception. But the constitutions give little indication of the extent to which urban communities are under-represented in the state legislatures. One is reminded in this connection of John Stuart Mill's statement that " All trust in constitutions is grounded on the assurance that they may afford, not that the depositaries of power will not, but that they cannot, misemploy it." [9] He may not have been thinking of the United States when he made this observation, but, at any rate, it accurately describes the typical American attitude toward constitutional law. We seem to take it for granted that the principles recognized in our constitutions can not be disregarded by the officials to whom their administration is entrusted. This childlike faith in the efficacy of constitutional provisions, for which we are indebted to the legal profession, will be rudely shattered when political literature comes to be written from the viewpoint of a more sympathetic understanding of the needs and ideals of democracy. The more or less prevalent American belief that constitutions have some peculiar and inherent potency by which they effectively control legislatures and other governmental agencies, belongs to the kindergarten stage of democracy. Our political literature still begins and ends very largely as a study of constitutional provisions. What is needed is to relate our study of constitutions to the actual facts of political organization. If this were systematically and thoroughly done, it would dispel for all time this naïve political superstition concerning the efficacy of mere constitutional provisions. A comparison of the facts relating to

[9] *Representative Government,* ch. VIII.

the actual apportionment of representation with the constitutional requirements to which they should, but do not, conform, would be sufficient to disillusion even the most uncritical.

There are at the present time thirteen state constitutions [10] which require the taking of a state census at the middle of every decade and which also require the legislature to reapportion representation according to population after each federal and state census. A few facts concerning the situation in these states are sufficient to show that something more than a democratic constitution is necessary to ensure political democracy. In only four of these states [11] was the state census taken in the year 1915 as required by the constitution. North Dakota is apparently the only state in which this provision has been continually enforced. In several of these states, such as Utah and Washington, the constitutional provision for a state census has been entirely ignored.

The legislative attitude toward reapportionment is reflected in the failure to make provision by law for the state census, since the purpose of the census, as specified in the constitution itself, is to make it possible to reapportion representation according to population at the following session of the legislature. In several of the states, the constitutional rules governing the times and the manner of reapportioning representation have been flagrantly disregarded.[12] The

[10] Colo., Iowa, Kans., Minn., Mont., Neb., Ore., N. Y., N. D., S. D., Utah, Wash., and Wyo.

[11] N. Y., N. D., S. D., and Wyo.

[12] The state of Washington offers a rather striking example of the nullification of such constitutional provisions by public officials. Not only does its constitution provide for a state census at the middle of every decade, but it also requires a reapportionment of both houses strictly according to population after each federal and each state census, or every five years. The last reapportionment was the one following the census of 1900 and this did not conform to the constitutional requirement. By thus ignoring the reap-

large cities are, as a rule, denied their fair share of representation in one or both branches of the legislature. In
some cases this discrimination is authorized by the constitution itself; in others it is brought about by the legislature
without the sanction and even in violation of the constitution. The situation in many of our states is strikingly
similar in kind and degree to that recently existing in
Germany where the city of Berlin had only six members in
the Reichstag, when, on the basis of population, it should
have had twenty. Nor is the motive which has been responsible for withholding adequate representation of urban communities in the United States essentially different from that
of the German Junkers who opposed a reapportionment
which would, by giving the cities more representation, have
increased the political influence of the radical party.

The obvious purpose of constitutional provisions making
it the duty of the legislatures of the states to reapportion
representation according to population at certain specified
and frequently recurring dates, was to guarantee that state
legislatures would at all times be representative of the public
opinion of the states. From the viewpoint of political democracy, these provisions are fundamental, as much so,
indeed, as those relating to the suffrage itself. To ignore
them, as state legislatures have repeatedly done, is to overthrow the majority government established by the constitution and to make the minority the controlling power in the
state. It allows the legislature to nullify the one basic constitutional guaranty of democracy — that the majority in
the legislature shall be elected by, and be representative of,
the majority of the voters. If there is any case where the

portionment provisions of the constitution, rural control of the legislature
has been perpetuated in a state in which the majority of the people now
live under urban conditions.

public need to be protected against the abuse of governmental power, it is that of the non-use or misuse by the legislature of the power to apportion representation. Yet in this matter, which involves the very existence of the form of government established by the constitution, the judiciary has generally held that the legislature can not be compelled to reapportion representation as required by the constitution.

If the courts fail us at the very point where their aid as guardians of the constitutions is most needed for the preservation of democracy, it may be due in some measure, perhaps, to lack of sympathy on the part of judges with the principle on which provisions of this sort rest. Had courts been as anxious throughout our history as a nation to encourage and defend majority rule as they have been to prevent it, it is altogether probable that they would have been able to discover means by which legislatures could be made to obey constitutions. The principle that our American courts have acted upon in declaring laws null and void might have been used quite as effectively for democracy as against it. A legislature elected after the constitutional mandate to reapportion has been ignored has not been legally chosen and does not represent the people of the state in the way required by the constitution. The courts could have refused to recognize the right of such a body to exercise the general lawmaking power. No doubt lawyers would reply that there must be a *de facto* legislature, since if this were not the case there would be no agency available for the enactment of such a reapportionment measure as the constitution requires. But though the necessity of recognizing the competency of some body to exercise certain functions of the legislature which are in a sense administrative, such as the enactment of apportionment and needed appropriation laws, may be admitted, it does not follow that such a body must be regarded as having general lawmaking power. The courts could have refused to recognize the right of an illegally organized legislature to exercise this power, by declaring such general acts null and void. By this means, they could have compelled the legislative branch of the state government to obey the apportionment provision of the state constitution. This, however, has not been the attitude of the courts. Indeed, they have shown as little sympathy with political democracy as the legislatures have, and this is, perhaps, the chief reason why the people have had so little assistance from the judiciary in their effort to make the reapportionment provisions of state constitutions effective.

The effects of the situation above described are not confined to the state governments, but extend even to the national House of Representatives. The members of this body are, by the Constitution of the United States, apportioned among the various states according to population, and, by act of Congress, the Representatives are to be elected in each state from " districts composed of contiguous and compact territory containing as nearly as practicable an equal number of inhabitants." It is the duty of the state legislature to create the congressional districts from which the Representatives assigned to that state are elected. The federal law governing the matter of the creation of congressional districts by state legislatures is clear and explicit in requiring that representation shall be apportioned according to population. Nevertheless, this rule has been quite generally, and in many instances flagrantly, disregarded by state legislatures.

It is significant that the large congressional districts, like the large state legislative districts, are generally urban, while

the small districts are as a rule rural. The over-representation of rural population in the state legislatures has thus
had the effect of bringing about a similar over-representation
in the federal House of Representatives.

Until the adoption of the Seventeenth Amendment in
1913, providing for the direct election of United States Senators, the members of the upper house of Congress were no
more representative of the popular majority in the various
states than were the local legislative bodies by which they
were chosen. Indirect election of United States Senators
would, no doubt, have been less unsatisfactory if state legislatures had been so apportioned as to make them representative of the majority of the voters.

This general practice of discriminating against the majority in the apportionment of representation has made the
amendment of both state and federal constitutions more
difficult, since the people must look to these unrepresentative
legislative bodies for the submission of proposed amendments and, in the case of the federal Constitution, their
ratification.

As pointed out above, the extension of the suffrage
alarmed the well-to-do classes in the cities, and brought their
influence to bear on the state government for the purpose of
protecting their interests against the non-property holding
voters in the large urban communities. In the decades immediately following the extension of the suffrage, the well-
to-do classes regarded the problem of city government as
one mainly of taxation and expenditure. This made them
view with favor any increase in state control over cities and,
at the same time, ensured their support for the practice of
giving cities, with their large non-property holding vote,
less than their proportionate share of representation. They
looked upon such discrimination against cities as a proper
and necessary safeguard against democratic abuses. In

this way, it was thought, the irresponsible radicalism of the cities could be controlled. The conservatism of the state government would be guaranteed through the over-representation of the rural population, and state interference would offer a remedy for the evils inflicted upon cities by the extension of the suffrage. If the old restrictions on the right to vote and to hold office had been retained, it would have been much less difficult to secure or to maintain for cities a reasonable measure of local self-government. The extension of the suffrage aroused a feeling of apprehension among conservatives which had much to do with the unfriendly attitude that legislatures and courts have shown toward local self-government as applied to urban communities. It is quite clear that in many instances state interference in municipal affairs was proposed and defended on the ground that the municipal taxpayer needed protection against the propertyless voters.

Speaking in support of a proposal to allow only tax-payers who owned property to the value of at least $1,000.00 to vote for members of the board of aldermen, a member of the New York constitutional convention of 1867–68, representing the business interests of the city of New York, said: " If these safeguards . . . be not adopted, then, for one, I shall feel constrained to vote against every proposed increase of governmental power to cities. . . . Now, sir, what has produced this condition of things? Sir, it was produced by the fact that when the whole of the administrative departments of the city were in the hands of officials chosen by the electors of the city, it was found that the taxes for local purposes were rapidly augmenting. . . . The citizens naturally looked to the Legislature for relief. The Legislature responded by creating these State commissions of which we have heard so much." [13]

[13] Opdyke, N. Y. Const. Conv., 1867–68, *Debates*, vol. IV, pp. 2976–77.

Another speaker asked: " Is there any reason . . . why the ignorant masses which largely preponderate in our large cities should hold the lives, property and health of our better class of citizens in their hands? . . . Why should that mass of people be allowed to determine the amount of taxes and what proportion each man shall pay . . . ? " [14] Here we find frankly stated the reason which, more than any other, made the well-to-do classes in the cities favor state interference — the desire to keep the control of local policies out of the hands of the newly enfranchised masses. This was clearly the predominant motive during the decades immediately following the extension of the suffrage.

Another phase of this same struggle is seen in the constitutional provisions limiting the right of cities to incur indebtedness. They represent, generally speaking, a somewhat later development of state interference, appearing just at the time when municipal utilities, such as water, gas, and transportation, were coming to be recognized as offering a lucrative field for the investment of private capital. Such restrictions on the borrowing power of cities were doubtless due in part, though not wholly, to the desire of the well-to-do for protection against high taxes. Another influence which probably had an important share in bringing about the adoption of these provisions was the fear on the part of certain interests that cities would utilize their credit for the purpose of municipal ownership. Evidence in support of this statement may be found in the proceedings of constitutional conventions of that period.

The Pennsylvania Constitution of 1873 contained a provision which limited the debt of any county, city, or borough to seven per cent of the assessed value of its taxable property. Speaking in support of this restriction on the borrow-

[14] Hand, N. Y. Const. Conv., 1867–68, *Debates,* vol. IV, p. 3017.

ing power of cities, a member of the convention which framed the document said: " Now, I am ready to admit that water works are to be built and that gas works are to be built, when a town or municipality will warrant such expenditures. But in all such cases persons will come forward ready to invest their money if they see profit in it, and those works will be built by private corporations. And let me say here . . . that all these works are better managed, more economically managed, by private corporations . . . than they can be by any municipal corporations." [15]   Other speakers expressed similar views though the reason generally given for favoring the proposed restriction was the desire to extend protection to the property holders in the cities.

The preference for private ownership expressed by some members of the convention may have been largely mere prejudice on the part of the business class against any policy that would restrict the field of private initiative, though it is probable that the public utility corporations were behind much of this professedly disinterested opposition to municipal ownership. The attitude of the taxpaying class with reference to the question of public or private ownership was, no doubt, largely determined by the fact that it no longer felt sure of its power to control municipal elections. In view of this situation, there was little chance that public ownership of municipal utilities could be used to lighten the taxpayer's burden. Indeed, it was likely to increase it by diminishing the amount of taxable property in the community. The opposition to public ownership voiced by chambers of commerce and other business organizations in our cities is due much less to any sentimental objection to this policy than to the fact that they are no longer confident of their ability to control it. Under a restricted suffrage, it is

[15] M'Allister, Penn. Const. Conv., 1872, *Debates*, vol. III, p. 283.

conceivable, in fact probable, that the well-to-do class would have little prejudice against public ownership or extended powers of local self-government for cities. The favor with which this same class has regarded public ownership in Prussian cities may be accounted for by the fact that, under their suffrage system, control of local affairs has been until recently securely in the hands of the property owning class. The democratization of the suffrage, which was brought about at the close of the World War, will probably have the effect of making the well-to-do class in Prussia much less sympathetic with the policy of municipal ownership.

Never heretofore have the interests opposed to democracy been so thoroughly organized, so powerful, or so difficult to cope with. The centralization of economic and financial power in the hands of a small class representing the public utilities and the large business interests has enabled organized wealth to exert an influence upon governmental institutions, which, though somewhat indirect and disguised, is much more effective than is generally supposed. The tremendous power which has been acquired by those who control the trusts, the public utilities, and the closely affiliated interests of the country, would not be permitted in a thoroughly democratized political society. For this reason, every effort to establish real self-government for a city, or to make the legislature of a state representative of the majority, encounters the opposition of interests that are nation-wide in the scope of their activities and influence.

It must not be supposed that it is only in the United States that it is difficult to secure a fair apportionment of representation. The practice of counteracting the effect of a widely extended suffrage through over-representation of the more conservative rural population is, in fact, more or less general. Even in remote Australia, famed for its supposed democracy, may be found discrimination against cities in the apportionment of representation no less flagrant than that by which the influence of urban population in the Reichstag was curtailed under the German Empire.[16] Indeed, the ruling class is everywhere quick to recognize that this is an expedient method of circumventing the advocates of political democracy. It does not necessarily require the enactment of any unjust or discriminatory apportionment legislation. Mere inaction on the part of legislatures, or failure to pass reapportionment laws, is all that is needed in most modern states where urban population is rapidly increasing, to ensure over-representation of the conservative rural minority.

The opposition to adequate representation of urban population and to municipal self-government comes to-day, primarily, not from the rural communities, but from the wealthy class in the cities, as it did in the period immediately following the extension of the suffrage. The present-day city is supposed to contain too many voters who are infected with radical political and economic ideas, to make it safe, from the viewpoint of the capitalist, to permit it to exercise a large measure of self-government, or to grant it the representation in the legislature to which its population would entitle it.

The policy, so widely supported by organized wealth, of seeking to control legislation by manipulating the apportionment of representation has been favored as a safeguard against radicalism; but, as a matter of fact, it could be employed by any minority, plutocratic or proletarian, that chanced to come into possession of political power, for the purpose of perpetuating its control. Indeed, the Constitu-

[16] *The Melbourne Herald*, July 25, 1922, gives many examples of gross discrimination against cities, showing that 303,766 metropolitan voters had the same representation in the Parliament of Victoria as 59,935 rural voters.

tion of the Russian Soviet Republic, adopted in 1918, expressly provides that urban population shall have five times as much representation as an equal amount of rural population. The radicals who drafted this Constitution were familiar with the method by which capitalistic countries deprive their popular majorities of the power to control the legislatures, and promptly adopted it for the purpose of perpetuating the power of the very class against which it had hitherto been invoked. Modern capitalism, in seeking to maintain for its own advantage an artificial, conservative majority in legislative bodies, may yet discover that it has established a dangerous precedent, one which can be used as easily to ensure control by a radical as by a conservative minority.

Chapter V

THE CONSTITUTION–INTERPRETING POWER IN THE
PERIOD IMMEDIATELY FOLLOWING THE
ADOPTION OF THE CONSTITUTION

The Constitution of the United States was adopted as a result of the conservative reaction which followed the American Revolution. It was framed supposedly on the theory that all power should be limited. It checked political authority by balancing the organs of the federal government over against one another, the federal government as a whole against the governments of the states, and the government, federal and state, against the people. Nevertheless, the most significant feature of the Constitution was the elaborate system of checks imposed on the will of the majority and the foundation that was thus laid for the development of the powers of the general government.

The chief concern of the framers of the Constitution was to guard against the development of popular sovereignty in the sense of untrammeled majority control. It was popular rather than governmental aggression that they feared. If the majority were permitted to control the government, it was argued, the rights of the minority would be overridden. To check the power of the majority, the framers of the Constitution sought to place political authority more largely in the hands of the federal government and, at the same time, to make the latter an effective check, both on the more democratic state governments and on the people of the country as a whole.

The framers of the Constitution were greatly impressed by the danger to liberty which they believed to be inherent in political democracy. A government controlled by the majority was in their opinion the greatest possible menace to the rights and liberty of the individual. It was more dangerous than monarchy or aristocracy because of the physical force of numbers behind it. In the very nature of the case, a government organized as a political democracy would be subject to no effective check. In monarchies and aristocracies, the potential resistance of the masses served in greater or less degree to temper governmental policies; but this moderating influence would be inoperative in a political democracy, where governmental authority was under the control of the majority.

The partisans of the Constitution, conservative by inheritance, education, and interest, made the most of their opportunity to discredit democracy. Their attempt to make it responsible for the evils which followed the Revolutionary War was, of course, merely a familiar conservative artifice, which would have reacted against the proposed Constitution, had the people generally possessed a higher degree of political intelligence. To anyone acquainted with the restrictions on suffrage and officeholding and with the system of representation of that time, there would seem to be no justification for the Federalist charge that the evils of the day were due to an excess of democracy.

It may seem strange to us to-day that the framers of the Constitution should have been so much alarmed by the democratic abuses of the time, in view of the fact that suffrage and officeholding restrictions not only excluded the majority of the people from any share in political control but even limited the influence of the voting class. But their concern was due less to the advance actually made toward political democracy than to the possibility of popular control in the future. It was mainly for the purpose of arresting the tendency toward political democracy that the system of checks and balances in the federal Constitution was devised.

With the adoption of the Constitution, there was established a more effective political check on the governments of the various states. But in strengthening the authority of the central government there was no intention to make it supreme. Sovereignty, in the sense of supreme unlimited power, was not recognized by the founders of our government as properly belonging to any political agency. All authority was, in their opinion, limited, and necessarily so if individual liberty were to be maintained. In addition to the checks and balances operative within the governmental system, there was, back of the governmental organization, a system of law by which it was limited and to which it was required to conform.

This law was in part definitely formulated as a written constitution, in which the chief features of the government were supposed to be outlined and its relation to the people determined. In large part, however, it was unwritten, but none the less binding. Indeed, this unwritten law was regarded as more basic and fundamental than any written law, and to it all written law, both constitutional and statutory, should conform. With the development of the modern idea of constitutional government, there had grown up a conception of certain natural laws or principles, which might be called, not inaccurately, a natural unwritten constitution. The powers of the government were thus limited, not only by the division of authority within the government itself, but also from without, by the Constitution and by the still more basic law which found expression in the generally accepted doctrines of natural law, natural rights, the social contract theory, and the theory of individual liberty.

After the adoption of the Constitution, the great political issues continued to revolve, as they had done in the earlier stages of constitutional development, around the division, distribution, and limitation of political power. The advocates of liberty and democracy stood for the policy of restricting and limiting governmental authority, while the opponents of individual liberty and political democracy favored the centralization of political power.

The significance of this struggle, however, is not always understood by the public. The real issues often, in fact generally, lie far below the surface of political controversy and are either unsuspected by the people or but vaguely apprehended. It requires exceptional intelligence to see more than the direct and immediate effects of political causes, although such effects may be of slight importance in comparison with the indirect and ultimate consequences. For this reason the vital questions of politics are often outside the field of popular interest.

The course of political development, even in a society organized as a political democracy, is thus only superficially and in no determining sense subject to popular control. There is a high degree of continuity in institutional development, in legislation, in governmental policies, which at any given time operates to restrict the choice of both means and ends. Only those who see far ahead, who understand ultimate consequences as well as immediate effects, are likely to have an appreciable influence in determining the direction of political development. Theoretically, public opinion is the final arbiter in a democratic state, but, in practice, commonly accepted opinion, even under a purely democratic form of government, can hardly be regarded as a determining political force. Popular control will never become an actuality until the people generally acquire a much higher degree of political intelligence than any community has thus far possessed. Effective control of the state means much more than the dependence of public officials on popular approval for continuance in office.

The political situation at any given time is infinitely complex. It is the outcome of innumerable forces, tendencies, and conditions — economic, religious, social, political — which very largely determines the course of development in the immediate future.

Institutions and laws are not manufactured. They come into existence as a result of slow growth and development. The most radical innovations in institutional arrangements or in legislation are, after all, but slight adaptations to meet some change in viewpoint or purpose. No matter how democratic the form of the state, institutions and policies yield but slowly to the pressure of public opinion. Only those influences which persist through a considerable period of time are likely to leave a permanent impress upon institutional life. The significant movements may lie far below the surface of politics, unseen and unsuspected by those whose lives are destined in the end to be profoundly affected by them, or, if their influence is felt, they may seem to be due to purely natural causes and not to conscious human purpose. But in the growth of institutional arrangements, conscious planning and farseeing purpose have a much more important place than is generally recognized. This intelligent continuing purpose which leaves its impress on political development is less likely, however, to be that of a popular majority than of some small compact class-conscious group which realizes that no momentary effort can achieve permanent results. Significant movements are likely to represent the viewpoint and interests of intelligent and active minorities and may be wholly opposed to the real interests of the popular majority.

But few people possess the political intelligence and capacity for sustained coöperative effort required in those who influence the course of public affairs. The interest of the ordinary person in politics is largely confined to the present and the immediate future. He does not realize how largely control of the state as a going concern is conditioned by the past, and that present political control is less effective for the purpose of securing immediate results than for determining the direction of future development. It is the direct and immediate results of political control that interest the majority, yet these may be of minor importance compared with the indirect and ultimate consequences which only a few foresee. Such control of political development as is possible is, in fact, less a control of the form and functions of the state as it now is than as it will be in the future. Little may be done in the way of bringing about immediate reforms in the state or its policies; but much may be accomplished in laying the foundation for future changes and in giving direction to future development. It is here, however, that democracy is weak. Popular interest is focused on that part of the political field which yields immediate results, but in which present control is least effective, leaving the evolution of the state to chance, or to the guidance of interested minorities.

The history of the United States, hardly less than that of the older countries of Europe, is an example of the potent influence of minorities. Minority control has in this country, however, been so skillfully clothed in democratic forms that it has been less obvious than in countries where the outward form of the old order still survives. But that it has been highly effective here can not be doubted. This, of course, does not mean that public opinion has been without influence, or that the minority has been able to have its way about matters in which the general public were actively interested. But because the minority sees farther ahead than the majority, is looking to the indirect and ultimate results in which the mass of the people have little or no interest, it is generally able to plan and guide the course of events so as to accomplish its purpose in the end. This is illustrated in all the greater outstanding events that mark the course of our political development.

No political doctrine was more generally accepted at the time of the Revolution and in the period immediately following than the idea that all political power should be strictly limited. The application made of this doctrine in framing the Constitution of the United States emphasized the limitation of the power of the popular majority. The government itself, which in the main was designed to represent the minority, was set over against the people as a check on their power. This situation foreshadowed, and made inevitable, a movement toward governmental absolutism. The minority, represented by the officeholding class, and the influential groups most active in politics, were naturally desirous of augmenting their own influence by strengthening the government and weakening the popular checks which restrained it. This struggle between governmental and popular authority began with the adoption of the Constitution and has continued in one form or another ever since.

When the government was established under the Constitution, its powers were supposed to be limited thereby. Just how the limitations were to be enforced was a matter to which public attention had not been directed and which even the framers of the Constitution themselves had largely ignored. There were some influential members of the federal constitutional convention who hoped that eventually the function of enforcing the Constitution would devolve on the federal judiciary. But there is no ground for believing that this viewpoint was accepted by the convention as a whole, or even by any influential class of that time, such as the legal profession. It would be a serious mistake to assume that the value which the fathers attached to written constitutions was in any way associated in their minds with the exercise of this power by the courts. They recognized the fact that a written document is necessary where there is a break with the past, as in the American colonies after the Revolution. The various elements of which society is composed can be harmonized and brought into orderly coöperative relations only on the basis of a definite written agreement or constitution.

According to the political thought of the time, there were two ways in which the limitations of a written constitution could be enforced. One was through public opinion operating upon the government from without. The other was the check and balance plan of organization, under which, it was assumed, any attempt by any organ of government to exercise authority not clearly conferred upon it by the constitution would be resisted by the other branches of the government, or, if attempted by the federal government as a whole, by the united opposition of the various state governments. Each branch of government, under the theory of checks and balances, was conceived to be charged with the duty of interpreting and enforcing the constitution. Its interpretation did not, however, become authoritative until acquiesced in by the other coördinate branches of the government. The check and balance idea, consistently applied, would have made the constitution-interpreting power, no less than statutory enactment, subject to constitutional limitations.

Soon after the adoption of the Constitution, the struggle between those who wished to extend governmental control, and those who sought to enlarge popular control, began to turn on the method of interpreting the Constitution. The Alien and Sedition laws, enacted by the Federalists, were opposed by the Anti-Federalists as unconstitutional. This immediately brought the question of the method of enforcing constitutional limitations into the arena of political controversy. It was obvious that where a provision of the Constitution was designed to limit the powers of a governmental organ, it could be effectively nullified if its interpretation and enforcement were left to the authorities it was designed to restrain. Clearly, common sense required that no organ of the government should be able to determine its own powers. To take any other view of the matter would enable public officials to override the checks on their powers imposed by the Constitution.

A fair interpretation of the general purpose of the framers would deny, not only to any branch of the general government but to the federal government as a whole, the right to determine its authority under the Constitution. Had they intended that any branch of the federal government should have the right to determine its own powers, or that the federal government as a whole should interpret and enforce the constitutional limitations on its authority, and had they made this intention clear in the wording of the Constitution, it can not be doubted that the plan of government proposed would have been overwhelmingly rejected. Limitation of authority was the basic principle of the document. It was designed in good faith to impose not nominal but actual checks, not upon the various branches of the federal government alone but upon the federal government as a whole.

It was assumed by the people that the new government was to be actually limited by the Constitution. If such were to be the case, the federal government could not be permitted to determine the limits of its own authority, since this would make it, and not the Constitution, supreme. If, then, in enacting the Alien and Sedition laws the general government had exceeded its authority, how were the constitutional restraints to be made operative? This question the Constitution did not answer. But in the absence of any express provision in the Constitution itself concerning the method of enforcing its limitations, it was necessary to find suitable means of making them effective.

To have suggested, when the Constitution was submitted for ratification, that the federal government itself was the proper instrument for enforcing the checks on its own powers would have been regarded as too absurd to merit consideration. Of course, the plan of government provided for in the Constitution made each of the coördinate branches a check on the others, and this check and balance arrangement might have served the purpose of enforcing constitutional restraints imposed upon a single coördinate branch of the government; but when the question pertained not to the checks imposed on an individual branch of the government but upon the government as a whole, it was necessary to look beyond the federal government for the means of making them effective. Each branch might be expected to exercise such powers as it possessed to protect itself against assumption of undue federal authority by any other branch; but when it was not merely a matter of the distribution of powers within the federal government itself, but rather the scope of federal authority — the limitations imposed to prevent it from encroaching upon the powers reserved to the states, or to the people of the United States — neither the federal government as a whole nor any of its organs could be safely entrusted with the enforcement of the constitutional restraints.

The enforcement of the constitutional limitations imposed upon federal authority was dealt with in a rather vague and indefinite manner in the Federalist papers. In number forty-six of *The Federalist,* Madison discusses the question of keeping the federal government within the limits fixed by the Constitution. The only means of opposing federal aggression mentioned in his discussion of the matter are the disquietude, disapproval, and resistance of the people on the one hand, and of the state governments on the other. He maintained that the state governments were advantageously situated for the purpose of resisting any undue extension of federal powers and that, secure in the loyalty of the people, their opposition would be such that the " federal government would hardly be willing to encounter " it.

The Virginia Resolutions (1798), drawn by Madison, declared " that, in case of a deliberate, palpable, and dangerous exercise of other powers not granted . . . the States . . . have the right and are in duty bound to interpose for arresting the progress of the evil, and for maintaining within their respective limits the authorities, rights, and liberties appertaining to them."

In the Kentucky Resolutions of 1798, it was affirmed " that whensoever the general government assumes undelegated powers, its acts are unauthoritative, void, and of no force: . . . That the government . . . was not made the exclusive or final judge of the extent of the powers delegated to itself; since that would have made its discretion, and not the Constitution, the measure of its powers; but that as in all other cases of compact among parties having no common Judge, each party has an equal right to judge for itself, as well of infractions as of the mode and measure of redress." In the original draft of these Resolutions, written by Jefferson, it was asserted that where the federal government assumes powers not delegated to it, nullification by a state of such unconstitutional acts is the rightful remedy. This was omitted from the Resolutions as adopted, but the Kentucky Resolutions of 1799 embodied the substance of Jefferson's proposal. They declared " *That a Nullification by those sovereignties* [the states], *of all unauthorized acts done under color of that instrument is the rightful remedy.*"

There were some among the members of the federal constitutional convention who, like Hamilton, desired to centralize authority in the general government; but this was not the generally accepted view of that body. Conservatives as they were, the members of the convention nevertheless believed in the limitation of governmental powers. They certainly wished to construct a constitutional barrier which democracy could not override; but this did not imply a belief in, or desire to establish, governmental supremacy. The framers of the Constitution as a whole accepted without question the eighteenth century belief in the system of checks and balances, and the Constitution must be regarded as an attempt to adapt this theory to what they conceived to be the needs of the country. The greatest need, as they viewed the situation, was for the limitation of governmental authority. But it was, they believed, the state governments whose powers most needed to be restrained. And this could be accomplished only by creating a general government strong enough to function as an actual check on the states.

That the Constitution was designed to limit the powers of the state governments and increase those of the general government can not be denied. The Articles of Confederation had effectively closed the door against the assumption of undelegated powers by the general government, through the declaration that " each state retains its sovereignty, freedom and independence, and every power, jurisdiction and right, which is not by this confederation expressly delegated to the United States in Congress assembled." [1]   This clearly limited the powers of the general government to those expressly conferred, and thus placed an almost insurmountable obstacle in the way of the growth of federal authority at the expense of the states.   By omitting the word " expressly," the framers of the Constitution of the United States laid a foundation for the doctrine of implied powers, through which the authority of the general government may be extended practically without limit.   It is fair to assume, however, that their purpose was not to make the federal government supreme, but to make it a more effective check on the power of the states.

The framers of the Constitution appropriated the name " Federal " as descriptive of the plan of governmental organization which they favored.   And so far as all public discussion at that time indicated, they meant by this to make the division of powers between the states and the general government such that neither would be able to encroach on the other.   Certainly this was the view of the proposed Constitution presented to the public by those who urged its ratification.   But while the fathers believed in federal government, they did not believe in a loosely organized political system, such as existed under the Articles of Confederation, which left the separate states without adequate central check.   In making provisions for needed restraints on the powers of the states, however, they were not seeking to establish a general government with unlimited authority.   The

---

[1] Article II.

very name, " Federal," which they adopted, whether descriptive of their purpose or not, was intended to imply, and was understood by the people to imply, such a balanced distribution of political powers between the states on the one hand and the general government on the other, as would make it possible for the former to oppose successfully any attempt on the part of the latter to exercise powers denied to it by the Constitution. If " federalism " was anything more than a political catchword to secure the support of the people by misrepresenting the purpose of the Constitution, it meant that the authority of the general government was restricted no less than that of the states.

It was John C. Calhoun who later developed this view of the Constitution, in treatises which for convincing argument have never been equaled in all the literature dealing with constitutional interpretation.[2] He assumed that the Constitution was designed, as the Federalists proclaimed it was, to establish a balance of power not only between the several branches of the general government, but also between the general government on the one hand and the states on the other. Being a fundamental law which was to control both the federal government and the states, it must, of course, he interpreted in a manner calculated to give effect to this purpose. It was obvious that neither the state nor the general government should have the final and exclusive right to interpret the law which limited its own powers. Since the Constitution was a law made not by, but for, the government, its interpretation could not be left to any governmental organ, or even to the government as a whole. Constitution-interpreting power was in essence constitution-making power, and should be under the control of those

[2] *Disquisition on Government and Discourse on the Constitution and Government of the United States, Works,* vol. I.

agencies in which the Constitution itself had lodged the power of amendment. The federal government would, of course, be in a sense a constitution-interpreting agency, but its interpretation would not be final if contested by the states. Should a state regard as unconstitutional a law passed by Congress it could declare such a law null and void within the limits of its jurisdiction. Such action on the part of a state would require the federal government to abandon the law in question or appeal to the only tribunal which the Constitution provided for making important changes in the system of government. Unless mooted constitutional questions were to be finally decided by the process of formal constitutional amendment, actual changes in the government could be made under the guise of mere interpretation. In order to preclude all changes except those approved by the regular process of amendment, the constitution-making authorities established by the Constitution must of necessity be regarded as the final tribunal for settling all doubtful questions of interpretation.

According to Calhoun, neither the state nor the general government was to be regarded as superior or inferior. Each had a field definitely assigned to it by the Constitution, upon which the other was forbidden to encroach. Although he referred to the states and the federal government as coördinate sovereignties, he did not think of them as in any sense really sovereign. This was precluded by the American theory of a constitution as a fundamental law to which the government itself was required to conform. The Constitution was made, and could be interpreted and amended, only by the concurrent action of the federal and state governments. Since every exercise of constitution-making power, whether by formal amendment, or less obviously by interpretation, involved the coöperation of both federal and state governmental agencies, it would be impossible for either to extend its powers at the expense of the other.

The framers of the Constitution, Calhoun maintained, intended that the powers of the general government should be strictly limited. This was clearly indicated in the check and balance plan of organization by which the states were to be an effective check upon the federal government.

From the very beginning of our political history, there has been a constant struggle between conservatism and liberalism. The line of demarcation between these contending forces has at times been somewhat blurred. Often the issues have been confused and misrepresented, but fundamentally it has been a struggle between those who would limit and diffuse political power and those who would centralize and extend governmental authority.

The adoption of the Constitution was, in form, a compromise between the advocates of centralization and decentralization, of class and mass rule. In appearance, the new government conformed to the avowed purpose of the founders in that it was strictly federal. It can not be doubted, however, that some of the more farseeing of the framers of the Constitution, such as Alexander Hamilton, much as they may have desired for practical reasons to be known as Federalists, were really seeking to lay the foundation for a government which they hoped would in time become essentially national. The Constitution, accepted as a purely federal document, could be easily adapted to the purposes of those who wished to give a national trend to political development, provided the states could be deprived of any share in the constitution-interpreting power. This question, which became a subject of controversy as soon as the Constitution was adopted, and was debated for more than half a century, was finally decided only as a result of the Civil War.

Chapter VI

THE ORIGIN AND SIGNIFICANCE
OF THE JUDICIAL VETO

It would be impossible to understand constitutional development in the United States without keeping constantly in mind the important fact that the Constitution was framed by lawyers and that its interpretation from the beginning has been under their control. In the course of English constitutional development, there had come about what may be called a deification of law as such. The conception of divine or natural law and the idea of the social contract implied the belief that all officials were subject to the fundamental law. This idea of the supremacy of natural law, which had its roots deep in religious and political thought, was extended by the courts and lawyers to include the common law. The body of rules constituting what was called the common law of England was represented as being made up of the unwritten usages and customs of the people interpreted and enforced by the courts. The assumption of popular origin conferred on the common law a prestige which it did not altogether deserve. Courts and lawyers sought to give to it a dignity and basic importance by ascribing to it a purely popular origin, such as was by the social contract theory imputed to the state itself. This emphasis on the assumed popular origin of the common law did much to exalt it in the estimation of an uncritical public.

It could not be seriously contended that the lawyers and judges of seventeenth century England were devoted to the cause of popular government as implied in the social contract theory of the state. They were advocates, rather, of the supremacy of law as interpreted and applied by the courts. It may be assumed, too, that they were under no illusion as to the significance of judicial interpretation of the common law; that they recognized that the exclusive right to interpret an unwritten code involved the right to enact and amend; that the common law (nominally the people's law) was, in fact, the expression of the will of the courts. Nevertheless, the effort made in the formative period of modern constitutional development to exalt the common law may be regarded as part of the larger struggle to limit all political power. It had as its basic assumption the subordination of all officials, including the judges, to the common law. In theory, at least, it supplied a check on the various branches of the government.

As a matter of fact the supremacy of the common law meant very largely the supremacy of those who controlled its interpretation. In the Tudor and Stuart periods, the real power behind the courts was the king; but after the Revolution of 1688, which deprived the king of his control over the judicial branch, Parliament, through its power of removal, actually controlled the courts and the common law. At the time the Constitution of the United States was framed, the legal profession, as represented by the judicial branch of the government, had been distinctly subordinated to Parliament in England.

In a general way, the plan of government outlined in the Constitution was modeled after the English government of the eighteenth century. But once the new government was established, the earlier English conception of judicial supremacy had a potent influence upon the interpretation and

development of the Constitution. The survival of the idea
of judicial supremacy in American political theory was,
of course, largely the work of the politically conservative
but influential members of the legal profession. They took
the English conception of the common law as a fundamental
popular law and sought to adapt it to the Constitution of
the United States, though there was, in view of the way in
which this document was framed and adopted, no justification for the claim that it was an expression of the popular
will. And just as the English lawyers had formerly looked
upon the courts as the interpreters and guardians of the
common law, so the conservative American lawyers sought
to vest the interpretation and guardianship of the Constitution in the federal courts. If they had little faith in democracy, they doubtless felt that they were justified on the
ground that the people generally were insufficiently informed
and liable to be misled. The leaders of the so-called Federalist party clearly understood, and took advantage of, this
lack of general political intelligence, for the purpose of
moulding American political institutions in harmony with
their own views.

The Constitution as adopted was not, in the opinion of the
more conservative Federalists, a sufficient protection against
the dangers of democracy. It was not possible to ensure
such protection without conservative control of constitutional interpretation. Gradually and skillfully the way was
prepared for the exercise of the constitution-interpreting
power by the judicial branch of the federal government. As
the result of a carefully directed educational campaign appealing to the popular belief in the necessity for checks on
governmental authority, a popular conception of the American system of government finally emerged, which envisaged
the Constitution as a fundamental law imposed by the people

upon the government and enforced for them against the latter by the courts.

It is undisputed that only conservatives who held the legalistic view of political institutions, such as Hamilton and James Wilson, supported the proposal to give the courts the power of interpreting the Constitution in the beginning. It was clearly recognized by Federalist leaders that this could not be accomplished until a suitable attitude toward the judicial branch of the federal government had been created — a popular conception of the Supreme Court identical in its essential elements with the implicit faith which the loyal subject formerly had in the king, or the devout Catholic in the infallibility of the Pope. That the Supreme Court of the United States exercises a function in the American governmental system similar to that performed by the Pope in the Catholic Church is recognized by an eminent Catholic authority:

" What, then, is the real doctrine of Infallibility? It simply means that the Pope, as successor of St. Peter, Prince of the Apostles, by virtue of the promises of Jesus Christ, is preserved from error of judgment when he promulgates to the Church a decision on faith or morals.

" The Pope, therefore, be it known, is not the maker of the Divine law; he is only its expounder. He is not the author of revelation, but only its interpreter. . . .

" In a word, the Sovereign Pontiff is to the Church, though in a more eminent degree, what the Chief Justice is to the United States. We have an instrument called the Constitution of the United States, which is the charter of our civil rights and liberties. If a controversy arises between two states regarding a constitutional clause the question is referred, in the last resort, to the Supreme Court at Washington. The Chief Justice, with his Associate Judges, examines into the case, and then pronounces judgment upon it; and this decision is final, irrevocable and practically infallible." [1]

The Declaration of Independence by its indictment of the old order and its emphasis on individual rights, and the Constitution of the United States by the very form of political organization which it provided, reflected distrust of governmental agencies. Yet those who favored judicial supremacy were under no misapprehension as to its nature and its ultimate effect on the American system of government. Though not such professedly, the proposal to give the courts the constitution-interpreting power was in reality a plan to centralize and strengthen governmental authority, and to make it more or less independent of the people. The problem was to find a way of giving this power to the judiciary which would satisfy those who had a sentimental but undiscriminating faith in popular government.

To accomplish this was less difficult than would have been the case had the Revolution brought about any profound changes in the intellectual and moral basis of the state. After the excitement and enthusiasm of the War had subsided, the people were but little influenced in their political ideas and attitude by the fact of independence. The elimination of king and hereditary nobility, which had long been essential parts of the political order, did not mean a corresponding change in the political outlook of the ordinary citizen. The passive attitude toward government which characterized loyal subjects of monarchy was an inevitable though unfortunate inheritance of the democratic state. Faith in public officials and governmental agencies, though shaken temporarily by the Revolutionary movement, was not destroyed.

[1] James Cardinal Gibbons, *The Faith of Our Fathers*, ch. XI.

The advocates of judicial supremacy were careful to support it not as a conservative safeguard, but as a means — assumed to be necessary — of protecting popular rights and enforcing the constitutional checks on public officials. Every effort was made to create the impression that the Supreme Court of the United States was designed to protect the people, and, by its position under the Constitution, was admirably fitted to serve as the authoritative interpreter of their will. Much was said about the Constitution as the people's law, about the danger of governmental encroachment on the rights reserved to individuals in the Constitution, and the need of a protecting agency that would stand between the people and the government and annul such acts of the latter as were in conflict with the Constitution of the United States.

In all this propaganda in support of the extension of judicial authority, it was tacitly assumed that the judiciary was something outside of, and apart from, the regular machinery of government; that it was merely the mouthpiece or instrument of the law itself; that to give to the Supreme Court the final power of interpretation would, in effect, make the people's will, as expressed in the Constitution, self-enforcing. This notion of the Supreme Court as an impersonal organ of the Constitution, uninfluenced by prejudice, passion, or interest, was gradually and adroitly insinuated into the public mind by the conservatives who wished to make the Constitution yield not to popular, but to ruling class, sentiment. It was the method of selecting federal judges, their life tenure, the security afforded them by the Constitution against removal, their independence of public opinion, which made it seem desirable to conservatives of the Hamiltonian type to bring about general acquiescence in an interpretation of the Constitution which would lay the foundation for judicial supremacy. It is obvious that if the Constitution had made judges directly dependent upon the people through direct election, short term of office, or an easy method of removal, there would have been no conservative movement to extend the political power of the courts.

It is an interesting commentary on the state of general political intelligence that a small, shrewd minority, by the repeated avowal of democratic aims, could successfully carry out a design which, in effect, profoundly modified the Constitution as it was represented to, and understood by, the public at the time of its adoption. There is probably no other instance in the whole history of constitutional development where public opinion has been so misled as to the fundamental nature of a political arrangement. The ostensible purpose in advocating the assumption of the veto power by the courts was to provide a means of enforcing constitutional restraints; but the real purpose was to centralize political authority largely in the Supreme Court of the United States, and, through the power of final interpretation, to make the Constitution an adequate bulwark of conservatism. By all legalistic writers, this power has been and still is defended as one naturally and necessarily belonging to the courts wherever there is a constitution of the check and balance type. How, they ask, can a system of checks and balances really restrain public officials, unless there is some one organ of government whose duty it is to enforce these limitations? This line of argument is, no doubt, more or less effective with those who still retain an essentially monarchic attitude toward government. It appeals to that large number of politically inactive and undiscriminating citizens who profess belief in democracy without understanding its significance, and who readily accept the comforting suggestion that the Supreme Court is the natural guardian and protector of their constitutional rights.

It seems almost unbelievable that in a community accepting the political theory of checks and balances, there could have been developed a general belief in judicial supremacy. In all their essentials these two ideas are inherently opposed. The former is in essence the theory that political power should be divided and diffused in order that it may be effectively limited. The latter centralizes authority in the Supreme Court, where it is subject to no effective political limitation. By grafting the idea of judicial supremacy upon the system of checks and balances, the conservatives virtually destroyed the form of government they professed to be conserving. The redistribution of powers thus brought about effectively subordinated the democratic element in the government, and placed predominant authority in that branch which was so constituted as to be safely beyond the reach of public opinion.

In laying the foundation for the acceptance by the public of the doctrine of judicial supremacy, much use was made of the idea that the people were the ultimate source of political power. Strictly speaking, this did not imply popular sovereignty as that term is now understood, since, as explained above, all political power, even that of the people themselves, was conceived to be limited. But though a rather vague and indefinite notion, it was assumed that the authority of the people, even if limited by natural law, was superior to any other authority in human society.

The courts, which under the conservative plan were to be the final interpreters of the will of the people as expressed in constitutions, regarded themselves as entrusted with the duty of enforcing those basic principles implied in the term, natural law, not only against the other branches of the government, but even against the people themselves. It was largely this conception of natural law in relation to human authority which in the early decades of our history supplied the courts with a pretext for claiming the right to declare laws null and void. If they were the guardians of this higher law, it followed logically that they should refuse to enforce any statute which was in conflict therewith. This left the way open for the development of the judicial veto, regardless of the powers held to be conferred upon the courts by constitutions.

That judges were feeling their way as the guardians of natural law toward the exercise of the veto power is clearly revealed in many decisions of the pre-Civil War period. In the Georgia land grant case of Fletcher v. Peck, decided in 1810, the unanimous opinion of the United States Supreme Court, written by Chief Justice Marshall, may be regarded as indicative of the early judicial attitude. In this case the Court held that " the state of Georgia was restrained, either by general principles which are common to our free institutions, or by the particular provisions of the constitution of the United States." [2] Apparently, the Court itself had some doubt at that time as to the best way of justifying the exercise of the veto power. The Constitution had not then been deified; its future was more or less uncertain; and the position and powers of the federal judiciary were problematical. This, no doubt, explains the Court's reference to, and emphasis on, " general principles " as a ground for its decision. Justice Johnson, in a separate opinion, makes it clear that he did not look to the Constitution, but to general principles as the source of the Court's power to declare the statute in question null and void. " I do not hesitate," he said, " to declare that a state does not possess the power of revoking

2 6 Cranch 87. See also Calder v. Bull, 3 Dallas 388 (1798).

its own grants. But I do it, on a general principle, on the reason and nature of things; a principle which will impose laws even on the Deity. . . . I have thrown out these ideas, that I may have it distinctly understood, that my opinion on this point is not founded on the provision in the constitution of the United States, relative to laws impairing the obligation of contracts."

Legalistic thought of this period was strongly influenced by the belief in an overruling law of nature which it was the duty of the courts to recognize and enforce. Property rights were conceived to be protected by natural law, even against the government itself. Story, who was appointed to the Supreme Bench the year following the decision in Fletcher v. Peck, says: " Whether, indeed, independently of the constitution of the United States, the nature of republican and free governments does not necessarily impose some restraints upon the legislative power, has been much discussed. It seems to be the general opinion, fortified by a strong current of judicial opinion, that, since the American revolution, no state government can be presumed to possess the transcendental sovereignty, to take away vested rights of property." [3]

Although no device that ingenuity could suggest was overlooked in the effort to convince the uncritical public that courts must be clothed with the power to annul legislation in order to enforce compliance on the part of the other branches of government with the will of the people as expressed in the fundamental law, court decisions, both state and federal, have indicated a pronounced distrust and fear of democracy. This attitude was clearly revealed about the middle of the nineteenth century in a series of opinions on the referendum, which arose in connection with the attempt

[3] Commentaries on the Constitution of the United States, sec. 1399.

to enact temperance legislation of the prohibition or local option type. Legislatures were unable to resist the popular pressure for anti-liquor laws, but in passing them they hit upon the device of making their validity depend upon the approval of the people, as expressed by a direct vote on the proposed law. All general state statutes referred by legislatures to the voters, and by them approved, were held by the courts to be null and void.

The grounds upon which these decisions were based reflect pronounced hostility to direct popular control of governmental policies. One of these cases, Parker v. Commonwealth, decided by the Supreme Court of Pennsylvania in 1847, involved the validity of a local option law. The court held that inasmuch as the government of Pennsylvania was one of limited authority, " it is, therefore, not to be denied that the action of its legislature may be invalid, though it contravene no express provision of the constitution, if it be in violation of the spirit of that instrument, and the genius of the public institutions designed to be created by it." [4] This was followed by a long discussion of the evils and dangers involved in the submission of laws to popular vote, in which the court emphasized " the imminent danger that, in the absence of a sense of responsibility, the surest guaranty of social justice, the rights of the minority would be disregarded by a majority seeking only the gratification of its own desires or the advancement of its peculiar opinions."

The court evidently recognized the fact that the Constitution of Pennsylvania did not afford sufficient justification for the exercise of the judicial veto in the case of this particular law. Since the government of Pennsylvania was not one of enumerated powers, and the submission of this law to the people violated no constitutional provision, it was clear that

[4] 47 American Decisions 480.

the court could not defend judicial annulment without discovering some higher law or principle apart from the written constitution, with which the law in question could be held to conflict. The court supplied this need by assuming the existence of a more subtle and intangible thing than the written constitution, which it called the "spirit of that instrument" and which necessarily depended less upon the written constitution than upon the political and economic views of the judges themselves. Still farther removed from the realm of constitutional fact, and even more distinctly an emanation of judicial fancy, was the "genius of the public institutions designed to be created" by the constitution. The court in this case not only professed to be the guardian of the constitution, but, in effect, assumed the additional role of interpreter of its spirit and of what it called the genius of public institutions. The foundation which the court sought to lay in this case for the exercise of its legislative powers was sufficiently broad to bring practically all legislation under its control.

The principal proclaimed — that a law which does not violate the constitution may nevertheless be void — was one which had persisted in legalistic political thought from the beginning of our constitutional history. But with the progress of democracy and the growth of the belief that our constitutions are and ought to be the people's overruling law, the courts were more and more constrained to base the judicial veto upon purely constitutional grounds. In doing so, however, they did not propose to surrender any of the power which accrued to them under the earlier assumption that they could invalidate any law which they might hold to be in conflict with general principles. This attitude accounts for the extension of the constitution to include those sublimated products of judicial refinement — the spirit of the constitution and the genius of the institutions created by it.

In order to defend its position, the court had to show that the submission of laws to the voters, though not forbidden by specific constitutional provision, was, nevertheless, inconsistent with the nature and purpose of the government created under the organic law. This task was not an easy one, in view of the fact that the constitution of the state declared: " That all power is inherent in the people, and all free governments are founded on their authority, and instituted for their peace, safety, and happiness. For the advancement of those ends, they have at all times an unalienable and indefeasible right to alter, reform, or abolish their government, in such manner as they may think proper; " and " That no power of suspending laws shall be exercised, unless by the legislature or its authority."

These declarations of the Pennsylvania Constitution of 1838 are merely restatements of political principles formulated by John Locke in his *Two Treatises on Civil Government*. " The legislative," he says, " cannot transfer the power of making laws to other hands, for it being but a delegated power from the people, they who have it cannot pass it over to others. The people alone can appoint the form of the commonwealth, which is by constituting the legislative, and appointing in whose hands that shall be. And when the people have said, ' We will submit, and be governed by laws made by such men, and in such forms,' nobody else can say other men shall make laws for them; nor can they be bound by any laws but such as are enacted by those whom they have chosen and authorized to make laws for them." [5]

According to Locke's view, the people are in the position of a principal, and the legislature is merely their agent. It

[5] Bk. II, ch. XI.

follows that the powers of the lawmaking body are determined by the rules which govern the relations between principal and agent. One of these well settled principles is that the agent can not, without the consent of the principal, delegate the power granted to him as agent.

In American legalistic literature relating to the powers of the judiciary, we have a striking illustration of the way in which a doctrine that affirms the supremacy of the people has been employed to deprive them of effective political control. The doctrine that public officials are agents of the people lies at the very foundation of the whole theory of popular government. In this country, however, the doctrine has been so perverted by conservative legalistic writers that it has lost entirely its original meaning. From Hamilton's defense of the Supreme Court in *The Federalist* down to the present time, it has been the starting point of all the advocates of judicial supremacy. That the relation of the government to the people is that of agent to principal has been accepted by conservative writers as a convenient and useful political fiction, which has made it possible to secure public approval for institutional arrangements designed to prevent popular control. It is on the assumption that public officials are agents of the people and bound by their will as expressed in the constitution, that the courts have come to rest their claim to the veto power. What the public do not recognize and, indeed, are not expected to see is that the voice of a politically independent court is much less likely to be the voice of the people than is that of the more dependent legislative body. If the people generally could read and understand the opinion of the court in Parker v. Commonwealth and other similar cases, it would tend to destroy the prevalent American political superstition that judicial supremacy is a means of enforcing the popular will.

" To exercise the power of making laws delegated to the general assembly," says the court, " is not so much the privilege of that body as it is its duty, whenever the good of the community calls for legislative action. . . . Among the primal axioms of jurisprudence, political and municipal, is to be found the principle that an agent, unless expressly empowered, can not transfer his delegated authority to another, more especially when it rests in a confidence, partaking the nature of a trust, and requiring for its due discharge, understanding, knowledge, and rectitude. The maxim is, *delegata potestas non potest delegari.* And what shall be said to be a higher trust, based upon a broader confidence, than the possession of the legislative function? . . . It is a duty which can not, therefore, be transferred by the representative; no, not even to the people themselves; for they have forbidden it by the solemn expression of their will that the legislative power shall be vested in the general assembly. . . . An attempt to do so would be not only to disregard the constitutional inhibition, but tend directly to impress upon the body of the state those social diseases that have always resulted in the death of republics, and to avoid which the scheme of a representative democracy was devised and is to be fostered."

No one who will intelligently read these decisions can be under any illusion as to the attitude of the courts toward popular control of governmental policies. The political maxim that delegated powers can not be redelegated has been shorn by American judges of all its original significance as a democratic doctrine. It was used by Locke to support control by the people; American judges have employed it in their attempt to justify the limitation of popular authority. Locke denied the power of legislators, elected by and responsible to the people, to pass their authority to make laws on to others not thus designated by their principal, the people. But American courts under the pretense of enforcing this doctrine have generally held that it does not permit the legislature to refer a proposed law to the voters of the state. The only exception to this attitude was the recognition by the courts in a number of states of the right of the legislature to submit laws of the local option type.

Judge Cooley says with reference to these earlier referendum decisions: " May not any law framed for the State at large be made conditional on an acceptance by the people at large, declared through the ballot-box?   If it is not unconstitutional to delegate to a single locality the power to decide whether it will be governed by a particular charter, must it not quite as clearly be within the power of the legislature to refer to the people at large, from whom all power is derived, the decision upon any proposed statute affecting the whole State?   And can that be called a delegation of power which consists only in the agent or trustee referring back to the principal the final decision in a case where the principal is the party concerned . . . ? " [6]

According to Locke, " the legislative is the supreme power " in the state and to it the other branches of the government are distinctly subordinate. He assigned this place to the legislature as the direct and responsible agent of the people; but under the guidance of conservative thought, American political development has subordinated the legislative branch, ostensibly to protect the people against misrepresentation, but in reality to limit their power by limiting that of the governmental organ most responsible to their will.

It is this judicial hostility to popular control that has been largely responsible for the rapid increase in recent decades

[6] T. M. Cooley, *Constitutional Limitations*, p. 141, 6th ed.

in the size of state constitutions.   The refusal of the courts
to allow legislatures to refer proposed laws to the people
has led to the amendment of a number of state constitutions,
by which the people have expressly conferred upon themselves the powers denied to them by the judiciary.   Since the
courts had abandoned the right, originally claimed, to veto
laws held to be in conflict with general principles, and had
come to acknowledge constitutions as the source of their
authority, judicial opposition to popular government could
be overcome in many cases by a more detailed enumeration
of the powers of the legislature and the people.   The bulky
state constitutions of the post-Civil War period are to be
attributed in no small degree to this cause.   Had the constitution-interpreting power been more amenable to public
opinion, it is unlikely that our state constitutions would have
approximated their present size.   The effort of the courts to
control legislation led the advocates of popular supremacy
to favor constitutions which, by elaborate and detailed provisions, minimized judicial control of fundamental law.
This practice of enumerating in detail the powers of the
people and the legislature is, of course, much criticized by
conservatives, who desire to preserve intact the source of
judicial supremacy.   They would have a constitution include
only general provisions, thus giving to the courts large
powers of interpretation through which they could mould the
constitution in conformity with their own political ideas.

This method of limiting judicial control has, however,
little importance except in the strictly subordinate field of
state legislation.   The federal Constitution is so difficult to
amend that the Supreme Court of the United States very
rarely has its power of interpretation interfered with in this
way.   Only two amendments designed to correct what was
conceived to be judicial misinterpretation of the Constitu-

tion have been adopted since our present form of government was established in the eighteenth century. The Eleventh Amendment was the response of the states' rights advocates to the United States Supreme Court decision in Chisholm v. Georgia. The Sixteenth Amendment, adopted in 1913, overruled the Supreme Court's interpretation in the Income Tax decision of 1895.

CHAPTER VII

GOVERNMENTAL SUPREMACY UNDER THE GUISE OF POPULAR SOVEREIGNTY

The judicial veto as a means of centralizing political power and extending and strengthening governmental authority acquired a new significance with the distinction between state and government which political scientists of the conservative school attempted to make near the end of the nineteenth century. This distinction, which is characteristic of the viewpoint and method of American legalistic writers on political science, has been serviceable in the effort to provide a plausible justification for the legislative powers of American judges, and in augmenting the authority of the general government. The credit for this distinction is generally given to Professor J. W. Burgess, who may be regarded as the chief academic champion of judicial supremacy.

According to Professor Burgess, the government is controlled by the Constitution, which determines the nature and scope of its authority. Back of the Constitution is its creator, the state, clothed with sovereignty, which he defines as " original, absolute, unlimited, universal power over the individual subject and over all associations of subjects." [1] The state as distinguished from the government, which is merely an organ of the state, consists of all those agencies and instrumentalities through which the people exercise the constitution-making power.

This conception of the state always assumes, before it

[1] *Political Science and Constitutional Law*, vol. I, p. 52.

reaches the public in diluted popular form, the attractive garb of popular sovereignty. And, indeed, it is the fact that the public can be easily induced to accept the sovereignty of the state as synonymous with the unlimited power of the people themselves, that has given the purely artificial distinction between state and government an important place in recent political discussion.

If institutional arrangements are to endure, they must retain the support of public opinion. But so-called public opinion is usually created for the people, rather than by them. The great majority have little more rational foundation for their political opinions than for their religious beliefs. For this reason, it is safe to assume that they will not discover inconsistencies and contradictions that lie below the surface of political discussion. That the people politically organized constitute the state, that their power thus organized as the state is unlimited, that their will as expressed in the Constitution is the supreme law by which all public officials are governed, is a conception that tends to inspire confidence in the representative character of our governmental sytem. It also flatters the vanity of the ordinary citizen by acknowledgment of his position as joint-proprietor of an all-powerful state.

The assumption on which this distinction is based will not, however, bear careful analysis. Pleasing as it may be to think that the Constitution is the expression of the will of the people, the facts concerning the framing, adoption, amendment, interpretation, and enforcement of this instrument furnish no substantial basis for this belief.

Our first constitution, The Articles of Confederation, was framed by the Continental Congress and ratified by the state legislatures. The people, as distinguished from the government, had no part whatever in its adoption. It was wholly a governmental creation and could be regarded as an expression of the people's will only in so far as public opinion might be reflected in the acts of their federal and state legislative bodies. This constitution was as truly a legislative product as is ordinary statute law.

It was the federal legislature, the Congress of the Confederation, that called the convention which framed the Constitution of the United States, and it was by the legislatures of the several states that the members of that body were appointed. Hence, the only opportunity which public opinion had to exert any influence was when the Constitution was submitted to the states. And although the members of the state conventions ratifying it were elected by the qualified voters, their power was limited to the question of accepting or rejecting the Constitution as submitted.

All amendments to the Constitution are, in practice, proposed by the federal legislature and may be ratified either by the state legislatures or by conventions, as Congress may direct. The choice of ratifying agencies being left to Congress by the Constitution, that body has followed the invariable practice of requiring ratification of amendments by the state legislatures. All formal changes in our constitutional system have been made, as our first federal constitution was framed and adopted, by the federal and the state legislatures. Moreover, the Constitution as originally adopted and all amendments since made have been interpreted wholly by governmental agencies. Any influence that the people have had upon the Constitution as it was originally framed, upon the amendments thereto, or upon the interpretation and enforcement of its provisions, must of necessity have been exerted solely through the medium of governmental agencies. And since the Constitution has become what it now is more largely by the process of interpretation than by formal enactment, the greater part of it may be regarded as mainly an expression of the will of that branch of the federal government which is independent of public opinion.

It would appear from an inspection of state constitutions that they are in much larger measure under direct popular control than is the federal Constitution. But as hereinbefore shown, constitutional provisions can not be accepted at their face value. Their enforcement depending as it does so largely upon the coöperation of the very officials whose powers would be limited thereby, we find not infrequently that they are either enforced in a manner designed to defeat their purpose or entirely ignored.

In the framing of a state constitution, except in such states as have the constitutional initiative, any influence which the public may have in determining the content of the constitution as submitted for ratification depends entirely upon the representative character of the convention. This body, brought into being for the sole purpose of framing a constitution or amendments thereto, is generally supposed to be more representative of the people than is the legislature. The facts, however, do not justify this view. There are fourteen state constitutions which make no provision for a constitutional convention.[2] But whether the constitution expressly provides for the calling of such a convention or not, the extent to which the body when called will be representative of the people is very largely under the control of the legislature. Nearly every constitution which contains a provision relating to apportionment of representation in the constitutional convention requires that it shall correspond either to that of the house or senate. But we have seen that in a majority of the states there are constitutional restric-

[2] W. F. Dodd, *Revision and Amendment of State Constitutions*, p. 69.

tions on apportionment of representation in one or both houses. Moreover, we must remember that where a constitution requires apportionment of the legislature strictly according to population we may, nevertheless, have a legislature that is in no true sense representative of the people of the state.[3] American legislatures have not as a rule shown much regard for the principle of apportionment according to population. Even where this rule is enjoined by the constitution, the legislature may disregard it and in practice frequently has. And in those states which impose constitutional restrictions on the representation of the majority, the legislatures in apportioning their members are likely to aggravate the effect of these restrictions. It is therefore not to be expected that the apportionment of the members of a constitutional convention will be such as to make it a better medium of public opinion than the state legislature. And since the constitutional convention is usually representative of the majority only in a limited sense, it is safe to assume that a constitution framed by such a body will not reflect in all its provisions the public opinion of the state.

But assuming that the convention does omit certain provisions which a majority of the voters wish to see included and incorporates others to which they are opposed, the people, as the ultimate source of authority, are supposed to have the right to accept or reject the work of the convention as a whole. But since only seventeen of our forty-eight state constitutions contain provisions requiring the submission of new constitutions to the people, it would seem that this supposition is hardly borne out by the facts.[4]

Although a few of the early state constitutions were submitted to the voters, the use of popular ratification was

[3] *Supra.*
[4] W. F. Dodd, *Revision and Amendment of State Constitutions*, p. 69.

negligible until after the extension of the suffrage. The early Federalists' view as to the proper method of ratifying constitutions was expressed by Chief Justice Marshall in McCulloch v. Maryland. Referring to the ratification of the Constitution of the United States by conventions chosen by the voters, he said that this was " the only manner in which they can act safely, effectively, and wisely, on such a subject." [5] The earlier enabling acts by which Congress provided for the admission of new states did not require popular ratification. It was not until 1857, in the enabling act for Minnesota, that the desirability of popular ratification was recognized by Congress, although for nearly twenty years prior to this time all new constitutions had been submitted to the people. Since the Civil War, however, every enabling act has required popular ratification. This condition imposed by Congress applies only to the constitution under which a state is admitted. Once admitted, a state may adopt a new constitution without submission to the people, unless some provision in the original constitution makes this procedure so clearly necessary that the courts will be compelled to enforce it.

It is, however, by no means certain that we can rely upon the courts to enforce provisions requiring popular ratification. A provision of this type would naturally be regarded by the conservative legal mind such as we generally find in our higher courts as an undesirable, even if at times necessary, concession to public opinion. The attitude of courts, both federal and state, toward the question of majority control in general and the referendum in particular has not been such as to warrant the expectation of hearty judicial approval of the constitutional referendum. If courts have been hostile to the submission of statutes to the people,

[5] 4 Wheaton 316.

they would be even less sympathetic with the policy of popular ratification of constitutions.

It may be doubted whether, even in those states the constitutions of which expressly and unequivocally provide for popular ratification of both constitutions and constitutional amendments, submission to the people would under all circumstances be enforced by the courts. Since the courts would probably not be in sympathy with the policy involved in submitting constitutional law to a vote of the people, they would intervene to declare a constitution not thus submitted void, only if required to do so by the clearly established and generally recognized principles of constitutional interpretation.

It would probably be quite generally assumed that a constitutional provision clearly defining the method by which an existing constitution might be amended or replaced by a new one would be respected by all governmental agencies, including the courts. A study of American constitutional history, however, will show that this assumption is not altogether supported by the facts. Our first federal constitution, the Articles of Confederation, provided that no change should be made in the system of government at any time, " unless such alteration be agreed to in a Congress of the United States, and be afterwards confirmed by the Legislatures of every State." [6] This provision was entirely ignored in framing and adopting the Constitution of the United States. The reason for disregarding it was the purely practical one that adherence to this method would probably have made the adoption of the new Constitution impossible. Hence, it was proposed that ratification by nine states should be sufficient for the establishment of the Constitution between the states so ratifying.

[6] Art. XIII.

It was recognized by the framers that this procedure was irregular and needed some special justification, although at that time constitutional provisions did not have the high place in public esteem which they later acquired. The Articles of Confederation concluded with the declaration that they " shall be inviolably observed by the States we respectively represent, and that the Union shall be perpetual." [7] The provision in the new Constitution that ratification by nine states was sufficient to dissolve the old Union and supplant it with the union between the states thus ratifying, was so obviously in violation of the Articles of Confederation that even the framers admitted it. Madison writing in defense of the method by which the new Constitution was to be adopted said:

" Two questions of a very delicate nature present themselves on this occasion: 1. On what principle the Confederation, which stands in the solemn form of a compact among the States, can be superseded without the unanimous consent of the parties to it? 2. What relation is to subsist between the nine or more States ratifying the Constitution and the remaining few who do not become parties to it?

" The first question is answered at once by recurring to the absolute necessity of the case: to the great principle of self-preservation; to the transcendant law of nature and of nature's God, which declares that the safety and happiness of society are the objects at which all political institutions aim, and to which all such institutions must be sacrificed." [8]

This is the argument always advanced in defense of revolution or revolutionary procedure. It is stressed in the Declaration of Independence and in various public documents of that time. The general principle that institutional arrangements must be sacrificed when the safety and happiness

[7] Art. XIII.　　　　　[8] *The Federalist*, No. 43.

of society require it is incontrovertible as a purely abstract proposition. It is the basis of the right of revolution implied in the social contract theory of the state, and has served a useful purpose by providing an ultimate popular check on irresponsible governmental authority.

In political theory, the right of revolution was a purely popular right — one which the people in extreme cases could exercise against the government itself, but never one which would justify governmental organs in ignoring the constitutional checks imposed upon them. Only the people themselves could brush aside the restraints imposed by political institutions, and they would exercise this power only when " the great principle of self-preservation " required it.

To permit governmental organs, professing to act as the agents of the people, to ignore constitutional limitations on their authority, is to make the will of the government itself virtually supreme. To defend, as the Federalists did, disregard of the provisions of the established constitution in order to supplant it with one more to their liking was to lay an insecure foundation for the constitutional structure which they hoped to perpetuate; to ignore existing constitutional requirements in altering the form of government was to establish a precedent which future constitution-makers might follow, as much better suited to their purpose than the method of amendment or revision which the Constitution required. What is to prevent some party in the future, in possession of the governmental organization and pledged to bring about certain important changes in our constitutional system, from disregarding the amendment provision of our present Constitution, as its makers disregarded that of the constitution which it superseded? Certainly, a constitution which could not have been adopted except in violation of the one which preceded it can not be regarded as itself adequately protected against the danger of change by revolutionary procedure. Some time in the future when those in control may wish to change the form of government and find that it can not be done by following the difficult method of amendment prescribed in the Constitution, they may, like the federal constitutional convention, disregard the requirements of constitutional law and appeal from the Constitution to the " transcendent law of nature " in justification of their act.[9]

It was, perhaps, a recognition of this danger which led Madison to search for an additional justification of the course pursued in adopting the Constitution. An appeal to revolutionary procedure afforded precarious support for a constitution designed to secure stability and permanency in political arrangements. It was highly desirable to give to the new Constitution the appearance of legal regularity. This probably explains why Madison, after defending its adoption by revolutionary procedure, attempted to show that there was, after all, no irregularity in the adoption of the Constitution. His contention was that the Articles of Confederation did not have the binding force of constitutional law. " It has been heretofore noted among the defects of the Confederation," he said, " that in many of the States it had received no higher sanction than a mere legislative ratification; " and since it had been ratified by the state legislatures, it enjoyed no higher validity than a treaty.[10] He did not mention, of course, that the Constitution he was defending might be justly criticized on the same ground. Although the method proposed for the ratification of the

[9] South Carolina at the beginning of the Civil War justified her withdrawal from the Union on the ground that the American Revolution had established " the right of a people to abolish a government when it becomes destructive of the ends for which it was instituted." *South Carolina Declaration of Independence*, 1860.

[10] *The Federalist*, No. 43.

Constitution was by conventions; all future amendments were to be ratified either by conventions or legislatures, as Congress might direct, and legislative ratification has, in fact, been required in all instances. It was, to say the least, inconsistent to claim that the Articles of Confederation lacked the binding force of constitutional law because of legislative ratification, in order to justify the proposed method of adopting a constitution which expressly provided a similar method of ratification for all amendments.

If it be held that it is necessary in adopting a constitution to follow the method required by the constitution which it is to supersede, it would also be necessary to hold that our present federal Constitution was illegally adopted. The only way out of this dilemma is to assume with Madison that constitutional restraints on the power to amend may be disregarded if they conflict with the higher law of necessity; although this assumption would, for all practical purposes, place those in control of the government above the Constitution which they are supposed to obey.

The faith which most Americans have in constitutional guaranties is difficult to explain in view of the actual facts of our political history. What the people have not yet learned is that the efficacy of constitutional provisions, under our American system, depends upon the government itself. Constitutional guaranties may be deprived of their original significance by the process of interpretation, or they may be entirely ignored.

The interpretation of the Fourteenth Amendment, adopted at the close of the Civil War, illustrates the dependence of constitutional law for its meaning and effectiveness on governmental coöperation. The construction placed on section 1 of this amendment offers a striking example of the way in which judicial interpretation may change the character of a constitutional provision. "No state," it reads, "shall make or enforce any law which shall abridge the privileges or immunities of citizens of the United States; nor shall any state deprive any person of life, liberty, or property, without due process of law; nor deny to any person within its jurisdiction the equal protection of the laws." A student of American history would realize that such limitation on the power of the state governments as this provision imposed was not designed to hamper them in their efforts to protect the interests and promote the welfare of their citizens. Indeed, it merely denied to the states the power to deprive " citizens " and " persons " within their jurisdiction of rights without " due process of law." Since it was stated in general terms, one could, of course, read into it much or little, according to the viewpoint from which it was interpreted. The general intention of the amendment, however, was obvious. It was to protect " citizens " and " persons " against governmental authority exercised in a spirit of unjust discrimination — to guarantee to them, in the language of the amendment, " the equal protection of the law." Neither in this amendment nor in any other part of the Constitution can be found anything that even remotely suggests that private corporations are to be regarded as persons or citizens.[11] Nor is there any reference either in the Constitution or in any of the amendments, to the corporate form of industry. Nevertheless, we find that this amendment, as interpreted by the courts, has been an important instrument for the protection of corporations against regulation in the interest of the public. Certain phrases in the amendment, such as " due process of law " and " the equal protection of the laws," have been made to do similar service in curtailing

[11] For a different view see Roscoe Conkling's argument in B. B. Kendrick, *The Journal of the Joint Committee of Fifteen on Reconstruction; Columbia University Studies in History, Economics and Public Law*, vol. LXII.

the power of the states to give real protection to their citizens. It is this provision of the federal Constitution which has been made to supply the justification for a large number of United States Supreme Court decisions declaring unconstitutional, state laws designed to protect labor or regulate corporations. A careful study of these cases would reveal the true significance of the American doctrine of judicial supremacy. It would show how largely the effect of constitutional provisions depends upon the social, political, and economic opinions of the judges who exercise the final power of interpretation. The Court in these decisions has taken an amendment which clearly had in view the very definite purpose of protecting the former slaves, and, by a forced and undemocratic construction, given it an effect which no one could have foreseen at the time of its adoption. Designed to protect the rights of persons, it became in the hands of the Court the chief bulwark of corporate privilege.

Section 2 of the Fourteenth Amendment provided that where a state deprives adult male citizens of the right to vote its representation in the lower house of Congress is to be correspondingly reduced. This provision did not prohibit but was designed to discourage changes in the suffrage which would have the effect of disfranchising the Negro. Congress has the power, and the Constitution makes it its duty, to enforce this section by enacting the necessary reapportionment legislation. But notwithstanding the fact that its enforcement would strengthen Republican control by reducing Democratic representation, it has been entirely ignored.

The Fifteenth Amendment was designed to afford additional and more direct protection for the political rights of Negroes. It denied to the states the power to withhold the right to vote, " on account of race, color, or previous condition of servitude." This amendment, however, has become practically a dead letter. Moreover, it is not surprising that so conservative a body as our Supreme Court should have had little desire to enforce it. In the case of Giles v. Harris, it was claimed that the suffrage provisions of the Alabama Constitution of 1901, which included the so-called grandfather clause, violated the Fourteenth and Fifteenth Amendments. The Court, however, declared that " relief from a great political wrong, if done, as alleged, by the people of a State and the State itself, must be given by them or by the legislative and political department of the government of the United States." [12] That this grandfather clause found in some of the southern states has more recently been declared unconstitutional in one or two cases does not materially affect the situation inasmuch as there may be the grossest kind of discrimination against the Negro in the administration of suffrage provisions — such as the educational qualification — which in form apply to all alike. The attitude of the Supreme Court toward the disfranchisement of the Negro is probably fairly indicated in the case of Williams v. Mississippi. It was contended that the constitution and statutes of Mississippi deprived the Negro of rights guaranteed to him by the Fourteenth Amendment. The Court said with reference to these constitutional and statutory provisions: " They do not on their face discriminate between the races, and it has not been shown that their actual administration was evil, only that evil was possible under them." [13]

It is interesting to note in this connection how the constitutional provisions which deprived the Negro of the political rights guaranteed to him by the Fifteenth Amendment were adopted in some of the states. The Reconstruction constitutions under which the southern states were readmitted into

---

[12] 189 U. S. 475 (1902). Opinion by Justice Holmes.
[13] 170 U. S. 213 (1897).

the Union, though submitted to the people in compliance with federal law, were, unfortunately, somewhat indefinite concerning popular ratification in case of the adoption of new constitutions. The practice of submitting constitutions to the people, which had been uniformly followed in the United States from 1840 to 1860, had been largely abandoned in the South during the Civil War period, but was revived by the federal government during Reconstruction. These Reconstruction constitutions extended the suffrage to all male citizens twenty-one years of age or over, subject to a moderate residence requirement. All provided for popular ratification of amendments or changes. In seven of them, mention was made of the constitutional convention as a method of framing a new constitution. Six of the seven required that the proposal for a convention should be approved by the voters. But only one, Missouri, required that the constitution thus framed should be submitted to the people. The rest were silent concerning the way in which constitutional changes proposed by a convention were to be adopted. Five southern constitutions of this period contained no mention of the constitutional convention.

We have seen then that conservative opinion in the early period of our history did not regard popular ratification as either essential or desirable. Nevertheless, with the extension of the suffrage in the early years of the nineteenth century, this had become the general practice; and public opinion had come to regard ratification of state constitutions by the people as a necessary step in the process of adopting them. But regardless of public opinion concerning this question, six constitutions have been adopted since 1890 without popular approval. One of these is the Delaware Constitution of 1897, framed and adopted by a convention in a state in which neither constitutions nor constitutional amendments have ever been submitted to the people. The adoption of the present constitution of Delaware illustrates the fact that popular ratification is not necessary in the absence of a constitutional provision expressly requiring it.

Four Southern constitutions adopted without submission to the people raise the question as to the necessity for submission even when it is expressly required by the constitution in force. The Mississippi Constitution of 1868, which was popularly ratified, provided, under the heading " Mode of revising the constitution," that any " change, alteration, or amendment " should be submitted to the people. It contained no reference to a convention or the framing of an entire new constitution. But according to any reasonable interpretation of such a provision for popular reference, it would be held that a new constitution could not be legally adopted without ratification by the voters. The words, " any change, alteration, or amendment," if they mean anything at all, would include the proposal to supplant the existing constitution with a new one. This conclusion seems necessary, especially in view of the fact that the provision for amending was under the heading, " Mode of revising the constitution." Nevertheless, the Constitution of 1890 was adopted by a convention without ratification by the people. This new constitution repeated in substance the amendment provisions of the old constitution, but changed the heading from " Mode of revising the constitution " to " Amendments to the Constitution."

The Louisiana Constitution of 1868 had a title for its article on amendment which was identical with that of Mississippi's Reconstruction constitution, and like the Mississippi constitution it provided for popular ratification of amendments. Thus in spite of the fact that the Constitution of 1868 was silent concerning conventions or the framing of a new constitution, the promulgation of the Constitution of 1898 without reference to the voters was clearly a violation of the amendment provision of the earlier constitution.[14] It is interesting to note that two years before, a constitutional amendment restricting the suffrage had been submitted to the voters and rejected.[15]

The South Carolina Constitution of 1868 and the Virginia Constitution of 1870 in addition to requiring popular ratification of amendments also required that the question of calling a constitutional convention should be submitted to the electors. Both were silent, however, concerning the method by which a constitution framed by a convention was to be legally adopted. In consequence of this omission the South Carolina Constitution of 1895 and the Virginia Constitution of 1902 became operative without submission to the people.

The constitutions which were replaced by these four recent state constitutions had been framed by conventions and ratified by the voters. The fact that two of them did not refer to constitutional revision except in the title of the amendment section, and that the other two referred to it without stating how a constitution framed by a convention was to be adopted, can not by any fair interpretation be held to justify the omission of popular ratification. It would be unreasonable to assume that the conventions which framed, and the people who ratified, the earlier constitutions in these states did not intend that new constitutions should be submitted to the people. Their purpose was evident in the specific requirement that all amendments were to be ratified by the voters. Assuming that these constitutions were made and adopted in good faith, it would be preposterous to claim

[14] The Constitution of 1898 has been superseded by the Constitution of 1921, which was also promulgated without popular ratification.
[15] W. F. Dodd, *Revision and Amendment of State Constitutions*, p. 67.

that it was not the intention of the framers, and of the people who approved their work, to require the submission of new constitutions to the voters. Why should they have been so careful to specify that all amendments were to be submitted for approval or rejection by the people if they intended to exclude popular ratification of new constitutions? The inconsistency in admitting that no mere amendment to a constitution could be made without the formal approval of the voters and at the same time claiming that an entirely new constitution, which deprived them of their most fundamental political right — the right to vote — could be legally adopted without their consent, is too obvious to need discussion.

The attitude toward popular participation in the adoption of formal amendments which is implied in the failure to submit these constitutions to the voters is clear. It assumes that ratification by the people is not necessary in any case unless required by the constitution in force in language so definite and unmistakable that no other interpretation can be put upon it. The rule that amendments must be submitted to the people is, according to this view, but one of those concessions which the progress of democratic opinion has made necessary. Like all constitutional concessions to the demand for direct popular control, this concession should be interpreted in the light of the old Federalist belief that the people are incapable of performing any important political function, except through the medium of their governmental representatives. The old conservative view of representative government would have limited popular participation in public affairs to the election of the less important officers, leaving all vital matters of legislation and policy to be decided by the government itself. It was, according to conservative opinion, highly desirable that the people should not have the power to reject what a representative body had approved — especially in the case of fundamental law. The power of the people to veto a constitution would largely defeat the purpose of representative government by making constitutional law in some measure directly dependent upon public opinion. It might at times be necessary to make changes in the constitution for which the majority would not be able to see the need, and which they would be able to prevent, if popular ratification were permitted.

Such a situation obtained in the case of the four Southern states already considered. The chief object which the constitutional conventions in these states had in view was the disfranchisement of a large proportion of the legally qualified voters. The class of voters affected consisted largely, though not entirely, of Negroes. The devices employed to disfranchise them were property, taxpaying, and educational tests, and a high and complex residence requirement. Every voter was required to satisfy at least one of the first three tests, except where the constitution contained the so-called grandfather clause, and all were subject to the residence rule. The proposed restrictions on the suffrage would clearly not be confined to Negro voters, since many white men would feel the effect of property, taxpaying, or educational qualifications if these were fairly enforced, and a large number of white voters would be disfranchised by the high residence requirement, irrespective of their ability to meet a property, taxpaying, or educational test. Under these circumstances, to submit the constitutions to the people who were to be disfranchised thereby would probably have defeated the movement to abridge the suffrage.

No doubt, the leaders felt as Madison did when the present Constitution of the United States was adopted, that disregard by governmental agencies of specific requirements of the constitutions in force might be justified by the higher law of necessity. The motive for resorting to revolutionary procedure, as in the case of the adoption of the federal Constitution, was the desire to make governmental institutions less directly responsive to public opinion. If constitutions were in fact what the people have believed them to be — fundamental laws which protect them against abuses of governmental authority — the constitutional history of the United States would have been altogether different.

Legislatures and constitutional conventions would be powerless to enforce constitutions illegally adopted if they did not have the sympathy and coöperation of the courts. With their acquired power of veto, the latter could in any case brought before them, civil or criminal, which involved rights or governmental authority claimed under such a constitution or under the laws enacted by the government sought to be established by it, declare such a constitution without binding force and all official acts under it unauthorized and without legal effect. If the courts had assumed the attitude that a constitution could not be legally adopted without following the method required by existing constitutional law, they would have been under the necessity of refusing to coöperate with the legislative and executive branches of the state governments organized under such illegally adopted constitutions. Inasmuch as the courts have come to be entrusted with the duty of standing guard over our constitutions, their power of veto is admirably suited to the purpose of preventing legislatures and conventions from depriving the people of their constitutional rights by wholly unconstitutional methods. American experience, however, has abundantly shown that courts are not to be depended upon to protect the people in the enjoyment of the political rights guaranteed to them by the express terms of their fundamental law.

There are three important political rights which any constitution for a free people should guarantee, and which are, in fact, specified in practically all of our state constitutions — the elective franchise, the right to adequate legislative representation, and the right to pass on any change in the fundamental law.

Qualifications for voting should be definitely fixed in the constitution and not subject to modification at the hands of governmental agencies. Where the right of suffrage is not specified in the fundamental law, the legislature has the power to disfranchise the voters whom it is supposed to represent.

In order to make the right of suffrage a real power in the hands of the people a constitution must further guarantee that the legislature will be so apportioned as to make it representative of the voters. To leave this matter to the legislature itself would make it possible for that body to nullify the influence of a widely extended suffrage by so apportioning its members as to give to a minority of the voters an effective legislative majority. We have attempted in our fundamental law — federal and state — to protect the voters against this form of indirect disfranchisement by requiring that representation shall be reapportioned at regularly recurring periods and according to a plan contained in the constitution itself. But in spite of constitutional provisions of this sort, legislatures have continued to use large discretionary powers in relation to apportionment. They have ignored in many instances mandatory provisions designed to ensure a fair representation. Such a provision in the federal Constitution, as we have seen above, has never been enforced, and definite provisions of state constitutions which were intended to guarantee frequent and regularly recurring reapportionment of representation have been repeatedly ignored.[16]

In a state where the population is increasing more rapidly in some districts than in others, a lawmaking body, unless frequently reapportioned, will become unrepresentative of the state as a whole. Suppose, for instance, that in a state where the legislature is originally apportioned so as to be really representative reapportionment is not required until the end of a ten-year period. It is quite possible that before the term elapses the distribution of population may so change that the districts represented by a majority of the legislators will contain much less than half of the population of the state. Having the majority in the legislature, these districts will still largely control legislation. A reapportionment made in compliance with the constitution would, however, deprive them of this control.

The reasons for disregarding constitutional provisions requiring a reapportionment of representation are easy to discover. The parts of the state which would lose political power through reapportionment are almost always predominantly rural, while the communities which would be benefited by redistribution are usually largely urban. Compliance with the constitution would therefore mean the surrender of political control by the interests in possession of the state government, and the substitution of urban for rural ascendancy. Confronted by such a contingency, the legislative majority is likely to feel that strict enforcement of the apportionment provision of the constitution would be so unwise as to justify sufficient disregard of constitutional requirements as to make possible the continuance of rural

[16] See ch. IV.

supremacy. There may also be a more distinctly selfish reason for disregarding the constitution. Reapportionment as required by the constitution would leave many members of the legislature who come from the over-represented parts of the state without constituencies to represent. Not only would some members be deprived of the chance to be re-elected, but a much larger number would be disturbed by the fear that their chances of reëlection would be diminished. In the case supposed, it would be exceedingly undesirable from the viewpoint of the members of the legislature to have a general rearrangement of house and senate districts. Moreover, the members are likely to feel that they represent districts rather than the state as a whole, since they were chosen by single districts and must look to them for reëlection. The majority of the members being dependent upon constituencies that are over-represented would naturally be slow to enact reapportionment legislation depriving that part of the state which they represent of its controlling influence in the legislature. Their disinclination to act in this matter would be even more pronounced if it meant the transfer of control over legislation to another and in some respects opposing group of interests, as would be the case if reapportionment involved the supplanting of rural by urban control.

It is obvious that the effectiveness of a widely extended suffrage may be greatly impaired by the neglect or refusal of the legislature to apportion representation as required by the constitution. Thus, in spite of constitutional provisions designed to safeguard the suffrage by guaranteeing to each voter his proportionate share of representation, legislatures have often indirectly disfranchised the majority through their control over apportionment. Both the right to vote and the right to be adequately represented, even though guaranteed by the constitution, are subject to legislative impairment.

There is, moreover, no assurance that the constitution will continue to recognize these rights unless the people have the additional right to veto proposed changes in the constitution. Popular ratification of all constitutional changes, whether proposed by a legislature or a constitutional convention, and whether in the form of an amendment or a complete revision of the constitution, is absolutely necessary if the constitution is to afford the people any protection in the enjoyment of their political rights. If the requirement of popular ratification can be disregarded and a new constitution can be framed and adopted by purely governmental agencies, it is obvious that the political rights of the people depend less upon formal constitutional guaranties than upon the caprice of legislative bodies.

If courts were in fact what they profess to be — the guardians of constitutional rights — we would expect them to regard governmental abridgment of these rights as a suitable occasion for the exercise of the judicial veto. We have seen that in the case of Williams v. Mississippi, referred to above, the Supreme Court of the United States refused to interfere. This body is, however, the recognized protector only of such rights as are guaranteed to the people by the federal Constitution. It is to our state courts that we must look for the enforcement of those rights which are guaranteed only in our state constitutions. Nevertheless, the appeal to state courts for protection against violation of the above mentioned political rights has been futile.

A study of the cases in which the validity of these constitutions was a point in dispute makes it quite clear that the courts were in sympathy with the main object of these constitutional changes. Their chief concern seems to have been to find a plausible reason for refusing to interfere. The Supreme Court of Mississippi in Sproule v. Fredericks, decided in 1892, based its decision upholding the procedure in adopting the new constitution on the theory that a constitutional convention is a sovereign body. " The sole limitation upon its powers," according to the opinion of the court, is that imposed by the Constitution of the United States, which requires every state to maintain a republican form of government.[17] In relation to the government, the existing constitution, and the people of the state, the constitutional convention is, according to this view, a sovereign body. Starting with this assumption, the court found it easy to justify the omission of popular ratification. As a sovereign body, the constitutional convention can not be regarded as legally bound to follow the requirements of existing constitutional law. The court does not say this in express terms, but it is clearly implied.

In the Virginia case, Taylor v. Commonwealth, the Virginia Supreme Court of Appeals evaded the question as to whether the constitutional convention had the power to promulgate the new constitution. " We do not wish," said the court, " to be understood as acquiescing in the contention of the prisoner that the convention of 1901–2 was without power to promulgate the Constitution it ordained. We have expressed no opinion upon that subject for two reasons: (1) Because the library at hand is not sufficient to enable us properly to investigate and consider the question; and (2) because, if it were conceded that the convention was without power to promulgate the Constitution, it would not alter the result in this case, inasmuch as the Constitution of 1902 has become the fundamental law of the state, as already shown,

17 11 Southern Reporter 472.

by being acknowledged and accepted by the government and people of the state." [18]

This is equivalent to saying that the method by which a constitution has been adopted is immaterial provided that those responsible for its adoption have been strong enough to enforce it. It is evident that the court had serious doubts as to the possibility of finding in American constitutional law any justification for disregarding the amendment provision of the old constitution. But whether legally or illegally adopted, it had become in fact the constitution, according to the court, " by being acknowledged and accepted by the government and people of the state." The court did not assert that the constitution was legally adopted, but based its decision wholly on the fact that it was acknowledged and accepted as such by the government and the people. The opinion said, in effect, that it was immaterial how the constitution might have been adopted, provided that a successful government had been established under it.

One might very properly ask what the court really meant when it said, in defense of its decision, that the constitution in question had been acknowledged and accepted by the government. Did it mean the state government as organized under the old or under the new constitution? On the supposition that the new constitution was illegally adopted and consequently void, the government organized under the old constitution would retain all lawful authority. But there was not even the remotest possibility that a government which had initiated and actively aided in carrying through the movement to establish the new constitution would refuse to acknowledge and accept it. Nor could it be expected that a government elected and organized under the new constitution would challenge its own right to exist. Moreover, it

[18] 44 Southeastern Reporter 754.

was the main purpose of the new constitution to ensure continued control of the state by the interests which were in possession of the government under the old constitution, this control being made more secure through the withdrawal of political rights from that class of citizens most likely to oppose it.

It was not, however, governmental acceptance of the constitution that the court emphasized, but rather its acceptance by both the government and the people. How then could the question of acceptance by the people be determined? There was but one method recognized in the constitutional law of the states and that was popular ratification or rejection. The refusal to respect the constitutional provision requiring submission to the people was in itself sufficient evidence that the leaders in this movement wished to make sure of the adoption of a constitution which might be rejected if a direct expression of public opinion were permitted. And since the people were deprived, by the convention which framed and promulgated the new constitution, of the only means by which they could have legally expressed their approval or disapproval prior to its promulgation, it would be interesting to know what the court had in mind when it referred to acknowledgment and acceptance by the people. After promulgation of the constitution by the convention, the only possible way of preventing its enforcement was to induce the court to declare it illegally adopted. This body refused, however, to consider the method of adoption on the ground that, even though not submitted to the voters, it had been recognized and accepted as the constitution of the state. The court did not tell us what constitutes recognition and acceptance by the people, but it is a fair inference from its decision that it found the proof of this fact in the maintenance of orderly government throughout the state during the period of transition from the old constitution to the new. Recognition and acceptance as evidenced by the absence of actual resistance is, of course, a very different thing from approval by a majority vote. In view of the fact that the new constitution was supported by the organized political and business interests of the state and enforced by the government, submission to it was the only peaceful course open to those who would have voted to reject it. For exactly the same reason which led the court to evade the question raised concerning the method of adopting the new constitution, it would have punished as law breakers those who resisted the authority exercised under that document. And yet the court held in effect that by acquiescing in the new régime provisionally and appealing to the court for relief, the people were estopped from questioning the validity of the new constitution.

The adoption of these state constitutions and of our federal Constitution as well, exemplifies the method known in European literature of political science as the *coup d'état*. This is a revolutionary change in the political system, initiated and carried through either by a dominant branch of the government or by the government as a whole. It must not be confused with that to which we ordinarily apply the term revolution, since the latter always has a popular origin and is directed not by, but against, established authority. The distinguishing feature of the *coup d'état* is the refusal of officials in changing the form of the state to recognize and be governed by the established rules of constitutional law. We have been in the habit of complacently assuming that in this country we are safeguarded against such abuses of governmental authority. The facts mentioned above indicate, however, that there is little foundation for this feeling of security.

If there is no branch of state or federal government to which the people may appeal for protection against disfranchisement by constitutional changes illegally made, have they, as the ultimate source of authority in the state, the right to protect themselves by taking the constitution-making power into their own hands? This right was clearly affirmed in the Declaration of Independence, which proclaimed the " Right of the People to alter or abolish " the government " and to institute new Government, laying its foundation on such principles and organizing its powers in such form, as to them shall seem most likely to effect their Safety and Happiness."

It was the attempt of the people of Rhode Island to protect themselves through an exercise of the constitution-making power that brought on the collision between popular and governmental authority usually referred to as Dorr's Rebellion. The charter of Rhode Island, granted by Charles II in 1663, was continued by act of the legislature at the outbreak of the Revolution as the constitution of the state. Suffrage was restricted to freeholders, and the method of apportioning representation in the legislature guaranteed control of that body to the rural interests of the state. A number of efforts had been made to induce the legislature to approve the proposal for a constitutional convention, but without result. It was in the city of Providence and in the larger towns that the injustice of a system which disfranchised the bulk of the population and placed the state under the control of a small rural oligarchy was most keenly felt. Thomas W. Dorr, a lawyer of Providence, took an active part in bringing about an organized popular demand for the extension of the suffrage and the reapportionment of representation. The strongly intrenched oligarchy in possession of the state government refusing to move in this direction, a constitutional convention was called by the people themselves. The members of this body were elected on the basis of manhood suffrage. The constitution framed by this convention was submitted to the people and ratified in December, 1841, by a large majority, which included a majority of those entitled to vote under the old constitution. The convention promptly reassembled and declared it to be the constitution of the state. At the election held under this constitution, Dorr was chosen governor. The old government, however, appealed to the President for federal aid in suppressing the movement to enforce the new constitution. The intervention of the President in support of the old government defeated the plan of the reformers. In an effort subsequently made to have the United States Supreme Court declare the new constitution the fundamental law of the state, that body evaded the question by declaring that it was a matter to be determined by the political department of the government.[19]

In supporting this unrepresentative state government against the people of the state, the federal government did what it would doubtless do again under similar conditions. In any struggle between popular and governmental authority in a state, federal intervention is practically certain to be in support of the established government, since the people can not expect governmental support in a movement directed against governmental authority. The reactionary Rhode Island state government was strictly within its legal rights in refusing to modernize the constitution, while the people, though merely seeking to substitute a democratic form of government for the one set up by a Stuart king, were of necessity opposing established authority by methods essentially revolutionary. The government itself may

[19] Luther v. Borden, 7 How., 1.

disregard constitutional restraints imposed for the protection of popular rights; but if the people on their own initiative attempt to defend or regain rights which the government has refused to recognize, they are certain to be opposed by governmental authority. A state government may disfranchise the majority of the voters through the promulgation of a new constitution adopted, as in the case of the southern constitutions referred to above, in violation of established rules of constitutional law; but the majority, thus illegally disfranchised, would be regarded as in opposition to established authority and dealt with accordingly, if they should by a concerted movement undertake to ignore the constitution by which they were illegally deprived of the right to vote. Any such organized effort, directed to the end of bringing into existence a government that would represent them, would be regarded as rebellion against the authority of the state and would be repressed, if necessary, by the federal government.

We came into existence as a nation by exercising the right of revolution against established authority, and, in our early political documents, we proclaimed the right of the people to abolish the established government whenever in their opinion it failed to serve the purpose for which it was created. There was, however, no hint in the political documents of that period, of the right of the government to resort to revolutionary procedure in changing the form of political organization. It was a power claimed exclusively for the people. Nevertheless, in the development of American politics, this right, originally claimed for the people, has come to be exercised exclusively by the government for the limitation of whose authority it was proclaimed in the Declaration of Independence.

If the Constitution of the United States does not control

the government effectively in time of peace, it is much less of a restraint upon governmental authority in time of war. The Constitution provides that " The Privilege of the Writ of *Habeas Corpus* shall not be suspended, unless when in Cases of Rebellion or Invasion the public Safety may require it." Whether it is to be suspended by Congress or by executive proclamation, the Constitution does not indicate. In practice, however, both Congress and the President have exercised this power.

Whether we may or may not regard the practical suspension of constitutional guaranties during war as necessary, it is obvious that a constitution ought to safeguard the people against precipitate action by the government in declaring war. The power to involve a country in war is the one which, more than any other, governments have abused. This power is a constant source of danger in every powerful state, since war always enhances the authority of the government and relieves it of the restraints to which it is subject in time of peace. Nevertheless, no check is imposed upon our government when exercising this power, except the necessity for coöperation between the President and Congress. Complete control over this matter is lodged in the hands of the executive and a majority of the two houses. If, as conservatives from the time of Alexander Hamilton down to the present have contended, the judicial veto is needed to protect the people against unconstitutional laws, is not some effective check much more urgently needed to protect them against abuse of the power to declare war? [20]

The Constitution makes the President the commander-in-chief of both the army and the navy, whether in time of

[20] It is interesting to note in this connection that the Articles of Confederation required the concurrence of nine states for the purpose of declaring war, which was the number specified in the Constitution as necessary for its adoption.

peace or war. He thus has the power not only to involve the country in war but even to employ the armed forces of the United States against countries with which we are supposed to be at peace, as was done in the case of Russia after the Bolshevist revolution and in Haiti during recent years.

Only in a monarchical country such as Germany was before the recent war, can we find any parallel to the situation that exists in the United States. The German Emperor, like the American President, was head of the army and the navy. Whether he was really responsible for starting the World War, as was so insistently proclaimed by the Allied Powers, may be an interesting subject for historians to investigate in the future. Concerning one aspect of the situation, however, there is no room for doubt; where the civil head of the state is commander-in-chief of both the army and the navy, he has, in fact, the war-making power. This combination of civil and military authority in one person existed in the past under monarchy; but no great democratic country save our own places the control of its army and navy directly in the hands of its chief executive.

To confer supreme military authority upon one who, like the President of the United States, is subject during his term of office to effective control neither by the other branches of the government nor by the people, seemed, no doubt, much less dangerous to the framers of the Constitution than it would have appeared in the light of one hundred and thirty years' experience under the form of government which they devised. We had in the beginning no standing army, and the navy was negligible. Consequently, the President had little real military or naval power in time of peace. But with the organization and growth of the army as a permanent institution, and the development of a large and powerful navy, the war powers of the President have acquired a new significance. His constitutional position as commander-in-chief of the army and navy means under the conditions which now exist, the power to bring on war. Although it was the intention of the founders of our government to give to Congress the power to declare war, the President's influence is likely to be the determining factor. Since he represents the government in all its foreign relations, and controls all official sources of information in this field, he could ordinarily induce Congress to accept his decision; and even if he should fail in this, he could force war upon an unwilling Congress through his control over the army and the navy.

By the unchecked act of the government, the country may be placed in a state of war. Constitutional restraints upon governmental authority are then relaxed or entirely suspended. The government as such becomes for all practical purposes supreme. Where the government has the power to commit the country to war, it must also have the right to adopt such coercive and repressive measures as will place at its disposal for the purposes of war all the available resources in men and money. It may even continue the suspension of constitutional rights after the war is over and, under the pretext of a technical state of war, carry over into a time of peace a policy of repression which could be justified, if at all, only as a war-time necessity. That this is not a purely imaginary danger the situation in this country during the years immediately following the close of the World War has shown.

It is only since the close of the recent war that we have come to realize the full significance of the treaty-making power. We have recently seen a President take an active part in framing a constitution for a proposed super-government, and attempt to secure its adoption, so far as this country was concerned, through an exercise of the treaty-making power. And although the plan failed because of his inability to obtain the required number of votes in the Senate, it is indicative of the use which may be made of this power. It was contended, of course, that the League of Nations was not designed to, and would not, in fact, limit the sovereignty of the individual states. But its very purpose was to impose an external restraint upon the several countries of the world. If it did not limit the power of a state with reference to questions which vitally concerned other states, it would, of course, be useless. To the extent that it possessed the power to coerce the individual state, the governments associated together under this larger political organization would occupy a distinctly subordinate position in relation to all matters placed under the jurisdiction of the League. It would follow that if the United States could be thus divested of some of its authority as an independent nation by an exercise of the treaty-making power, there would be no limit beyond which the President and Senate might not go in subordinating the country to external control. The proposal to associate the United States with other countries in a so-called League of Nations was as clearly designed to modify our governmental system as would be one to require popular ratification of a declaration of war. The latter, however, would have to pass through all the stages of the difficult process of constitutional amendment.

The distinction between state and government now made by conservative writers in this country may be regarded as an attempt to justify unlimited political power. It is in effect a repudiation of the basic principle of our system as it was originally established. Sovereignty in the sense of unlimited political authority was supposed to be incompatible with the check and balance theory of our governmental system. The law of nature was conceived as limiting not only every part of the government and the government as a whole, but also the power of the people. In fact, the chief purpose of the Constitution was to safeguard the country against either governmental or popular supremacy. As the United States Supreme Court said in Loan Association v. Topeka: " The theory of our governments, state and national, is opposed to the deposits of unlimited power anywhere. . . . There are limitations on such power which grow out of the essential nature of all free governments, implied reservations of individual rights, without which the social compact could not exist, and which are respected by all governments entitled to the name." [21]

It is evident from the debates in the federal constitutional convention that what the framers most feared and were most desirous of limiting was the power of the popular majority. But in defending the form of government which they established, it was the limitations imposed on governmental authority which they emphasized. Intelligent conservatives may have regarded and probably did regard the checks imposed on the people as the chief merit of the Constitution. But in the organized propaganda to create a public opinion that would preserve it, this feature was discreetly kept in the background. Prominently in the foreground were two assumptions: (1) that the Constitution was an embodiment of the will of the people and (2) that it could not be disregarded by the government.

The fiction that the Constitution was made by the people and was the instrument through which they controlled the government was designed to win popular support rather than to enlighten the people as to its true purpose. This fiction was constantly reiterated by federal judges, by the leaders

[21] 20 Wallace 663.

of the legal profession, and by all conservatives, who devoutly believed that it was necessary to have effective checks on popular authority. Even Chief Justice Marshall in McCulloch v. Maryland, decided in 1821, says: " The government of the Union . . . is, emphatically, and truly, a government of the people. In form and in substance it emanates from them. Its powers are granted by them." [22]

It is the acceptance by the people of the notion that our Constitution is an expression of their will and so designed as effectually to subordinate the government, that constitutes what is often referred to as the deification of our political system. Other nations, particularly the English, have believed in what may be called the supremacy of law; but they have recognized the all-important fact that law does not enforce itself — that in practice it becomes very largely what those who control its interpretation and enforcement may desire to make it. As a matter of fact it was the realization that a so-called reign of law may serve merely as a mask for governmental irresponsibility, that was the chief factor in bringing about the parliamentary form of government. We enjoy the somewhat doubtful distinction of being the only modern nation in which the belief largely prevails that those who govern not only do not, but can not, disregard the fundamental law. It is not strange, however, that the uncritical public should believe this, since it is the very essence of the legalistic view of our political system, adopted by all our conservative writers on political science and even incorporated in elementary textbooks on civics.

Referring to some foreign criticisms which point out the sophistry involved in the assumption that our Constitution is a fundamental law imposed upon the government and which it can not disregard, Woodrow Wilson says: " They

[22] 4 Wheaton 316.

emanate from men for whom all law is the voice of government and who regard the government as the source of all law, who can not conceive of a law set above government and to which it must conform." [23] He refers again in the same work to the power exercised by the federal Supreme Court as having " made our system, so far, a model before all the world of the reign of law." [24] He fails, however, to keep this basic assumption constantly in mind, for he tells us that " Constitute them how you will, governments are always governments of men, and no part of any government is better than the men to whom that part is intrusted." [25] " Every government," he admits later in the same work, " is a government of men, not of laws, and of course the courts of the United States are no wiser or better than the judges who constitute them." [26] But in spite of occasional statements such as the last two above quoted he may be regarded as a stanch defender of the legalistic view of the American Constitution.

From the very beginning of our history under the Constitution, we have attempted to distinguish between constitutional and statute law. Courts and writers on the American constitutional system, regard the government as the source of ordinary law, while constitutional law is represented by them as deriving its sanction from the people. According to this legalistic theory of our government, constitutional law is an expression of the will of the people, while statute law reflects the will of their agent, the government. It follows logically that in all cases of conflict between the will of the people as expressed in the Constitution and the will of the government as expressed in statute law the latter must yield to the former.

The conservatives who actively disseminated this purely

---

[23] *Constitutional Government in the United States,* p. 161.
[24] *Ibid.,* p. 172.   [25] *Ibid.,* p. 17.   [26] *Ibid.,* p. 165.

fanciful idea of the Constitution had two definite practical objects in view. They hoped to preserve the Constitution by having it accepted as the voice of the people; and they wished to provide a justification for the exercise of the judicial veto by attributing to it a popular origin. And since the judicial veto was defended as necessary for the enforcement of the people's will as expressed in the Constitution, the conservative interpretation of our governmental system came to be accepted as an application of the doctrine of popular sovereignty. It is quite clear, however, that the conservative lawyers who had the leading part in framing the Constitution and developing it by interpretation, did not believe in the sovereignty of the people. Ample proof of this is supplied by the form of government which they established; and, although the legal theory of the Constitution may seem to the superficial reader to imply popular sovereignty, it is, in fact, a denial of the supremacy of the people. Nevertheless, it is around the legal view of the Constitution that the prevalent opinion of it as the instrument of popular sovereignty has crystallized.

The distinction between state and government which has been so much emphasized in our recent literature of political science is not really new. It is clearly implied in the legal theory of the Constitution; it has been made by conservatives ever since the instrument was framed; it found expression in the Federalist papers, even before the instrument was ratified by the states. Burgess and other recent writers have merely given the name, state, to the power back of the Constitution, which had before been vaguely thought of by some as the people, and by others as that combination of governmental agencies entrusted with the constitution-making power.

The significance of this distinction, so far as recent writers are concerned, is to be found in the use made of it. Formerly, it served the purpose of justifying the limitation of political authority, but it is now advanced in support of the unlimited power of the state.

" The authority of the State," says W. F. Willoughby, " is unlimited; that of the government only such as the people acting as a body politic, that is as a State, choose to confer upon it. The State is the principal with inherent unlimited powers; the government an agent with only such powers as its principal may choose to confer upon it and those powers moreover it can exercise only in the manner prescribed by the State." [27]

There has been a marked recent tendency in the more popular books on political science, and especially in those of the college and high school textbook type, to repeat and emphasize the assumption that the people are sovereign and the government strictly subordinated. Thus in a college textbook we read:

" One of the most striking features of the Constitution of the United States, and one which distinguishes it most clearly from the constitution of Great Britain, is the sovereignty of the people. In England, Parliament is legally sovereign. . . . It has the power not only to pass any and all legislation but also to alter and amend the very constitution under which it acts. . . .

" Such power in the United States resides not in Congress, nor in any department of the government, nor in the states, but in the people. The first sentence of the Constitution clearly expresses the American theory in sharp contrast to the English theory: ' We the people of the United States . . . do ordain and establish this Constitution for the United States of America.' " [28]

[27] *The Government of Modern States*, p. 15.
[28] Everett Kimball, *The National Government of the United States*, p. 47.

In a widely used high school textbook under the topical
heading, " The Essential features of American Government," we are told:

" In order, however, that the form and the powers of the
governments shall remain the same until the people wish
them changed, the people of the Nation have adopted the
very important document called the Constitution of the
United States, and the people of each State have adopted a
similar constitution for their State. . . . They cannot be
altered by the *governments*, neither can the governments
make any change in their own powers. *All changes in an
old constitution must be made by the people, who made that
constitution, and who may abolish the old constitution and
have a new one in its place.* Since, therefore, the people
may change their old constitutions and make new ones, we
say *the people are sovereign;* that is, the people have the
supreme power which governments and individual citizens
are obliged to obey." [29]

In another book on civics written for high school classes,
we find the following:

" In the United States political power everywhere flows
from the people. The President of the United States, the
Congress, and the national Supreme Court, all receive their
powers from the Constitution of the United States, and this
Constitution is a creation of the people of the United States;
. . . Thus in the United States the will of the people prevails not only in the country taken as a whole but in all its
parts as well. This is the fundamental principle of the
American government.

" The people govern by a political device known as *majority rule.* When a question of government is to be decided, or when an officer of government is to be chosen, an

orderly vote is taken and the will of the majority is regarded as the will of all. The majority rules and the minority submits to the will of the majority; this is a necessary and unavoidable feature of democratic government. The minority, right or wrong, must bow to the will of the majority." [30]

The statements above quoted are representative of much of the literature used for civic instruction in the United States. Even where popular sovereignty is not expressly affirmed, it is nearly always tacitly assumed. By emphasizing the more democratic features of our governmental structure, by keeping its essentially conservative character in the background, and by misrepresenting the nature of our judicial system, a constitution designed mainly to subordinate the popular majority has come to be accepted by the people as a means of enforcing popular sovereignty.

The distinction between state and government, now generally made in this country by conservative writers, is not supposed to be susceptible of general application. In no country except the United States, we are told, is there the degree of separation between state and government which this distinction implies. It is the contention of Professor Burgess that by separating state and government and subordinating the latter to the former, we have reached a stage of political development in the United States which has been approached in no other country.

" I think the difficulty which lies in the way of the general acceptance by publicists of the principle of the sovereignty of the state," he says, " is the fact that they do not sufficiently distinguish the state from the government. They see the danger to individual liberty of recognizing an unlimited power in the government; and they immediately conclude that the same danger exists if the sovereignty of the

[30] S. E. Forman, *Advanced Civics,* p. 9.

state be recognized. This is especially true of European publicists, most especially of German publicists. . . . In America we have a great advantage in regard to this subject. With us the government is not the sovereign organization of the state. Back of the government lies the constitution; and back of the constitution the original sovereign state, which ordains the constitution both of government and of liberty. We have the distinction already in objective reality. . . . This is the point in which the public law of the United States has reached a far higher development than that of any state of Europe." [31]

It is in the veto power of the courts that Professor Burgess finds the distinctive superiority of the American political system, since it is through the exercise of this power that the government is prevented from encroaching on the sphere of the state by enacting laws that violate the Constitution. The federal state, although conceived to be entirely distinct from the federal government, is, as he defines it, a mere combination of governmental agencies; it makes, interprets, and enforces, the Constitution; its power is unlimited by any higher law or external authority. In reply to those who hold that the power of the state is limited, he says:

" But who is to interpret, in last instance, these principles, which are termed laws of God, laws of nature, laws of reason, and laws between nations, when they are invoked by anybody in justification of disobedience to a command of the state, or of the powers which the state authorizes? Is it not evident that this must be the state itself? " [32]

Those who follow Burgess in attempting to make this distinction between state and government generally confuse

<hr />

[31] *Political Science and Constitutional Law*, vol. I, p. 57.
[32] *Ibid.*, vol. I, p. 53.

the state with the people. By thus confusing the popular mind, it becomes comparatively easy to create a prevalent sentiment that will support unlimited political power under the guise of popular sovereignty. The general acceptance of the idea that the people, organized as the state, have unlimited power, would change profoundly the character of the political system originally established by breaking down restraints on governmental authority.

As we have seen above, there is really nothing new in the conception that there is an authority back of the Constitution and working through it which controls the government. Nor is there anything new in the contention that the people constitute the ultimate source of authority. The only new feature in this distinction between state and government is the unlimited power which is attributed to the people politically organized as the state. This is directly opposed to the earlier American view, which refused to recognize the sovereignty of either the government or the people. The dependence of the government on the governed was proclaimed in the Declaration of Independence. But since the majority of white men had no vote, they were not included in the state as that term is defined by these recent writers. The right of revolution, claimed for the people in the Declaration of Independence and in various state constitutions of the period, recognized this disfranchised majority as a restraint on the power of the state.

The adoption of the Constitution was the outcome of a movement to bring about what the framers believed to be a better distribution and balance of powers between the federal and the state governments and between the government as a whole and the people. The latter as a result of the Revolution had, it was thought, become too largely a direct source of political power. The framers believed that one of the chief problems which confronted them was to provide adequate protection against the excesses of democracy. This situation they hoped to remedy by the more effective system of checks and balances which the Constitution was supposed to provide. It was only in a strictly limited and negative sense that they thought of the people as being a source of political power. Indeed, the only political power directly conferred upon them was that of choosing the members of the least important branch of the government — the House of Representatives. With the single exception of the right to vote for members of the lower house, the people as such could act politically only through the government. Even this restricted right was at that time withheld from the majority.

The Constitution was framed and adopted by representative bodies and ever since the federal government was established under it, all constitutional law has been made by the federal and the state legislatures and interpreted and enforced exclusively by the federal government itself. Only through their governmental representatives were the people thought to be capable of exercising satisfactorily any important political function. Nothing, in fact, was farther from the minds of those who framed the Constitution than the idea of creating an organization distinct from, and entirely outside of, the government, which would control the Constitution and through it all officials who exercised political power.

" The person or body of persons," Professor Burgess tells us, " who in last resort interpret the will of God or of the superhuman spirit or the idea for a given people, and who give their interpretations the force of law, constitute the state." [33] For most purposes this final authority under our

[33] *Political Science and Constitutional Law*, vol. I, p. 75.

system of government is the United States Supreme Court. This leads him to call the governmental system of the United States the " aristocracy of the robe." [34]   Although he distinguishes between state and government, he does not attempt to identify the state with the people of the United States as many of his followers have done.   The state as he defines it is an aggregate of purely governmental agencies and for different purposes is differently constituted.   For amending the Constitution, it consists of two-thirds of each house of Congress and a majority in both houses of the legislature in three-fourths of the states.   For the purpose of interpreting and enforcing the Constitution, the Supreme Court is the state, except where under the established practice of our governmental system this function devolves on the executive or on one or both houses of Congress.   And since the Constitution is amended, interpreted, and enforced only by governmental agencies, Burgess' constant reference to the American state as organized wholly outside of the government, and to the government as controlled by the state, may be regarded as an attempt to make sovereignty or unlimited power acceptable to those who believe that governmental authority should be strictly limited.   He appears to hold the view that the government is controlled by the state through the Constitution; but the state as he defines it is a mere *alter ego* of the government itself.   Since there is so little basis for this distinction between state and government in the actual organization of American politics, it should perhaps be regarded, like the legal view of the Constitution, of which it is only a restatement, as a plausible method of reconciling the belief in limited government with the fact of governmental supremacy.   And just as the earlier legal view of our political system laid the foundation for the growth

[34] *Political Science and Constitutional Law,* vol. II, p. 365.

of governmental authority by envisaging the Constitution as a supreme law which the government could not disregard, so this distinction between state and government may be regarded as an attempt to defend governmental supremacy under the guise of popular sovereignty.

It was John C. Calhoun who with unanswerable logic exposed the sophistry in the conventional legal view of the Constitution. Starting with the assumption that the Constitution, as proclaimed by its framers, was designed to limit the power of the federal government, he maintained that it should be so interpreted as to give effect to its avowed purpose. It was with reference to the relation of the general government to the constitution-interpreting power that he opposed the legal view of the Constitution. He insisted that it was absurd to hold that the Constitution limited the powers of the federal government and at the same time to allow that government to interpret the restrictions on its own authority. He contended that there was a source of authority higher than the federal government or any of its organs — that which had been entrusted with the constitution-making power. This included the legislative branch of the general government, since Congress by a two-thirds majority proposed all constitutional amendments; but before any amendment thus proposed could become a part of the fundamental law, ratification by representative bodies (legislatures or conventions) in three-fourths of the states was necessary. We thus had the constitution-making power lodged in a group of governmental agencies so arranged as to impose an effective check on the federal government. This provision of the Constitution was obviously designed to prevent the general government from increasing its powers at the expense of the states. And since constitution-interpreting power was but a phase of the constitution-making power, it should be controlled by that group of governmental agencies having the power to amend the Constitution. To give effect to the declared purpose of the Constitution, it was necessary that the power of the federal government to interpret should be as effectively checked as was its power to amend, since if it had entire control of constitutional interpretation, it could relax and finally remove all restraints on its authority.

It is obvious that the distinction made by Calhoun between the federal government and the group of state and federal governmental organs having the power to amend the Constitution, corresponds exactly to Burgess' distinction of half a century later between the federal government and the federal state. But, unlike Calhoun, Burgess does not logically and consistently apply this distinction. He defines the state in terms of constitution-making power and recognizes interpretation as a function of the state, yet he defends the system under which a branch of the federal government, the Supreme Court, controls constitutional interpretation. Clearly, the explanation of Burgess' inconsistency in this respect was his desire to advance governmental supremacy under the guise of the sovereignty of the federal state.

The propaganda to which we are indebted for the prevalence of the belief that the government is effectually subordinated under our scheme of political organization, though originally designed to preserve the Constitution by deifying it, has actually tended to increase governmental independence of constitutional restraints. General acceptance of the fiction that all officials are controlled by the fundamental law, means in its practical application that this law is assumed to be self-enforcing. A people once thoroughly permeated with this notion would not be inclined to take a very active part in politics, since they would not see the need of it. Nothing could be devised that would tend to ensure public officials greater freedom to ignore constitutional requirements, than the belief that the government, even though it might wish to disregard the Constitution, is powerless to do so. The acceptance of such a notion precludes an intelligently critical attitude toward politics.

CHAPTER VIII

NATURAL LAW AND NATURAL RIGHTS AS CHECKS ON GOVERNMENTAL AUTHORITY

A conspicuous feature of political thought in recent decades has been the repudiation of the basic democratic ideas which supported the early constitutional movement and served to justify the American Revolution. This change of attitude is not confined to the United States. It is apparently due to influences which have been operative in all the more democratic countries. The extension of the suffrage, the disappearance of some of the more obvious checks on the people, and the consequent spread of the belief that political democracy has been attained, have removed the main ground for distrust of governmental authority. It is thus in part through the growth of belief in the new doctrine of popular sovereignty that these early democratic ideas have been discredited.

At the beginning of our history as a nation, we refused to recognize either the sovereignty of the government or the sovereignty of the people. We held tenaciously to the idea that all political power is limited by natural law, natural rights, and the principle of the social contract. Under the Constitution, as it was understood at the time of its adoption, the political power of the people, no less than that of the government, was supposed to be limited. The way was prepared for the conception of unlimited power by the legalistic view of the Constitution. Advanced by Hamilton in *The Federalist*, and later adopted by conservatives generally, it defined the doctrine that all governmental power is strictly limited by the Constitution, and represented the people as the source of constitutional law and of all political authority. But during the early period under the Constitution, the people, though vaguely conceived to be the highest and final source of political power, were not conceded to have unlimited authority. They, no less than the government itself, were supposed to be restrained by the fundamental principles to which all human authority should conform.

The belief in natural law and natural rights gradually declined as the people came to regard themselves as the final source of power in the state. So long as the government had been looked upon as an irresponsible institution, there was a recognized need for some external restraint on its authority. When, however, it came to be believed that the people themselves controlled the state, such ideas as natural law and natural rights lost much of their former prestige. The people readily saw the advantage of limiting the power of an irresponsible government, but they viewed with less favor any limitation of their own authority. They were willing to accept the idea that the government was limited by the Constitution, but less willing to admit that in making and interpreting constitutional law, the people were in like manner restrained by the higher law of nature. Though emphatic in denying sovereignty to the government, they were not unwilling to claim unlimited power for themselves. Political majorities, no less than public officials, are prone to take into their own hands as much power as circumstances permit.

With the growth of the idea of political democracy, the legalistic interpretation of the Constitution was modified to bring it into conformity with the new doctrine of popular sovereignty. Recognition of the people as supreme was incompatible with the idea that their will, as expressed in the Constitution, was limited by the fundamental principles implied in such terms as natural law and natural rights. According to the earlier view, the Constitution was not in fact the supreme law, since it was itself subject to a higher unwritten law. Although as the supposed expression of the people's will, it limited the powers of the government, the people themselves, in making constitutional law, were subject to the restraints imposed by the higher law of nature. The rights of the individual, as against the state, were really secured to him by natural law. The Constitution might recognize and enumerate these rights, but they were not derived from it, nor were they in any real sense guaranteed by it. All rights of this sort must, in the very nature of the case, depend for their protection and enforcement upon non-governmental agencies. As originally conceived, these rights were more fundamental than the Constitution and were not to be regarded as subject to abridgment by either the government or the people. But the idea of popular sovereignty, as it came to be generally accepted, superseded natural law and natural rights as a check on governmental authority. Individual rights, which, according to the earlier view, were derived from natural law, came now to be regarded as purely constitutional guaranties which the people might or might not recognize when exercising their sovereign function of making constitutional law.

No one can understand fully this change in attitude toward natural rights, without keeping in mind the contrast in purpose between the early and the later phase of the modern constitutional movement. Down to the time of the American Revolution, the interest in constitutional government revolved around the problem of limiting irresponsible power. Throughout this earlier period, limitation of political authority was regarded as the essential feature of constitutional government. This view was, in fact, carried over into the democratic state, and found expression in the system of checks and balances and in the continuation of natural law and natural rights as checks on popular authority. It was only at a much later time, as the idea gradually developed that the majority will is the final source of power in the state, that natural checks on political authority fell into disrepute.

The belief that there are certain fundamental principles or laws of nature by which all human authority should be restrained served a useful purpose in the development of constitutional government by enlisting popular support for the limitation of irresponsible political power. All opponents of monarchy could coöperate in disseminating the idea that rulers were subject to the checks implied in such doctrines as the social contract, natural law, and natural rights. But when the constitutional movement assumed in the nineteenth century a democratic character, the basic political ideas acquired a new significance.

The most important of these doctrines is the social contract theory of the state. This was the main support of the constitutional movement down to the time of the American Revolution and became the recognized basis of American political organization. It had an important place in political theory, not as an explanation of the origin of the state, but because it was supposed to formulate the principles to which governmental organization should conform. It supplied a criterion by which then existing governments were to be judged, and it held up an ideal which would in time, it was hoped, profoundly modify the form of the state. It was in reality an indirect and covert attack on the monarchical system of government.

The social contract theory was presented under the guise of an historical account of the origin of government. There were two reasons for this method of procedure. To have advanced the social contract as an ideal would have been an obvious and direct attack on monarchy, and would, moreover, have been ineffective. It assumed the disguise of history in order to minimize opposition and to render it more sacred. To discover the original social contract in the remote past, was to guarantee to it an influence upon the people which it could not have had if presented as a mere ideal. The writers who advanced this theory were but following the rather common practice of intelligent advocates of institutional reform, in making the new and untried more acceptable by representing it as very old.

The modern writers whose names are most conspicuously identified with the social contract theory of the state are Hobbes, Locke, and Rousseau. Hobbes wrote in defense of monarchy and can not be regarded as a supporter of the social contract theory, although he recognizes it as one of the ways in which states have come into existence. Government originates, he thinks, in two ways: " One by natural force, as when a man maketh his children to submit themselves and their children to his government, as being able to destroy them if they refuse; or by war subdueth his enemies to his will, giving them their lives on that condition. The other is when men agree amongst themselves to submit to some man, or assembly of men, voluntarily." [1]

That he repudiated the divine right doctrine and made the social contract idea the foundation of his defense of the monarchical system of government is indicative of the trend

[1] *Leviathan*, ch. XVII.

of public opinion in his time. He saw clearly that the divine right theory was no longer an adequate support for royal power, and that any acceptable defense of monarchy must recognize the people as the source of royal authority. By assuming that monarchy had its origin in an original social contract, he sought to give it the appearance, at least, of legitimacy. But his lack of sympathy with the substance of the social contract theory is clearly indicated by the way in which he sought to make it serve as a defense of monarchy. He made the authority of the king depend upon the consent of the people, as expressed in an original covenant by which they agreed among themselves to institute monarchy. This contract, he held, was binding upon the people but not upon the king, since he was not a party to it. Monarchy, though in the beginning established by the people and deriving its powers from them, became, once it was established, independent of them and was thenceforth the lawful possessor of supreme and unlimited power. Under the guise of recognizing the social contract as an explanation of the origin of monarchy, Hobbes made it clear that he opposed the essence of the social contract idea of the state.

The doctrine was given a new expression by Locke who asserted that it was the consent of the people, or in other words the social contract, " and that only, which did or could give beginning to any lawful government in the world." [2] A government which did not originate in this way, or recognize its dependence upon the people, was not in his opinion a lawful government. He did not contend that the social contract was the origin of all governments, but merely of all legitimate governments. It is evident that the emphasis which he placed on the social contract as an explanation of

[2] *Civil Government*, bk. II, ch. VIII.

the origin of government was really prompted by the desire to enhance its popularity and thus make it more effective in the struggle against irresponsible power. A fair interpretation of his political philosophy justifies the assumption that any part which the social contract may have had in the remote past in the creation of political institutions was, in his opinion, of minor importance in comparison with the significance of the social contract doctrine as a theory of political organization.

Rousseau, who is more frequently referred to as an advocate and exponent of the social contract theory than any other modern writer, apparently assumed in his *Contrat Social*, as other liberal thinkers had done before him, and, no doubt, for the same reason, that government had its origin in this original agreement of the people. It can not be said, however, that he believed that all government had been established in this way. In his *Discourse upon the Origin and Foundation of Inequality among Mankind,* published several years before the *Contrat Social,* after sketching the formation of government through the supposed original agreement of the people, he says: " Such was, or must have been had Man been left to himself, the origin of Society and of the Laws." [3]   Here, he clearly recognizes that men were not permitted to live in a so-called state of nature until such time as they could voluntarily agree to unite in setting up a state.

We find frequent reference in the recent literature of political science to David Hume, as an eighteenth century critic of the social contract theory. A conservative in his political philosophy, he was quite naturally opposed to some of the democratic implications of the social contract doctrine. But in so far as this theory may be regarded as an

[3] English tr. of R. and J. Dodsley, London, 1761.

explanation of the origin of government, it is evident that he did not altogether reject it.

"When we consider," he says, "how nearly equal all men are in their bodily force, and even in their mental powers and faculties, till cultivated by education; we must necessarily allow, that nothing but their own consent could, at first, associate them together, and subject them to any authority. The people, if we trace government to its first origin in the woods and deserts, are the source of all power and jurisdiction, and voluntarily, for the sake of peace and order, abandoned their native liberty, and received laws from their equal and companion. The conditions, upon which they were willing to submit, were either expressed, or were so clear and obvious, that it might well be esteemed superfluous to express them. If this, then, be meant by the *original contract*, it cannot be denied, that all government is, at first, founded on a contract, and that the most ancient rude combinations of mankind were formed chiefly by that principle." [4]

Although Hume traced the origin of government to what may be called a social contract, he assumed, as did Locke, that this antedated recorded history. "Almost all the governments," he tells us, "which exist at present, or of which there remains any record in story, have been founded originally, either on usurpation or conquest, or both, without any pretence of a fair consent, or voluntary subjection of the people." [5]

His essay, *Of the Original Contract,* is entirely free from the partisan bias which characterizes most of the literature that has grown up around this subject. His discussion of this highly controversial question is probably as good an example of the disinterested scientific attitude as could be

---

[4] *Of the Original Contract.*   [5] *Ibid.*

found in the entire literature of political science. It is incorrect to classify him, as many less disinterested writers have done, as an opponent of the social contract theory. It would be quite as reasonable to say that he defended it, for with certain qualifications he accepted it as an explanation of the beginning of government and as a speculative principle applicable to contemporary politics.

" As no party, in the present age," he says, " can well support itself, without a philosophical or speculative system of principles, annexed to its political or practical one we accordingly find, that each of the factions, into which this nation is divided, has reared up a fabric of the former kind, in order to protect and cover that scheme of actions, which it pursues. . . . The one party, by tracing up government to the Deity, endeavour to render it so sacred and inviolate, that it must be little less than sacrilege, however tyrannical it may become, to touch or invade it, in the smallest article. The other party, by founding government altogether on the consent of the People, suppose that there is a kind of *original contract,* by which the subjects have tacitly reserved the power of resisting their sovereign, whenever they find themselves aggrieved by that authority, with which they have, for certain purposes, voluntarily entrusted him. . . .

" I shall venture to affirm, *That both these* systems *of speculative principles are just; though not in the sense, intended by the parties:* And, *That both the* schemes *of practical consequences are prudent; though not in the extremes, to which each party, in opposition to the other, has commonly endeavoured to carry them."* [6]

He assumed that the most satisfactory form of government was to be found in the compromise between the divine and social contract ideas of the state which was the dis-

[6] *Of the Original Contract.*

tinctive feature of the English political system in his day. Having no sympathy with the doctrine of divine right as a defense of absolutism, he nevertheless believed that institutional arrangements which had long existed and had everywhere been generally accepted ought not to be lightly attacked. He believed that monarchy, though not a divine institution in the sense implied in the doctrine of divine right, was at least natural, as shown by its prevalence throughout the world during historic times.

Hume did not regard monarchy in its pure form as a desirable kind of government, but he believed that it was preferable to a republic. Since he was opposed to absolute government, whether of the monarchical or popular type, he had no sympathy with those who so interpreted the social contract theory as to make it support the unlimited power of the people. He apparently accepted the social contract idea in so far as it supplied a needed check upon king and aristocracy, but rejected it entirely as a doctrine of popular sovereignty.

The nineteenth century attack on the social contract was, for the most part, an attempt to discredit it by representing it as a theory of the origin of the state. Hume, who is often cited by recent critics of the doctrine as a supporter of their position, clearly recognized what these more recent opponents of the theory have generally ignored — that it was a "philosophical or speculative system of principles," designed to serve as a justification for the limitation of political power.

As in Hume's time this doctrine was the foundation of the argument for constitutionalism, so in the nineteenth century it became the chief theoretical support of the democratic movement. It is largely because of this relation to present day democratic tendencies, that the social contract idea has become the target of so much conservative criticism. The real motive behind this criticism is evident to anyone familiar with the history of the doctrine and its relation to the modern political movement. The fact that criticism has been focused so largely upon a minor and really non-essential feature of the social contract theory, is to be explained by the desire to attack the doctrine at what is conceived to be its weakest point.

The opposition of recent conservative writers to the social contract idea is clearly a reaction against the ultra democratic interpretation of it as a doctrine of popular sovereignty. The distinct trend, during the latter part of the nineteenth century, toward the supremacy of the popular majority caused conservative thinkers in all the more democratic countries much uneasiness. It seemed to threaten the overthrow of the entire system of constitutional checks which centuries of struggle had built up. Democracy was insistently claiming the supreme power, of which the king had been deprived through the growth of constitutional government; and it was feared that in order to gain such power the majority would remove every constitutional restraint in its way.

When a minority opposes a movement of this sort, which has behind it the physical force of the community, it is more expedient and more effective to attack indirectly, by undermining the speculative foundation without which it could not be justified. The modern writers who regard the sovereignty of the popular majority in much the same way as the advocates of constitutional government thought of the sovereignty of the king, are disposed to criticize and discredit the social contract doctrine for the same reason that it was supported by those who opposed royal supremacy. And just as many of the earlier writers refrained from attacking monarchy directly, but did, nevertheless, seek to inculcate ideas which were incompatible with the sovereignty of the king, so these recent writers, instead of attacking the social contract as a theory of democracy, have assailed it as an explanation of the origin of the state. The opposition to the doctrine from those who favor an effectively limited democracy is augmented by those who would entirely subordinate popular influence. The pronounced tendency on the part of conservative political writers since the middle of the nineteenth century to disparage the social contract philosophy is in fact an attack not only on the very foundation of democracy, but on that of the constitutional system which preceded it.

The essential principle in the social contract conception of the state is the subordination of the government to the people. According to this theory, political power is conceived to be derived from them, to be exercised under their sanction and for their benefit, and those to whom it is entrusted are thought of as immediately, or at least ultimately, accountable to them. The repudiation of this doctrine by political thinkers, if generally concurred in by the public, would profoundly influence the course of political development in the immediate future. It is, of course, designed, and would naturally tend, to bring about a reaction in political thought against the basic principles of democratic government.

If government depends upon the consent of the governed, as the social contract theory assumes, then it follows as a necessary deduction that where it persistently disregards the rights of the people, revolution is a justifiable method of redressing grievances. In the first flush of enthusiasm for independence, the American nation proclaimed the doctrine of revolution to be one of the unalienable rights of the people. But in the reaction against the democratic political philosophy of the American Revolution, which found expression in the new Constitution, the doctrine that the people have the fundamental right to overthrow an unjust government, was regarded by the dominant class in American politics as having outlived its usefulness. It had served as a means of justifying the Revolution, but it was a dangerous intellectual weapon for the people to possess, especially when, as the conservatives planned, the new Constitution was to deprive them of that controlling place in the state to which they were entitled under the social contract theory. Theoretically, if not actually, revolution was a method of redress which could be invoked successfully only by the majority. Its usefulness as a political doctrine was to be found in the fact that it supplied a check upon the government, which is most needed where the principle of political responsibility is inadequately recognized in the organization of the state. The general acceptance of such an idea by the people, no government, however strong, could afford to ignore. The attitude which it implied toward the state was, moreover, peculiarly incompatible with the purpose of the framers of the Constitution — the establishment of a strong government in which majority influence would be effectively subordinated.

The right of revolution as a protection against governmental oppression being a necessary inference from the social contract theory of the state, it is evident that the conservative reaction which brought about the adoption of the Constitution was, in fact, if not openly, opposed to the essential features of the social contract philosophy. All the interests in American political life which coöperated in imposing more effective checks upon the majority, naturally coöperated in the effort to give permanence to the system which they established, by discrediting first the so-called right of revolution and finally the entire social contract theory. Thus, by a process which is not difficult to comprehend if we remember that political theory is often the handmaid of practical politics, the doctrines which constituted our defense of the Revolution declined in popularity with the ruling class, as they came to be used more and more in support of manhood suffrage and other democratic reforms.

In countries where the democratic movement succeeded in breaking down the system of checks and establishing the supremacy of the numerical majority, as in England, the social contract theory lost its significance as a restraint on governmental authority, no less than in the United States. As a programme of the majority, it was serviceable in the movement to establish constitutional government. But when control of the state passed from the few to the many, the social contract idea ceased to function as a check upon governmental authority and became instead a justification of it.

No idea has been more closely identified with the modern democratic movement than the doctrine of equality. It is as much a part of what may be called the democratic creed, as inequality is of monarchy or aristocracy. Indeed, the idea of equality, like the social contract theory, was in the beginning largely a protest against the prevailing system of inequality.

Christianity gave to the world the idea of spiritual equality; but though it was the religion of the lowly, it made no attack upon the political, social, and economic inequalities of this world. This abstraction probably explains why it survived. Had its ideal of equality been one that clearly applied to this as well as to the next world, it would have encountered repression everywhere at the hands of the ruling classes. It is only because Christianity has upon the whole actively supported the established inequalities of society, or at least passively accepted them, that it has been permitted to expand and become the religion of the Western World.

From the viewpoint of the ruling classes, the chief function of the church in its relation to this-world affairs has always been that of inculcating respect for the established order. Control of the many by the few would have been extremely difficult, if not impossible, without the support of the church, which has given the appearance of divine sanction to the political and economic inequalities of existing societies. Any political system based upon inequality is of necessity insecure. Being opposed to the real interests of the many, its preservation depends upon the general acceptance of the belief that inequality in human society has divine sanction. This belief the church has encouraged by its passive attitude toward, or active defense of, existing inequality.

The adaptation of religious doctrines to the fact of class control is an inevitable consequence of the environmental influences under which Christianity developed. In all its relations to this world, the church has been, generally speaking, a supporter rather than an opponent of existing inequality. Even its dogmas have served this purpose. It long defended the institution of slavery, and its emphasis on the virtue of patience and resignation in this life, with the hope of reward in the world to come, has been a potent influence in silencing protests against political and economic inequality.

But notwithstanding the fact that the church, as a mainstay of law and order, has quite consistently supported the state in combating the leveling tendencies of the democratic movement, it is to the Christian idea of spiritual equality that modern democracy most largely owes its origin. It was this idea which prepared the way for the attack upon the doctrine that the king ruled by divine right. If men were really equal before God, how could monarchy be defended as a divinely ordained institution? Was not spiritual equality incompatible with the idea that the most conspicuous inequality in human society had divine sanction? Not only did the conception of spiritual equality tend to weaken popular reverence for monarchy, but it discredited the entire system of special privileges claimed by the ruling classes.

The doctrine of equality was really implied in the social contract theory of the state, which, as usually interpreted, assumed a preëxisting state of nature, in which men lived without distinctions of rank. It would be strictly logical to assert that the social contract theory, in so far as it offered an explanation of the origin of the state, was but an inference from the assumed equality of men in a state of nature. Consequently, those who accepted the social contract idea were inclined to regard men as, by nature, approximately equal. The inequalities which existed in society, they attributed to injustice.

" Nature," says Hobbes, " hath made men so equal in the faculties of the body and mind, as that, though there be found one man sometimes manifestly stronger in body or of quicker mind than another, yet when all is reckoned together the difference between man and man is not so considerable as that one man can thereupon claim to himself any benefit to which another may not pretend as well as he." [7]

Although defending monarchy, Hobbes attempted to reconcile it with the doctrine that men were by nature equal. " The inequality that now is," he tells us, " has been introduced by the laws civil. . . . If Nature therefore have made men equal, that equality is to be acknowledged; or, if

[7] *Leviathan*, ch. XIII.

Nature have made men unequal, yet because men that think themselves equal will not enter into conditions of peace but upon equal terms, such equality must be admitted." [8]

The natural equality of men was generally accepted by the advocates of the social contract theory. Even Hume asserted that because of this natural equality it was reasonable to believe that government had its origin in voluntary agreement.[9] The Declaration of Independence, in proclaiming as a self-evident truth " that all men are created equal," merely expressed what was an essential part of the political creed of liberal thinkers throughout the seventeenth and eighteenth centuries.

This widespread enthusiasm for the doctrine of equality was due less to its democratic than to its anti-monarchic and anti-aristocratic implications. Liberals were then much more interested in sweeping away the prerogatives of monarchy and aristocracy than in establishing a society in which all men would share equally in the exercise of political power. As the social contract theory had served a useful purpose in the long struggle against irresponsible power, so the idea of equality was employed by the middle class as an intellectual weapon to level down the privileged orders if not to level up the lower classes.

The leaders of the movement to establish American independence saw in the doctrine of equality an even more effective instrument of propaganda than was supplied by the social contract theory of the state. This doctrine made a strong appeal not only to the great majority of the people, who were then outside the pale of political rights, but also to the majority of the property owning class, who felt themselves discriminated against by the high officeholding qualifications and the social distinctions of the time. The

[8] *Ibid.*, ch. XV.   [9] *Supra*, p. 169.

importance of the principle of natural equality in the political philosophy of the American Revolution is indicated by the fact that it is the first of the " self-evident truths " mentioned in the Declaration of Independence, and that it stood first in the Massachusetts Declaration of Rights. There is, however, no ground for believing that those who framed and promulgated the philosophic defense of the Revolution really believed in equality as a practical political principle. Like all eighteenth century liberals, they gave lip-service to the idea of equality, but they had no desire to apply the principle in the practical organization of the state. Middle class advocacy of equality might be unqualified in a war document such as the Declaration of Independence, but it assumed a more cautious form of expression as the problems of political reconstruction came to receive critical attention.

The political significance of the doctrine of natural equality was unmistakable. If all men were created equal, the then existing restrictions on the right to vote and to hold office were clearly unjust and should be abolished. It was this implication which, perhaps more than any other, made the political leaders of the Revolutionary period realize, that however useful might be the formal acceptance of the idea of equality for the immediate purpose of establishing independence, it would later become a source of trouble. This probably explains why only one state constitution of the Revolutionary period, that of Massachusetts, contained a declaration of natural equality. The equality of all freemen was affirmed in the Kentucky Constitution of 1799, but no other state accepted the idea that all men, or even all freemen, were equal, until after 1835, when property qualifications for voters and for officeholders had been largely abolished. Up to the time of the Civil War, but three southern states [10] had declared in their constitutions that all freemen were equal and only two northern states [11] had followed Massachusetts in proclaiming the natural equality of all men. After the Civil War the doctrine of equality was included in the Reconstruction constitutions of five southern states.[12] But of the seventeen states admitted into the Union since 1850, only two [13] have recognized the principle of natural equality, and at the present time only seven state constitutions [14] contain the declaration that all men are equal.

It is interesting to note that the Massachusetts Constitution of 1780, which contained the declaration of natural equality, was the only one adopted during the Revolutionary period which actually increased the property requirements for voters. The fact that such qualifications were raised fifty per cent is a more trustworthy indication of the ruling class sentiment than the glittering generality that " all men are born free and equal."

The declaration in the Virginia Bill of Rights of 1776 that " all men are by nature equally free and independent " was designed to, and, no doubt, did in a measure satisfy the undiscriminating popular demand for governmental recognition of the principle of equality. Men may be equally free and independent, however, without being equal. To declare that " all men are by nature equally free and independent " is, in fact, merely to assert belief in the principle of individual liberty. Properly interpreted, it is to declare, not that all men are equal, but only that they have equal right to freedom and independence. Seventeen of our present

---

[10] Kentucky, Florida, and Arkansas.
[11] Iowa and Indiana.
[12] Alabama, Florida, Louisiana, North Carolina, and South Carolina.
[13] Idaho and Nevada.
[14] Idaho, Indiana, Iowa, Kentucky, Massachusetts, Nevada, and North Carolina.

state constitutions contain such a declaration, while in eighteen there is no reference to equality in any of its applications.

Both De Tocqueville and Bryce have commented on the American passion for equality; but if this has been a distinguishing trait of the American people there is little in our public documents to indicate it. There has been at times emphatic disapproval of certain kinds of inequality which discriminated against the majority of the people. It may be seriously doubted, however, whether there has ever been in this country any widespread belief in the doctrine of natural equality. The existence of chattel slavery for nearly a century after the Declaration of Independence is a fact which can not be reconciled with the theory of equality or the idea of individual liberty. Belief in equality, in so far as it has existed, has been clearly subject to important limitations. It has never been regarded as applying to inferior races. Even in non-slave states, the Negro has been discriminated against. Delaware, from the establishment of independence, denied political rights to all except white men. The idea of equality was made to support the movement for the extension of the suffrage; but, coincident with the abolition of property qualifications, various states adopted constitutional provisions which either expressly limited voting to free white men, or, as in the New York Constitution of 1821, made it difficult for colored voters to exercise this right. Connecticut in 1818 limited the suffrage to white male citizens twenty-one years of age. Pennsylvania adopted a similar provision in 1838 and New Jersey in 1844.

The advocacy of white manhood suffrage did not necessarily imply a belief in the essential equality of all white men. The argument for a widely extended suffrage may, of course, be based on the assumption of natural equality. If all men are in effect equal, there can be no justification for a policy which confers the right to vote on some and withholds it from others. But, as a matter of fact, belief in the desirability of a widely extended suffrage is usually defended on altogether different grounds. It is not the theory of natural equality, but rather the conviction that both justice and expediency require the state to treat all alike, that is the main guaranty of a liberal suffrage policy. The doctrine of natural equality has, of course, often been used in the attack on class privilege. In fact, the emphasis on this doctrine was very pronounced during the movement in the first half of the nineteenth century for the establishment of manhood suffrage. The popularity of the doctrine of equality in that period was due, however, less to any profound conviction that all men are equal, than to the desire to deprive the ruling class of its control of the state. The prevalent attitude was one of hostility to privilege, rather than of acceptance of the theory of equality.

If there was any one idea which was generally accepted in the early period of American history, it was that of individual liberty. It found expression in various bills of rights in such phrases as " equally free and independent," " equal in rights," and " equal before the law." Although this conception did not imply natural equality, it was inconsistent with belief in special privileges of any sort. Moreover, the desired liberty for the individual could be assured, if at all, only through the extension of the suffrage. This is expressly recognized in the Wyoming Constitution, which contains a declaration in favor of equality in the enjoyment of natural and civil rights through political equality.

Down to the Civil War period, the trend of opinion had been clearly toward acceptance of the idea, not that all white men should be regarded as equal, but that they should have equal rights, civil and political. Moreover, there was a growing conviction that all men, regardless of color, were by nature " equally free and independent." It was this belief in individual liberty, rather than a doctrinaire acceptance of the theory of natural equality, that brought about the abolition of slavery. The prohibition of racial discrimination by constitutional amendment after the Civil War can hardly be regarded as a serious attempt to extend the principle of equality in political rights to the Negro. It did not reflect a sentiment that was clearly prevalent, even in the North, inasmuch as the doctrine of white supremacy was included in the constitutions of several northern states, where the Negro element in the population was unimportant. The lack of any effective public opinion in favor of the abolition of political discrimination against the Negro is plainly indicated by the general non-enforcement of the Fifteenth Amendment.

The eighteenth century democratic philosophy, which found expression in the Declaration of Independence, and practical application in the extension of the suffrage and the abolition of slavery, has declined in popularity since the Civil War. It is no longer necessary for a political party to proclaim its acceptance of the " self-evident " truths enumerated in the Declaration, as the Democratic party did during the period which intervened between the extension of the suffrage and the Civil War, and the Republican party, during the Civil War and Reconstruction periods.

This change in viewpoint is clearly reflected in American political literature. We have largely discarded the opinion, more or less prevalent in the first half of the nineteenth century, that suffrage is one of the natural rights of the citizen, and have returned to the old conservative position which holds that it is a privilege which the state may or may not confer. That voting is not a right of the citizen as such is now generally stressed in American books on political science, especially in those used in connection with high school and college instruction in politics.[15] A foundation is thus being laid for a conception of the state which is directly opposed to the political philosophy of the Declaration of Independence.

As a rule, no mention is made of the social contract theory in this type of literature, but it is attacked indirectly in the systematic effort made to discredit the natural rights doctrine. To attack it directly might be inexpedient, inasmuch as it is the recognized basis of American political organization. A less obvious and, in the end, more effective method of bringing it into disrepute is naturally preferred, as less likely to arouse formidable opposition. To attack the social contract theory through the doctrine of natural rights has two distinct advantages. In addition to being indirect, it strikes at the very heart of the social contract idea of the state. If the doctrine of natural rights can be brought into disrepute, the social contract theory will be made untenable. The doctrine of natural rights is not only implied in

[15] In a high school book on civics the reader is reminded that, " Whatever the qualifications [of voters] may be, it ought to be noticed that they are imposed by the government, and that the elective franchise is a privilege which may be granted or withheld, and is not a right which the citizen enjoys simply because he is a citizen." S. E. Forman, *Advanced Civics*, p. 103 (1906).

In a recent book for college and university classes in government, we are told: " Another political activity which is a privilege rather than a right is the exercise of the electoral franchise. It is true that advocates of suffrage extension have always been prone to represent voting as a natural, if not a constitutional right. . . . But political scientists are substantially agreed that the composition of the electorate is, in the United States no less than in other lands, a matter to be determined by considerations of expediency." Frederic A. Ogg and P. Orman Ray, *Introduction to American Government*, p. 198 (1922).

The statements quoted above are fairly representative of our recent textbook literature, which serves as the basis of college and high school instruction in politics.

the social contract conception of the state, but is, indeed, the very essence of it.   To maintain, as conservative writers now quite generally do, that there are no natural rights, that voting is a privilege which the state may withhold, that, as a matter of fact, the citizen has no rights which the state must respect, is in effect a repudiation of all that is essential in the social contract theory.

In this covert and indirect way, if not openly, the present generation is being taught that the earlier view of the state, which is reflected in our constitutional documents, both state and federal, and was held by liberals during the first half of the nineteenth century, is erroneous.   The entire system of eighteenth century political philosophy, with its conception of the social contract, individual liberty, natural law, and natural rights, is discarded as a check on the power of the state.   The citizen has been stripped by conservative interpretation of all those intellectual and moral safeguards against governmental aggression which the political philosophy of the eighteenth century supplied.   A new conception of the state is being evolved, which is, in fact if not in form, a doctrine of governmental absolutism.

CHAPTER IX

CENTRALIZATION AND POPULAR CONTROL

The growth of centralized control in the United States has been rapid, especially since the Civil War. In less than a century and a half, a group of loosely organized communities have been welded into what is essentially a national state. This has been brought about largely through federal control of the constitution-interpreting power. As we have seen in the preceding discussion, the early struggle between the advocates and opponents of centralization was over the right of the federal Supreme Court to act as the final interpreter of the Constitution of the United States. The acquisition of this power by the federal judiciary made the general government supreme. Thenceforth, it determined its own authority and that of the states as well. A foundation was thus laid for the assumption of powers by the federal government which might in time strip the local subdivisions of all authority and make the general government national in all but name. This process of centralization was retarded in the first half of the nineteenth century by the states' rights sentiment; but since the Civil War there has been a marked acceleration in the growth of federal authority.

There are two ways in which the courts have contributed toward the centralization of political power in the hands of the general government. Both depend upon the right of the Supreme Court to act as the final interpreter of the federal Constitution. By the simple process of interpretation the

Court has read into the Constitution a larger grant of power to the general government than was originally intended or previously recognized as properly belonging to it. In this way, there has come about a vast accession of federal authority. The other way in which the judiciary has aided in the growth of federal power at the expense of the state has been indirect and no doubt often unintended. The Constitution denies to the states certain powers, as in the provision concerning laws " impairing the obligation of contracts " and in the Fourteenth Amendment. Through the interpretation which the judicial branch of the federal government has placed upon these provisions, the power of the states as regulative and protective agencies has been seriously impaired.[1] Moreover, by depriving the state governments of the power to enact much urgently needed legislation, the Court has compelled the people to look to the general government for relief. The immediate purpose of this limitation of state authority by judicial construction was probably in most instances to prevent the contemplated regulation; but the final result of this restriction on the powers of the states has been a compensating increase in the regulative authority of the federal government. The people, thwarted in their effort to secure adequate state regulation, have turned to the general government for protection, since its powers are not abridged by the Fourteenth Amendment or the constitutional provision concerning laws " impairing the obligation of contracts."

There is another aspect of the movement toward centralization, which has to do with the relation between state and local government. Just as the general government has in recent decades been rapidly extending its powers at the expense of the states, so have the various states themselves

[1] See ch. VII.

been taking more and more power away from the purely local governmental units.

Generally speaking, conservatives favor a centralized form of government while those who believe in popular control wish to keep political power largely in the hands of local authorities. This was true even at the beginning of our history under the Constitution. It was perfectly logical for Jefferson with his democratic viewpoint to desire a weak general, and strong local, government, as it was for Hamilton with his pronounced aristocratic bias to be the apostle of centralization.

The liberal political philosophy of the eighteenth century was fundamentally opposed to centralized control. The very essence of this philosophy — the doctrine of individual liberty — could be reconciled only with a decentralized form of government. The belief in self-determination for the individual was based on the assumption that he was better able to judge concerning his own interests and needs than was any external authority. The theory of individual liberty recognized that in any properly organized society self-determination was subject to certain limitations and restraints imposed in the interest of the general welfare. But in the choice of governmental agencies to protect the public against the abuse of individual liberty, the principle of self-determination required that political power should never be removed farther from those affected by its exercise than the extent of the interests involved made necessary. According to this principle, local government should have as much power and the central government as little as might be consistent with the safeguarding of the general public interests. Collective determination by governmental agencies would then be so exercised that the individual would have the largest possible influence in the imposition of necessary restraints on his liberty. To centralize political power would endanger individual liberty by placing all authority in those governmental organs farthest removed from effective popular control.

The opponents of popular control were not always in favor of centralized government. Intelligent conservatives at the close of the eighteenth century and the beginning of the nineteenth could, and many did, consistently believe in a large measure of decentralization. In fact, the main reason for conservative advocacy of centralization at the present time did not apply under the conditions which then existed. Local government was not then in the hands of the popular majority. The suffrage and officeholding qualifications of that time were a sufficient guaranty of the predominance of the property holding class in local affairs. And, inasmuch as the popular majority was effectively subordinated in local government, a centralized governmental organization was not necessary for the protection of property rights. Moreover, during the first half of the nineteenth century, the existence of slavery in the South made that section of the country pronounced in its support of state as opposed to central authority. The emphasis on state rights throughout the South during the pre-Civil War period was due, however, less to a belief in the theory of decentralized government than to the fear that federal authority might not be sufficiently representative of the slaveholding interests.

In the growth of governmental systems, the distribution of powers between central and local authorities is more likely to be determined by expediency than by the desire for logical consistency. Practice may be, and of course often is, determined by theory, but when the interests of the dominant class can not be reconciled with generally accepted doctrines, theory is certain to yield to practical considerations.

The early liberal view which associated individual liberty and adequate popular restraint on political power with the decentralized type of political organization is no longer predominant. More and more, the people are coming to accept the point of view implied in centralization of political authority. A number of influences have combined to bring about this change of attitude, chief among which has been the desire of the more conservative classes to safeguard the country in so far as possible against the supposed dangers of democracy, by removing political affairs as far as possible from the danger of popular control.

The attitude of the well-to-do classes toward local self-government was profoundly influenced by the extension of the suffrage. As shown in a preceding chapter,[2] the removal of property qualifications tended to divest the old ruling class of its control in local affairs. Thereafter, property owners regarded with distrust local government, in which they were outnumbered by the newly enfranchised voters. The fact that they may have believed in a large measure of local self-government when there were suitable restrictions on the right to vote and to hold public office, did not prevent them from advocating an increase in state control after the adoption of manhood suffrage.

American legalistic political theory has from the beginning of our history as a nation reflected the view that the state legislature is the source of all legislative powers both state and local, and that all local powers are conferred by the legislature and may be withdrawn at will. Local government, according to this conception, is a creature of the state government and, except for such rights as are granted by the state constitution, owes its existence and its powers to the state legislature. This view of the powers of the state legislature was, of course, merely an application to the state government of the English theory of parliamentary supremacy. After the extension of the suffrage the influence of this theory on local government was supplemented by judicial fear of the consequences of local democracy. Not only was all legislative power centralized in the state government, but the effort to decentralize it by constitutional amendment was largely nullified by hostile judicial interpretation. Our state courts have, in fact, persistently opposed local autonomy. Even the so-called home rule provisions included in some of our state constitutions to ensure municipal self-government have been largely ineffective, owing to the judicial construction placed upon them.

The refusal of the courts to recognize local self-government as a right has compelled dependence upon, and developed a habit of looking to, the state government for the exercise of many powers that ought to be under strictly local control. That we should distinguish more clearly than we have in the past between matters of general and matters of purely local concern is obvious to anyone who has given much attention to the question of political organization. The rapid increase in governmental functions during recent decades, the constantly growing volume of public business, and the consequent inability of the state government to deal in a satisfactory manner with the great number and variety of interests, general and local, for which it is responsible under any scheme of centralized control, make it necessary to relieve the state government of such functions as are purely local in character. It is clearly in the interest of economy and efficiency to leave the decision of all questions of local policy to the community directly concerned, subject, of course, as every exercise of local authority always is and of necessity must be, to such general supervision as may be needed to ensure adequate protection of the larger general interests.

If local self-government is to have any real existence in this country, we must find some way of securing, at the hands of legislatures and courts, recognition of the fact that cities are local communities with distinctly local interests, and that, as such, they are making only a reasonable demand when they ask that they be allowed to control their local affairs in their own way. Just where the line should be drawn separating local affairs from those subject to state regulation is a question about which there is at present much difference of opinion. But although it may be difficult to determine in some cases whether state or local control is the proper policy, there are some important functions so clearly local in character that the propriety of leaving them in the hands of local authorities is obvious. In matters of this sort, the policy to be pursued should be determined by the city or community concerned, the state having only such supervisory power on appeal from local determination as may be necessary for the protection of public and private rights.

The status of local government in the United States, though largely due to legal theory as it has been developed and applied by the courts, may be regarded as in some measure the consequence of purely historical facts. In continental Europe many cities had an independent existence before the states of which they are now a part were formed. In the process of political evolution, consequently, the extension of central control over cities has not entirely obscured the fact that the city was an original political corporation, and as such possessed and exercised all powers and functions suited to its needs. The tendency is to regard it as having, by virtue of its existence as a municipal corporation, and independently of any grant of powers by the central or state government, such authority as may be needed for the exercise of municipal functions. The question is not so much what powers have been delegated to the city, as what powers have been denied to it by the central authority. In America, on the other hand, the state as a political corporation antedates the city. It is in some measure due to this fact that the city is regarded by the courts as legally the creature of the state legislature which has granted it incorporation; that it has no clearly defined sphere of activity in which the state government may not intrude; that such powers as it may be permitted to exercise are delegated by the state government; and that, in exercising these, it is in legal theory acting, not as a local political corporation with original powers of self-government, but as a mere agent of the state government.

In America the state is the only local unit having original powers of self-government. Nevertheless, the state is a purely arbitrary division, while the city, on the other hand, is a natural and organic unit with interests peculiarly its own. For this reason, self-government is a question of supreme importance to cities — more important for the adequate protection of their interests than is self-government for the state.

No state government is competent to determine questions of local policy. This is particularly true where the state legislature is so apportioned as to overrepresent rural at the expense of urban communities. As our state governments are now organized, it is not infrequently the case that cities have very inadequate representation in the state legislature and are, therefore, at a great disadvantage as compared with the rural sections of the state.[3] This disproportionately small representation of urban population has not only facilitated the assumption of local functions by the state government, by depriving urban communities of the power to offer effective resistance to this extension of state authority, but it has also made the state legislature less competent to deal with local affairs. But a legislature even when properly apportioned is not, and can not be, representative of the various local interests of the state. It has a representative character in the true and democratic sense of that term only in so far as it deals with matters which concern the state as a whole. In all legislation relating to municipal affairs, rural members are politically responsible to no one. What interest, for example, do the people of a purely agricultural community have in legislation relating to municipal utilities? The people of such a community have no problem of this kind, it is not a matter which concerns them, and the part which their representative may take in the enactment of measures of this sort may not attract even so much as a passing notice. With respect to such legislation he can vote and act as he pleases without the risk of incurring the criticism or displeasure of his constituents.

Centralization of power has not only made government irresponsible in so far as implied powers are exercised, but it tends to make popular control ineffective even in the exercise of functions which democratic theory clearly assigns. The development of present day social and economic life has so greatly increased the demand for governmental regulation that even under a decentralized form of political organization, the volume of business entrusted to governmental agencies is too large and too complex for the public to follow intelligently. To load a government down with a

---

[3] *Supra,* ch. IV.

multitude of functions which it is not fitted to perform, tends to further confusion and renders it a less efficient instrument for the exercise of those functions which necessarily concern it.

The extension of the suffrage was followed, as we have seen, by a marked increase of state interference in local affairs. The underlying cause of this movement to centralize authority in the state government was the fear of municipal democracy. But the extension of the suffrage, so much dreaded by conservatives, did not after all make municipal government responsible in any effective way to the majority of the voters. Organized in many instances on the check and balance plan, like our state and federal governments, municipal government was a very unsatisfactory instrument of democracy. In response, however, to a popular demand for reform in the first and second decades of the twentieth century, cities were being reorganized in accordance with democratic principles. It is an interesting coincidence that just at this time a fresh impetus should have been given to the movement toward state control of local affairs. It was urged that local control of such matters as public utilities was inadequate and unsatisfactory. But the fact that this objection was not raised until after the movement to democratize local government had begun probably indicates to some extent, at least, both its true source and real purpose. Though ostensibly designed to give cities more effective protection against public utility abuses, it did not originate in any popular demand from urban communities. The initiative in this matter, however cleverly it may have assumed the guise of a popular movement, came largely from the interests which were opposed to effective regulation by either state or local authorities.

Satisfactory regulation is not, as seems to be implied in

much of the discussion favoring the substitution of state for local control, merely a question of placing this function in the hands of that governmental agency which has most power and prestige behind it. The power to exercise a particular function is of little consequence, unless there is an adequate guaranty that such power will be exercised in the interest of the local public for whose protection it is designed. It may be regarded as a well established principle of political science that to ensure a satisfactory and efficient exercise of a given power, it should be lodged in some governmental agency directly responsible to the constituency affected. Here, we find the weak point in the policy of centralizing control in the state government. A state agency, theoretically responsible to the entire state, may be safely entrusted with powers which concern the state as a whole; but when a state government assumes powers that are essentially local, it is not responsible in the sense that it is when it exercises powers in which the state as a whole is directly and vitally interested. The community or communities affected by its exercise of local authority lack the power to control it. It is for this reason that the extension of state control over local affairs fails to meet the requirements of democracy.

The assumption of local powers by the state government has greatly increased the opportunity for corruption in American politics. Advocates of centralization, however, have entirely ignored this aspect of the question. As a matter of fact, they have even defended the extension of state control over local affairs on the ground that it tends to remove the main sources of corruption in municipal politics. This argument was advanced in support of the recent public service commission movement by which cities have throughout the United States been largely deprived of the power to regulate local utilities. The contention that such a transfer of power would eliminate certain sources of corruption in local politics may be admitted, without conceding that it would be beneficial either to the local public or to the state at large. It is obvious that interests seeking privileges at the expense of the people would not be tempted to corrupt a local government which had no power to grant them. Instead of doing away with corruption, however, it would merely transfer that corruption to a larger political arena. And when a state government as such assumes and exercises purely local functions, it is much more liable to corruption than is a local government directly responsible to the local public. This is, no doubt, one important reason why public utility interests favor state control.

Democracy, in any true sense of the term, is possible only when there is the largest practicable measure of local self-government. This is evident from the fact that the problem of establishing and maintaining government responsible to the people is least difficult in the small local subdivisions. The difficulties in the way of effective popular control increase with the size of the governmental unit. Not only is the citizen's vote more effective in a local than in a state or national election, but the officials are more directly under his influence. Nor is his influence in the case of local government confined to election day. The town or city hall is near at hand and local officials may be easily reached by such as wish to voice approval or disapproval of official conduct. By reason of this proximity of the officials to the public they represent, local government is more likely to be influenced by the opinion of all important classes in the population, the poor as well as the rich, than is either state or federal government. The poor are, of course, always at a disadvantage as compared with the rich in making their influence felt, even in the case of local government. But the farther those entrusted with political power are removed from the people they are supposed to represent, the more likely they are to fall under the influence of organized wealth. So-called representative government is most considerate of those interests which keep constantly in touch with it through an effective organization. The large business interests have long recognized the fact that their profits are directly affected by governmental policies, and have consequently used the power of such organization to obtain desired legislation or to defeat measures to which they are opposed.

The farmers of the country, though representing more votes and more wealth employed in production than all other capital owning groups combined, have failed to exercise their due share of political influence through lack of effective coöperation for this purpose. This situation is due in part, no doubt, to the difficulty of securing united effort where large numbers of people are involved. Moreover, from the nature of their occupation, farmers are more individualistic than either business men or wage earners.

The influence of the average individual upon governmental policies may be regarded as negligible inasmuch as his interest in pending legislation is usually slight. He may think of a proposed measure as beneficial or harmful, but in either case the effects which he anticipates are not likely to be of sufficient importance to him to urge him to political activity. Generally speaking, the effort which he is disposed to make depends more largely upon the way in which he conceives his individual interests to be affected, than upon any consideration of what may be called the general welfare. The laboring man and the person of small means are as individuals unable to exert any appreciable influence over a government as far removed from the people generally as our

federal government is. Only by organization and coöperation is it possible for them to protect their interests, and this
is very difficult to bring about except where much in the way
of personal or property rights is believed to be at stake.
This probably explains why wage earners in many industries
have been more effectively organized than have farmers.
Their personal rights have been so clearly endangered by
organized capital that the organization of labor was seen to
be necessary for defensive purposes. The farmer was slower
to respond to this tendency, not only because of his more
pronounced individualism, but also because his need of organization was less urgent.

The preponderance of political influence exercised by
capitalistic groups is only in part due to the superior capacity
of business men for effective coöperation; it is in large measure due to the highly centralized economic control which has
become the rule in capitalistic industries. To some extent,
large scale organization may indicate coöperative ability,
but the highly centralized control which now prevails in so
many industries is no more the fruit of economic coöperation
than the highly centralized state is the expression of political
democracy. Indeed, coöperation and centralization are inherently opposed, inasmuch as the former implies diffusion
of power and would secure the necessary unification of effort
without resort to compulsion.

The public interests are likely to receive less consideration
at the hands of our national legislature than important
special interests receive, for the simple reason that there is
no adequate, continuing, active, popular support for the
former, while the latter are always represented by an active
and aggressive lobby. The purely financial interest of the
people as a whole in a proposed measure may be and usually
is much greater than that of the particular group that is

seeking to have it enacted at the expense of the public; but because the former is a widely diffused interest it is usually unrepresented, while the latter, because it is highly concentrated and more intense, exerts an influence out of all proportion to its real economic and social importance. In industries where ownership and control are highly centralized, the influence of business upon politics is certain to be greatest. In fact, it is the desire for power that has been one of the most important factors in bringing about centralized control of industry. This has not only greatly increased business influence in the field of politics, but has strengthened its power to dictate terms to labor and prices to the consumer.

To make centralization of economic power acceptable to the public, it has been represented as a means of achieving efficiency and economy in production. It has, moreover, always been assumed by the defenders of centralized industry that such benefits as are thereby achieved accrue in large measure to the general public. As a matter of fact, however, the concentration of economic control was no more designed to augment the wealth and income of the masses than centralization of political power was designed to increase popular control.

An intelligent democrat might be inclined to wonder how anyone could believe that centralization of economic and political power would tend to bring about a diffusion of economic and political well-being. But many who have a sentimental attachment to democracy have no adequate comprehension of the political philosophy upon which government by the people is based. If any considerable portion of the general public had all along possessed this intelligence, the sophistry and misrepresentation which have always had so large a place in the discussion and literature of politics would have been much less effective in misleading public opinion.

A highly centralized economic system is inherently opposed to decentralization in the government. If those who control industry are to be free to use this power for their own purposes, they must control the state, since political democracy would definitely subordinate economic power to restraints imposed for the protection of the public. Moreover, large scale industry, engaged as it is in enterprises that are national and even international in scope, is impatient of the diversity in laws and policies which is inevitable under any system of local regulation.

Chapter X

IMPERIALISM AND
GOVERNMENTAL SUPREMACY

Imperialism is a natural and inevitable consequence of our capitalistic industrial system.

No one can understand the significance of present day capitalism, who thinks of it merely as a form of industrial organization designed to ensure efficiency in production. More and more, the power to control distribution is becoming its outstanding feature. Profits may depend less upon efficiency in the production of wealth than upon the power to decrease wages and increase prices.

The orthodox defense of the capitalistic system assumes that distribution is regulated by natural law. Business men by virtue of their ownership of capital control production, but competition is supposed to determine the distribution of the social income. Modern economic theory has thus attempted to reconcile private capitalism with the individualistic philosophy, by showing that the distribution of wealth and income is automatically controlled by natural law. Capitalists themselves, however, have been unceasing in their effort to overcome the restraints imposed by competition.

The conception of industry as regulated by natural law, is an application of the political theory of checks and balances to the field of economics. It was no mere coincidence that liberal thinkers in the latter part of the eighteenth century who believed in the division and balancing of political power also believed in the competitive regulation of industry.

202

The essential feature of both their political and economic philosophy was the recognition of the need for restraints which would protect the people against misuse of irresponsible power. Competition was supposed to supply the needed protection in industry, as the check and balance type of governmental organization did in the state.

But in the business world as in politics, the struggle for power has resulted in the concentration of authority. Competition, which in the past was largely between individuals, is becoming more and more a struggle between economic classes. The capitalistic group, being the best organized and holding the means of production in their control, have become the chief source of economic and political power in modern society.

This centralization of power has made it possible for organized wealth to overcome in large measure the competitive and governmental restraints which are supposed to safeguard the public interests. Capitalistic imperialism has become, in consequence, a standing menace to the peace and well-being of the world. The burdens imposed by such a policy are borne by the public, while the benefits which accrue from it are monopolized by the capital owning class.

It is highly improbable that a democratic state in which the benefits and burdens of government were widely and equitably diffused would become imperialistic. Even if we assume that democracy is no less selfish than plutocracy, an adequate motive would be lacking, since, for the people as a whole, the burdens of imperialism would more than counterbalance the advantages. Moreover, democracy and imperialism are irreconcilably opposed. To annex territory and rule a subject population is to lay a foundation for modification of political ideals and growth of coercive agencies that must in the end overwhelm democracy at home.

In so far as imperialism has an economic basis, it is motivated largely by the belief that its effect on the distribution of the social income is advantageous to the capital owning class. Foreign markets as an outlet for surplus goods are needed for the protection of profits, since production can not continue under the capitalistic system unless there is an effective demand for the goods produced. This demand could, of course, be ensured by increasing the consuming power of the masses at home through higher wages and lower prices. Such a method of making demand balance supply would, however, mean a reduction in the capitalist's share of the social income. Since he benefits by keeping prices up and wages down in the domestic market, he quite naturally wishes to exclude foreign competition in the home market, and at the same time to have unimpeded access to the markets of other countries.

Imperialism is designed to increase the capitalist's income, partly at the expense of other classes in his own country and partly at the expense of weaker foreign countries. To inaugurate and carry out a policy of this sort presupposes a strong government, unhampered by too much popular control. It must be sufficiently amenable to capitalistic influence to protect the interests of that class even at the expense of the people generally, and strong enough to insist on an open door abroad while maintaining a policy of exclusion at home.

Imperialism could not, of course, be successfully defended on any such selfish and anti-social grounds. To ensure adequate popular support, it is necessary to give it a broadly humanitarian and ethical interpretation. This has not been difficult inasmuch as a large proportion of the professional and educated classes, including the great majority of those who represent higher education and the church, have been among its active supporters. However materialistic and mercenary the motives that have been chiefly responsible for the adoption of an imperialistic policy, it invariably assumes the guise of a great disinterested national effort to extend the blessings of free government and Christian civilization to the less fortunate regions of the world.

With the organized intelligence of a country so largely enlisted in its defense, it is not surprising that imperialism has been made acceptable to many who expect no material benefit from it, direct or indirect, and who, moreover, are under no misapprehension concerning the burden which such a policy necessarily imposes on the public. All too frequently the religious and ethical minded, but politically and socially unintelligent, are misled as to its real nature and purpose by the insistent though insincere emphasis on humanitarian duty and Christian responsibility.

The conventional defense of imperialism contains hardly a hint of the sordid motives that lie in the background. Even the interest which the stronger country has in exploiting the weaker is presented not as a selfish economic motive but as a sublimated desire for the promotion of well-being throughout the world. The capitalistic pressure to secure markets and privileges at the expense of weaker countries assumes at the hands of the pseudo-ethical and pseudo-religious apologists the guise of a high moral purpose. To justify this form of capitalistic aggression, even the foundation of private property is attacked. The less developed parts of the world should, we are told, be under the control of nations that can ensure an efficient use of their natural resources. Property may be a useful device for the purpose of encouraging industry and promoting well-being, but ownership, either individual or national, is subject to the implied obligation that the wealth thus owned shall be efficiently used. The world's natural resources belong ultimately to the people of the world as a whole. Individual or community ownership of wealth can not be ethically defended and need not be respected, except in so far as it is beneficial to the world at large. Backward nations in possession of valuable natural resources which the people of the entire world need and which are withheld from use or very inadequately utilized, may, according to this view, be justly brought under sufficient foreign control to guarantee that they will make an adequate contribution to the material wellbeing of mankind.

The philosophy of imperialism is in its essence but a restatement of the old argument for aristocracy. Few would now dare to advocate class control as such, since to do so would offend even the most superficial and uncritical adherent of democracy. The prevalent attachment to democracy is, however, to its external form rather than to its spirit and substance. The great majority of those who profess belief in democratic principles, rarely permit those principles to influence their everyday political conduct. Even the most enthusiastic advocates of democracy are likely to hold that it is a suitable form of government only for such communities as have reached a high stage of development. The so-called inferior races and communities are thought of as unfitted to assume the responsibilities implied in democracy. And since they are supposed to be incapable of governing themselves, it is declared to be the duty of the strong and more advanced nations to supply the kind of government which they need. Imperialism is thus justified as the manifestation of a larger patriotism which recognizes the cost of ruling the inferior races as " the white man's burden."

It is, of course, always tacitly assumed by the advocates of imperialism that any control exercised by their own gov-

ernment over weaker countries is for the benefit of all concerned. Imperialism is thus presented not in the garb of
greedy commercialism but as an agency of progress — political, social, economic, and even religious. The fallacy
in the argument of those who seek to justify imperialism
is the gratuitous assumption that a strong government
can be depended upon to use such power justly and
wisely.

It has always been assumed by the supporters of aristocracy that the ruling class can govern the people better
than they can govern themselves. Long continued experience has shown, however, that no class is fit to be thus
entrusted with power. A ruling class, however it may be
constituted, whether hereditary, ecclesiastical, or plutocratic,
inevitably makes its own interests the criteria by which to
determine the general welfare. The modern democratic
movement is convincing evidence that class control has been
found unsatisfactory. The few may know better than the
many what the real interests of the latter are, but if their
own interests happen to be opposed to those of the majority,
it could not reasonably be assumed that political power
placed in their hands would be exercised for the benefit of
the public.

But if control of a country by a ruling class is inimical to
the general welfare, such control as may be exercised over it
by an imperialistic nation is much more so. The authority
of a class government is always tempered by the fact that
the subject classes in the state greatly outnumber the ruling
element and, therefore, possess the potential power to overthrow the established government. Moreover, rulers and
subjects are of the same race, have the same language, literature, and religion, and enjoy a common social inheritance.
This conscious community of interests restrains to some ex-

tent the natural tendency of the ruling class to use its power for its own advantage. Where, however, the subject classes live, not in the same community with those by whom they are controlled, but in a remote colony, there is far greater danger of ruthless exploitation. In such a case, the state is dealing not with its own citizens but with an alien and supposedly inferior population. It is not likely, therefore, that public opinion will insist upon the same standards of governmental conduct which it demands at home. Moreover, even if public opinion within an imperialistic country were definitely in favor of the view that a colonial venture is in the nature of a trust to be administered for the benefit of those controlled, there is no assurance and little likelihood that this purpose would be consistently reflected in the colonial policies of the government. It is difficult enough for a subject population to bring its grievances to the attention of the ruling class when it is not widely separated geographically; but when it is isolated not only by distance but by differences in race, language, religion, and culture, the difficulties encountered by the colonial population in trying to secure a sympathetic consideration of its interests and needs by those theoretically responsible for its welfare are enormously increased.

The average citizen, who has never been outside of his own country, who neither buys nor sells abroad, and who has no foreign investments, is but little interested in the relation of his government to other countries. This largely explains the fact, more or less generally recognized, that foreign relations, even in the case of the most democratic governments, have not yet been brought under effective popular supervision. Class control is hardly less of a reality in the field of foreign affairs to-day than it was before the birth of modern democracy. Such matters are too far removed from the daily experience of the people generally, and do not have a sufficiently direct and obvious bearing upon their material interests, to attract much public attention. Democracy, feeble enough with respect to the internal affairs of the state, where the citizen comes into direct contact with the activities and policies of the government, has an almost negligible influence upon foreign relations. It is for this reason, doubtless, that no real progress has been made toward effective publicity in the management of the foreign affairs of present-day governments.

The organized business interests are in virtual control of the foreign office of every great modern state — a situation which seems to be inevitable under the capitalistic system. Those who represent organized wealth, unlike the great majority, are actively interested in the external relations of the government. This class knows more of the outside world by direct contact. Moreover, the desire for governmental assistance in protecting foreign investments, and in securing foreign markets and profitable concessions abroad, directs its attention to the field of foreign relations. But even if the people were sufficiently intelligent to have an active interest in foreign relations, they would find it difficult to make their influence effective. The huge aggregations of wealth are in a position to deprive public opinion very largely of the opportunity to be heard in relation to foreign policies, through their influence on the press and other agencies to which public officials are accustomed to look for the expression of approval or disapproval. Moreover, high public officials, influenced as they almost invariably are by the traditional aristocratic view that government exists primarily for the protection of property rights, are likely to look to this class for guidance, or at least for information and suggestions, wherever foreign policies affect its interests.

Although the professedly disinterested humanitarian and Christian motives so loudly acclaimed by the servitors of big business may be, and usually are, merely selfish capitalistic propaganda, many who actively defend the policy of imperialism are entirely sincere in their belief that the strong nation should assume its share of responsibility for the control and development of the more backward parts of the earth. The tendency is everywhere prevalent to deify all established institutional arrangements — economic, social, political, religious. This conception of our own society as representing the highest achievement and the nearest approach to perfection in all the important fields of human interest and endeavor, constitutes what may be called the moral basis for the belief in imperialism.

The Christian religion from its very nature is imperialistic. Since it is, according to its adherents, the only true religion, it is the only means of saving a benighted world. Inevitably, the fervent orthodox Christian is possessed by a missionary zeal to carry the gospel to all lands that are shrouded in spiritual darkness. All other religions being false, it becomes the duty of the devotees of the one true faith to have it recognized and accepted as such throughout the world. The conversion of non-Christian peoples thus becomes a definite end which the church keeps constantly in view. It is true that in its fight with paganism the church does not desire to employ force. It appeals to the individual on the assumption that he is likely to accept the Christian belief, once that faith is fully and fairly expounded to him. Orthodox Christians are, however, inclined to have little patience with communities so benighted as to regard the missionary as an intruder. Quite easily they come to accept the view that it is the duty of the state to make use of its power in laying a suitable foundation for the Christianization of the world. Hence it is not to be expected that the church will defend the right of non-Christian peoples to govern themselves in case they are menaced by the imperialism of a militant Christian state. Inasmuch as the spread of the true religion is the supremely important consideration, any form of governmental organization, even the most autocratic, which would tend to bring the world under Christian influences, would be preferable to self-government for non-Christian regions, especially if the latter meant the exclusion of Christianity or the retardation of its influence. Having as a fixed purpose the destruction of all competing religions and the establishment of the spiritual supremacy of Christianity throughout the world, the church may as a rule be counted upon to support the imperialistic plans of the state.

Missionaries no less than traders have served as advance agents of imperialism. Both are interested in having the flag follow their activities. The missionary may be less selfish than the trader, but he is not likely to be less patriotic in the conventional meaning of that term. He may be thinking only of the improvement and well-being of the people among whom he works; but inevitably he regards himself as the representative of a higher and better civilization and of the only true religion, and his government as the one best fitted to promote the material and spiritual interests of mankind. Holding to this view, it is perfectly natural that he should play an important part in the development of imperialism. Missionaries may have been untainted by the sordid commercial motives that have too often influenced business men; but they have in many instances actively coöperated with those who, for selfish or so-called patriotic reasons, desired to create colonies, protectorates, or spheres of influence, and thus establish the supremacy of their own government in regions hitherto independent.

Protection for missionaries in foreign countries may afford the pretext for an imperialistic policy, when the really determining factor is the influence of a dominant class bent only on exploiting a weaker people. It is, of course, to be expected that the representatives of an aggressively militant religion — one whose avowed aim is the spiritual conquest of the world — will occasionally encounter bitter opposition from the people whose religion they are seeking to supplant. But even the crimes of violence which are thus provoked and of which missionaries are the victims may serve a useful purpose, as in the case of Germany's acquisition of Kiaochau and the mining and railway privileges in Shantung, or France's claim to enormously valuable concessions in southern China.[1] The proselyting spirit of the Christian religion has thus made the church an unwitting ally of capitalistic imperialism.

Organized capital has been chiefly responsible for the rapid increase in military and naval expenditures during recent decades. It has supported the policy of national preparedness for the ostensible reason that a formidable navy and an adequate army are the only possible means of guaranteeing international peace. This " big stick " argument for militarism has had a prominent place in the literature of imperialism.

" That the organization of military strength," says a distinguished advocate of preparedness, " involves provocation to war is a fallacy, which the experience of each succeeding year now refutes. The immense armaments of Europe are onerous; but nevertheless, by the mutual respect and caution they enforce, they present a cheap alternative, certainly

---

[1] See Paul Reinsch, *Colonial Government*, ch. III.

in misery, probably in money, to the frequent devastating wars which preceded the era of general military preparation." [2]

The recent World War, however, with its appalling destruction of life and property and the train of evils — political, social, and economic — which have followed it, has, it seems, effectually disposed of the militaristic pretense that general preparedness for war tends to preserve peace. The competition in armaments between the great capitalistic nations is merely one phase of the struggle for economic advantage. Armies and navies are regarded by the capitalist class as indispensable for the protection and advancement of their interests. The stronger a country is in this respect, the more effectively it can serve the capitalists who control it. But unfortunately, the nation that believes it is best prepared is quite likely to assume a bullying attitude in dealing with other nations. The "big stick," professedly defended as a means of protection, inevitably becomes in practice a temptation to aggression. It would be too much to expect that a capitalistic state, conscious of its military and naval power, would not occasionally assume an aggressive attitude where the interests of its dominant class were involved.

Inasmuch as organized wealth very largely controls the agencies through which public opinion is made, it is easy to arouse popular enthusiasm for capitalistic aggression by misrepresenting it as purely defensive. This is clearly shown by the fact that the responsibility for starting a war is always charged by each belligerent nation against the other, and that the people whose government is the aggressor are no less convinced that they are engaged in a defensive war than are the victims of their aggression. If the

[2] A. T. Mahan, *The Interest of America in Sea Power, Present and Future,* p. 104. Published in 1897.

economic control which capitalism exercises is not of itself sufficient to ensure the prevalence of such a belief, it is always possible in an emergency of this sort to invoke governmental aid in the form of official censorship and propaganda.

Capitalistic belief in the desirability of military preparedness is not wholly a question of international politics. The advocates of this policy usually find it expedient to emphasize the need of adequate protection against external dangers, but often it is internal danger that arouses most apprehension and is the main, if not the avowed, reason for maintaining a strong military establishment.

" The means of defense against foreign danger," observed James Madison, " have been always the instruments of tyranny at home. Among the Romans it was a standing maxim to excite a war, whenever a revolt was apprehended. Throughout all Europe, the armies kept up under the pretext of defending, have enslaved the people." [3]

It was the general recognition of this fact which explains the pronounced opposition to standing armies in the early period of our history. A government under which the great majority of the people were disqualified to vote or hold public office should not, it was thought, be supplied with the means by which the ruling minority could permanently repress the majority. The extension of the suffrage, however, and the deification of the Constitution by misrepresenting it as the embodiment of, and the indispensable means of enforcing, the sovereignty of the people, brought about a fundamental change in the popular attitude toward governmental authority. The main reason for democratic distrust of governmental power disappeared as the people came to accept the fiction that popular sovereignty was an

[3] Debates in the Convention of 1787, *Documentary History of the Constitution of the United States of America,* vol. III, pp. 241–42.

accomplished political fact. The way was thus cleared for the growth of military power in the period of capitalistic domination which began after the Civil War.

The relatively small class controlling the means of production under present-day capitalism realize that they need the protection of a strong government friendly to their interests. From their point of view, government is needed not to protect the many against the few, but primarily to protect the well-to-do minority against the propertyless majority.[4] The old aristocratic conception of the state thus survives in the political thought of present-day capitalism. It is, of course, incompatible with the newer and widely accepted idea that government is, or at least ought to be, under the control of the majority. Consequently, the capitalistic view of the state is usually kept discreetly in the background. Indeed, the interests of capitalism are much more secure under a government which clothes class control in democratic forms than they would be if capitalists constituted a legally established and generally recognized ruling class.

The effort of labor, through organization and strikes, to make its influence felt in the control of industry is likely to be regarded by the large-scale employer in much the same way that the old ruling class viewed the early democratic movement. The tactical advantage of legality is almost invariably on the side of capital in the industrial struggle, as it was on the side of king and aristocracy in the long struggle for political democracy. Labor, in seeking to divest capital of the control over industry, is striking at the foundation of a system which, its beneficiaries believe, the government and all social agencies, such as school and

---

[4] For an excellent statement of this view, see *The Federalist*, Art. no. 10, by James Madison.

church, ought to defend against attack. All who oppose the control of industry by the capitalist class are certain to be regarded as dangerously revolutionary.

Capitalism, being a form of class control, could not survive without governmental support. Because of potential dissatisfaction with existing economic arrangements and the possible desire to change them even though the legal rights of those who own the means of production might thereby be abridged or abolished, the state needs to be ready at all times to compel any numerous body of its citizens to respect rights which they might wish to ignore. A permanent military force, therefore, is necessary to ensure adequate protection for capital in time of economic turmoil.

But a military establishment, no matter how large it may be, is not of itself sufficient to protect the interests of capital in the long run. Coercion may meet the needs of a temporary emergency, but if the majority are to be permanently controlled a less obvious method must be adopted. It is necessary to inculcate the viewpoint and philosophy of militarism through the various agencies which mould the opinion of the people. For this purpose, a system of military training which brings the great majority of the people under its influence is more important than a standing army. If wisely conceived and skillfully administered, it may be the means of profoundly modifying the viewpoint and attitude of the average citizen toward the state.

" Is it nothing," asks a devotee of the system, " in an age when authority is weakening and restraints are loosening, that the youth of a nation passes through a school in which order, obedience, and reverence are learned . . . ? Is it nothing that masses of youths . . . are brought together, . . . taught to work and act together, . . . and carrying back into civil life that respect for constituted authority which is urgently needed in these days when lawlessness is erected into a religion? " [5]

Militarism is, of course, incompatible with democracy. It is in fact diametrically opposed to everything for which democracy stands. It demands implicit faith in, and unquestioning obedience to, established authority as such. In so far as military training succeeds in creating this attitude, it paves the way for an irresponsible governmental absolutism. By teaching reverence for authority and developing the habit of obedience, it tends to prevent democratic innovation.

There is still another way in which the maintenance of a large military and naval establishment tends to benefit the capitalist class. Preparedness for war diverts vast quantities of wealth from productive to non-productive uses. This diversion is obviously disadvantageous to the public, but it tends to benefit the capitalist by making it possible for him to secure a larger share of the social income.

Capitalists as such are interested in making production more efficient, only in so far as improved methods tend to augment their income. They have no interest in efficiency in the broader social sense of that term, as a method of ensuring low prices for the consumer and increased consumption by the worker. The history of combinations and trusts abundantly proves that the interests of the capitalist class may make them favor curtailed production and high prices with resulting monopoly profits, rather than a greater degree of efficiency secured through enlarged production and increased popular consumption. Limitation of output, though often resorted to for the purpose of increasing profits, has, however, some recognized disadvantages. To restrict production is to diminish employment and thus reduce

[5] A. T. Mahan, *The Interest of America in Sea Power, Present and Future,* pp. 232–33.

the capacity of labor to buy. A method of augmenting profits which does not lessen the demand for goods is far more advantageous to the capital owning class. Their interests are more likely to be advanced by increasing demand, if this can be accomplished without increasing wages, than by raising prices at the expense of the wage earner's power to consume.

The unique advantage of the policy of preparedness, from the viewpoint of capital, is that it augments demand without increasing popular consumption. The huge expenditure for the construction and maintenance of fortifications and navies, and for the support of armies, has been advantageous to the capitalist in that it has tended to safeguard his profits against the danger of an over-supplied market, by providing a large and constantly increasing unproductive demand for goods. It does not require a great deal of imagination to be able to see that the enormous expenditure of capitalistic nations for military and naval purposes, during the last two or three generations, has altered the distribution of the social income to the advantage of the capital owning class. If the goods consumed in preparation for, and in carrying on, war had been devoted entirely to productive uses, it is clear that the capitalistic system could not have functioned without a sufficient rise in wages and decline in profits to ensure an adequate demand for the products of industry. As a result of such a readjustment, capital would have occupied a much less advantageous position in relation to distribution than it does at the present time.

The growth of militarism has provided the outlet for surplus wealth that capitalism needed to protect its profits. The vast sums expended for military purposes, obtained by loans and indirect taxes, constitute a burden which finally rests upon the masses of the people, and from which they derive no benefit whatever. For the capital owning class, however, such expenditures have been distinctly profitable. They have not only had the effect of augmenting demand and thus keeping profits high, but in so far as the funds thus expended have been secured through loans, capital has enjoyed the benefit of a peculiarly advantageous form of investment. Loans for this purpose are, from the viewpoint of the capitalist, money actually invested, inasmuch as they yield an income. Not only do they function as capital in this respect, but they do so without increasing the supply of consumption goods and therefore without lowering prices and profits. Loans for productive purposes, on the other hand, by augmenting the wealth-creating power of society, tend in the end to bring about a change in distribution advantageous to the masses of the people, through the necessity of finding a demand sufficient to absorb the increased supply of goods. Militarism has thus provided for the capitalist class a new field in which its surplus income may be invested with the comforting realization that its profits are not being endangered by the creation of new capital and new competition.

Heretofore there has been a decided advantage to the capitalist class not only in maintaining large armies and navies in time of peace, but also in the frightful waste of resources which actual war always entails.

What effect the recent world wide struggle will have on capitalistic militarism and imperialism can only be surmised. It will depend very largely, no doubt, on whether capital is upon the whole benefited or burdened as a result of the War. The World War should at least diminish capitalistic enthusiasm for government bonds as a form of investment. The appalling increase of public indebtedness, together with the destruction of wealth and the disorganization of industry which resulted from the War, has either seriously impaired or entirely destroyed the credit of many countries. Not only have the bonds of the defeated nations become practically worthless, but even many of the victors in the struggle have found it difficult to restore confidence in their ability to meet their obligations. One reason, no doubt, for the attempt to saddle the entire cost of the War upon the vanquished was the desire of the victorious powers to strengthen their own tottering credit.

Repudiation of public debts would, of course, strike at the foundation of the capitalistic system; nevertheless, not only would it seem that the terms imposed by the victors have made it inevitable with respect to much of the indebtedness of the defeated nations, but influential interests are behind a proposal to cancel all indebtedness between the Allies. The capitalists who hold large masses of Allied bonds are, as a matter of course, anxious to have the Allied governments placed in a position to pay their obligations to individuals and private corporations — a prospect which would be improved by the cancellation of all inter-Allied indebtedness. It would be extremely unwise for advocates of this policy to admit that they were even remotely influenced by such a consideration. Yet there is doubtless some significance in the fact that the international banking interests are actively supporting this proposal. It would, of course, be untrue to say that they are actuated in this matter by purely selfish motives, as it would be equally untrue to affirm that their object is purely disinterested. In this, as in most political questions, there is no doubt a blending of selfish and unselfish motives, although the former may be disavowed and the latter loudly proclaimed. Much might be said in defense of this proposal, but it is altogether likely that its most active and effective supporters are the big financial corporations which hold large quantities of the bonds of Allied nations and expect, by having it accepted, to increase the value of such bonds, especially those issued by the financially weaker and more heavily burdened countries.

Just so long as militarism benefits the capital owning class, the world will continue to suffer the ravages of frequently recurring wars. Small as this class is numerically, its economic power enables it effectively to constitute for all practical purposes a ruling group. The firm grip which it has on the agencies through which public opinion is formed enables it to implant in the popular mind that suspicion and fear of other nations which it utilizes so effectively in support of large military and naval establishments. Moreover, its influence in politics, particularly in the field of foreign relations, is a constant menace to peace. Either directly or indirectly capitalism has been responsible for nearly all our recent wars. Even in those instances where it may have favored peace it can not be regarded as blameless, since its active advocacy of militarism has helped to create a situation in which it is easy to start a conflagration of this sort.

If some way could be found of depriving capital of the advantages which it has, as a rule, derived from militarism, the most potent cause of war would be removed. For this reason, the inability of nations to pay debts incurred in the prosecution of war would not be an unmixed evil. If government bonds issued for this purpose and now held by the capitalist class were rendered practically worthless, this heretofore unique and, from the capitalistic viewpoint, desirable kind of investment would no longer be a menace to the peace of the world.

The crushing load of indebtedness which so many countries are struggling under as a result of the War makes it highly probable that much of this burden will ultimately be placed upon the capital owning class. This may not come about through formal repudiation; the method employed is likely to be less direct but probably not less effective. Depreciation of the money in which such obligations are paid may make government bonds an unprofitable investment. But even if there were no decline in the purchasing power of the monetary unit and government bonds were worth their face value, they might easily be made a burden upon, instead of a benefit to, the capitalist class. The tremendous increase in government expenditure as a result of the War, by compelling resort to new sources of revenue and to redistribution of the burden of taxation, has brought home to the capitalist the realization that he faces the danger of having to pay a large share of the cost of future wars.

A somewhat higher degree of popular intelligence and a more effective political democracy would probably enable the people to see the advisability of depriving the capitalist class of the opportunity to profit either by war or by preparation for it. This end could be accomplished by means of a system of taxation avowedly designed and maintained for the purpose of making the capitalist classes bear, in so far as possible, the entire burden of militarism. Government bonds representing expenditure for war would cease to be an attractive form of investment when it came to be the policy of the state to meet obligations of this sort through taxes levied on the capitalist class. To transfer to capital the whole or even a large part of the burden represented by militarism would be taking a long step toward international peace.

If the great mass of the common people throughout the civilized world were sufficiently intelligent to see the direction in which their interests lie, they could convert capital-

ism from a peace-distributing into a peace-conserving force.
But even though they may fail to understand the wisdom of
saddling organized wealth with the burden of supporting
militarism, financial necessity has compelled capital to bear
a large part of the burden imposed by the recent war. It
is to be hoped that this will be sufficiently heavy to make
capitalists as a class feel that militarism is no longer advantageous to them, but has become, instead, distinctly
burdensome.

Something of the spirit of imperialism has been characteristic of the United States from the beginning of its history
as a colonial possession of Great Britain. Chattel slavery,
maintained for nearly a century after the Declaration of
Independence, together with the long continued struggle to
dispossess the original inhabitants of the territory, quite
naturally gave the people a viewpoint which tended to make
them susceptible to the imperialistic propaganda that began in the Spanish-American War period and has continued
ever since. A people accustomed to regard Negro slavery
as a justifiable institution, and, after its abolition, to believe
in the desirability of a racial discrimination which deprives
the black man of a voice in the choice of the officials by
whom he is governed, or to justify mistreatment of the
American Indians on the ground that they are an inferior
race, have already acquired a psychology that is essentially
imperialistic.

The imperialism of the United States was quiescent, however, until capitalism in the closing decades of the nineteenth century became a determining force in national politics. The American people, it is true, had long been keenly
interested in the expansion of the national domain. But
this may be explained in part at least by the desire to safeguard themselves against external danger. The territory

annexed was all on the continent of North America, and, until Alaska was purchased from Russia after the Civil War, it was all contiguous to the United States. With the exception of that acquired at the expense of Mexico, it was obtained without resort to force and with the consent of the European nations laying claim to it. The main reason for acquiring it was the desire to escape the danger of having old-world monarchies for near neighbors. The vast region ceded to the United States by Mexico after the War of 1846–48 represented the spoils of incipient American imperialism, but an imperialism of the slaveholding agricultural, rather than of the present-day capitalistic, type.

It was not until, with the increase of population and the growth of industry, the western frontier had disappeared that the people of the United States began to yield to the lure of imperialistic philosophy. The country was then coming, through a consciousness of its great and rapidly growing population and its varied and abounding natural resources, to a realization of its latent political power. Up to this time, it had been too much occupied with problems of internal development, and, during the early part of this period, too sensible of its own weakness to be misled by dreams of colonial empire.

During the hundred years following the Declaration of Independence, the people were very largely under the influence of the liberal political ideas promulgated in that document. Their conduct may have been in many instances inconsistent with their philosophy, but such divergence between theory and practice is to be expected as a matter of course. In a general way, they accepted the Declaration as an authoritative pronouncement of fundamental principles to which the state, both in internal organization and external relations, should as far as possible conform; and this de-

spite the fact of flagrant violations in the matters of slavery
and suffrage restrictions. Admitting such shortcomings, it
can not be gainsaid that American policies were upon the
whole profoundly influenced during the early national period
by the liberal political philosophy of the Declaration.
Doubtless, this influence was more pronounced with respect
to foreign relations than in the field of purely domestic politics. The reason is not difficult to find. Practical considerations were regarded as sufficient to justify convenient
deviations from abstract principles in the internal organization of the state, but it was clearly expedient in the early
decades of our history to follow a strictly let alone foreign
policy. Menaced by dissension at home and aggression
from without, the new federal state could have followed no
other course without endangering its existence as a nation.
Moreover, the social compact philosophy of the Declaration
of Independence, with its assumption of natural equality and
its doctrine that government derives all authority from the
consent of the governed, was, in effect, a denial of the right
of any nation to interfere in the internal affairs of another
nation. It was obviously incompatible with an imperialistic
foreign policy.

The emergence of a highly developed capitalism in the
last quarter of the nineteenth century brought with it an
effective demand for a new type of political and economic
philosophy. It was no mere coincidence that the theory of
competition and the doctrine of equality were fundamental
concepts of the liberal political and economic philosophy of
the eighteenth century. They were complementary ideas
and an essential part of the social contract and natural rights
conception of society. The equality assumed in the social
contract idea of the state supplied the foundation to support
the theory of competitive regulation of business. Moreover,

the continuance of competition being clearly incompatible with any marked inequality between competitors, the acceptance of it as a regulative principle implied the belief that equality was not only desirable, but that it was in some degree an actuality, since if competitors were unequal competition would tend to disappear. This system of political and economic philosophy had in view the limitation of irresponsible political power. It was actively espoused by those who wished to free industry from the vexations and burdens of irresponsible governmental interference. The individual, they assumed, would thereby be protected against the government in the enjoyment of his natural right to industrial liberty. Capitalists, however, unlike the old landowning ruling class of the eighteenth century, were interested not in maintaining competition, but in suppressing it. By merging competing industrial enterprises in combinations and trusts and by controlling the agencies of transportation and credit, organized capital was acquiring the arbitrary power to fix prices and to appropriate a larger share of the social income than would have been possible under a régime of free competition. A theoretical defense of large scale business and monopolistic organization, with the resulting inequality in the distribution of wealth, was an urgent need. It was highly desirable from the standpoint of capital to have competitive regulation of industry thoroughly discredited, since this would remove the chief obstacle to effective capitalistic control.

Socialism had already prepared the way for a propaganda of this sort, by attempting to prove that competition is necessarily self-destructive and that capitalistic monopoly is a form of organization through which our industrial system must inevitably pass in the course of its development. By emphasizing the desirability and inevitableness of economic centralization, the earlier socialistic agitation did much to undermine popular belief in the efficacy of competitive regulation and to disseminate the myth that productive efficiency necessarily increases with the combination of competing concerns, reaching its highest development only under a régime of complete monopoly. Quite naturally all the servitors of capitalistic privilege came to the aid of the socialists in their attack on competition and their defense of industrial consolidation. The socialistic conception of efficiency in production was admirably adapted to the purposes of those who sought to defend private capitalism against the attacks made upon it by the advocates of competitive industry. The whole movement to preserve the competitive régime by the enactment and enforcement of legislation designed to counteract the monopolistic tendency of capitalism could be easily frustrated, if the socialistic conception of the superior efficiency of large scale organization could be insinuated into the popular mind.

It was not a difficult matter to create a more or less prevalent belief that the disappearance of competition through the growth of combinations was bringing into existence a less wasteful system of production. It mattered little that this decreased cost of production might not be evidenced in the price paid by consumers. The socialists themselves, though continually expatiating upon the evils of modern capitalism, were as much opposed to the restoration of competition as were the immediate beneficiaries of large-scale production. Thinking of private capitalism as but one of the ascending stages in the evolution of industry, they were willing to endure its evils for the time being, in order to reach that happy economic state in which private capital would be entirely superseded by government ownership and operation. The citizen who did not believe in the socialistic commonwealth, but who had been influenced by the pro-trust propaganda, became, like the socialist, a defender of industrial consolidation. He might realize that the benefits of combinations were very largely appropriated by the capitalist class; but in common with the socialists he expected to invoke the power of the state to make capitalism more effectively serve the public. He parted company with the socialists only when they came to the question of a suitable remedy for the evils of large-scale business. He wished to preserve private capitalism and merely subject it to needful regulation, while the socialists expected to have it taken over and administered by the state itself.

The popular attitude brought about through this socialistic and big business propaganda secured to capitalists practical immunity from all anti-monopoly legislation. The competitive system was thoroughly discredited and the idea instilled in the mind of the people that the movement toward centralized control of industry was natural and inevitable. The evils which accompanied this development came to be thought of as temporary and remediable, while the advantages of consolidation, it was assumed, would be permanent and would accrue ultimately, if not immediately, to the people generally. This change in popular attitude toward industrial consolidation permitted the virtual nonenforcement of existing anti-combination laws and ensured the defeat of all proposed legislation which would have prevented the suppression of competition through combination. Capitalists could now anticipate a period more or less prolonged, between the disappearance of competition and the ultimate establishment of effective public regulation, during which they would be able to enjoy monopoly profits without serious interference at the hands of the state.

The waning enthusiasm in this country for the democratic ideas of the Declaration of Independence is due in

part at least to the growing power of American capitalism
and its subtle influence on the agencies for moulding public
opinion. To this source must be attributed mainly the attack on equality and the defense of inequality. So long as
the United States remained predominantly agricultural, it
was, if not enthusiastic in its belief in equality, at least opposed to such inequalities as were due to special privileges
of any sort. But the ascendancy of the commercial and
manufacturing interests toward the end of the nineteenth
century, and the rapidly growing inequality in wealth which
marked the transition from rural to urban predominance,
made it highly expedient to undermine any surviving belief
in the doctrine of equality. This doctrine, so much emphasized in the beginning of our history as a nation, could not be
reconciled with the fact of glaring economic inequality. Privileged industry would not be secure against popular attack,
unless the people could be induced to accept inequality as
natural and justifiable. The great fortunes which were being rapidly accumulated were clearly incompatible with a
democratic conception of either politics or industry. The
popular reverence for the Declaration of Independence, with
its emphasis on natural equality, made it highly serviceable
in the attack on plutocracy. It was clearly necessary to
discredit this document, since no people really influenced by
its philosophy could be expected to tolerate the inequality
which capitalism was bringing about.

Conservatives in consequence rallied to the defense of
privilege against the subversive ideas of the Declaration of
Independence. Not only was the Declaration left in
the background in all conservative political and economic
discussion from this time on, but a systematic attempt
was made to disseminate the idea that inequality was a
perfectly natural and desirable feature of human society.

The lip-service to equality which had characterized the electioneering speeches of politicians and much of our political literature up to this time, gradually subsided, while the opposition to it which had been largely silenced during the preceding period of professed devotion to democratic ideals, became active and outspoken. The philosophy of the Declaration of Independence, which it had been the custom to eulogize on important public occasions as a beacon light to guide the ship of state, soon passed into eclipse.[6] The great man theory of society, which the democratic movement with its insistence on equality had apparently discredited, was brought forth from the limbo of discarded beliefs, decked out in the verbal finery of pseudo-science, and offered as an explanation and justification of inequality.[7] The great fortunes accumulated under the capitalistic system were represented, with few and unimportant exceptions, as the well earned reward which society had paid to its great industrial leaders. Economic inequality was assumed to be merely an indication of that more fundamental inequality of intelligence and worth. Progress in industry, it was said, had been due to the intelligently directed efforts of the outstanding few, who, notwithstanding their huge fortunes, had been but inadequately compensated for their contribution to the well-being of society.

As a result of this propaganda, the popular attack on

[6] This change of attitude is rather strikingly illustrated by a well known and widely used high school textbook on civics of this period: John Fiske, *Civil Government in the United States Considered with Some Reference to Its Origins*, 1891. Although dealing with the matter historically and attempting to trace the growth of our political institutions from colonial times, the author, a distinguished historical writer, did not so much as mention or even allude to the Declaration of Independence from the beginning to the end of this volume.

[7] One of the best statements of the great man theory, as it was used to account for and justify the rapidly increasing inequality of wealth, may be found in *Aristocracy and Evolution* by W. H. Mallock, a defender of British capitalism, published in 1898.

privileged industry, which began after the Civil War and continued through the seventies and eighties, was gradually abating by the close of the century. Not only were the people coming to accept the socialist and pro-trust contention that industrial consolidation meant increased efficiency, but the notion was being gradually and adroitly insinuated into the popular mind that inequality in wealth was indicative of a corresponding inequality in services rendered. The spread of this impression was materially aided by the constantly growing stream of benefactions which carried back to the public for schools and churches, for libraries and hospitals, for university pensions and missionary activities, a large amount, but after all a relatively unimportant part, of the wealth which had been unjustly appropriated by the beneficiaries of big business. It was, of course, too much to expect that the harshness of the earlier criticism of economic inequality would not be considerably softened or even entirely abated as the dependence on such benefactions, or the desire for them, came to be widely felt and generally diffused throughout the country. Philanthropy of this sort has in fact been an excellent investment for privileged industry, even though it may not have been intended as such.

It is true that belief in economic inequality might not be incompatible with the idea of political equality. We might think that great inequality in wealth is due to a corresponding inequality in character and intelligence, and yet believe that the only wise course for a state to pursue is to treat all men alike. We could favor political equality on the ground of expediency, without accepting the doctrine of natural equality. Nevertheless, belief in natural inequality not only serves to justify, but tends to lead to, political discrimination against those assumed to be inferior. The propaganda which discredited the political ideas of the Declaration of Independence thus opened the door to capitalistic imperialism.

Capitalistic propaganda, aided by the growing spirit of ambitious and aggressive nationalism, prepared the way for the acceptance of the imperialistic philosophy. It was the Spanish-American War, however, which first made it clear that the United States was rapidly becoming an imperialistic nation. This war was the occasion, rather than the cause, of the manifestation of the imperialistic sentiment which accompanied it and which has been steadily augmenting since. It marks the close of that period of American history during which the principles of the Declaration of Independence had a real, if not always controlling, influence upon politics, and begins a new epoch in which political thought and governmental policies have been profoundly influenced by the philosophy of imperialism.

The agitation for intervention in the struggle between Spain and her colonies sought to arouse the enthusiasm of the American public for the emancipation of a subject population from a harsh and despotic alien rule. To this extent, it made a direct appeal to all who might still be under the influence of the political ideas of the Revolutionary period. But the alleged humanitarian motives were reinforced by more practical considerations, such as the need for protection of American investments in Cuba and the injury to American business interests resulting from the disorder and anarchy which were continually recurring under Spanish rule. The propaganda for intervention, though ostensibly having in view the establishment of Cuban independence, reflected clearly enough the desire to protect the property rights and business interests of Americans against the dangers of political instability.

That the American public was not ready to approve a war of conquest is indicated by the fact that the war with Spain began with a joint resolution of Congress which expressly recognized the independence of Cuba and disclaimed any desire to bring it under the control of the United States. There was, however, strong conservative opposition to the fulfillment of the promise thus solemnly made by Congress, with the result that Cuba did not acquire the status of an independent state. The American government retained a large measure of control over Cuba's foreign relations and financial affairs, and reserved the right to intervene, among other purposes, for " the maintenance of a government adequate for the protection of life, property, and individual liberty. . . ." [8] Inasmuch as the government of the United States interprets these limitations on the sovereignty of Cuba and also determines when the facts justify intervention, it clearly has a large measure of control over both the internal affairs and the external relations of this so-called republic. A small country thus supervised by a strong state is merely a dependency of the latter, and any powers of self-government which it may exercise, it really holds on sufferance. The nominal independence of Cuba may for a time conceal its actual dependence, but sooner or later, with the growth of American imperialism, its political status will probably be generally recognized.

There is no room for misconception concerning the status of Porto Rico and the Philippines. Acquired as a result of the war with Spain, they became subject to the United States without becoming a part of it. The political and civil rights of their inhabitants were such as the American government saw fit to recognize. This annexation of foreign territory, to be held and ruled as colonial dependencies,

[8] Platt amendment to the army appropriation act, March, 1901.

marked the beginning of an avowedly imperialistic foreign policy.

Military and especially naval expenditures have rapidly increased. The Panama Canal, constructed, fortified, and controlled by the United States, is, of course, important as a highway of commerce, but its chief significance is political. With colonies in both the Atlantic and the Pacific, it would be difficult for the United States to defend them in case of war with any important naval power, unless the American fleet could be easily and quickly transferred from one ocean to the other as the need might arise. The Panama Canal may thus be regarded as an undertaking designed and carried through primarily for the purpose of increasing the efficiency of the American navy.

With the adoption of an imperialistic foreign policy, the Monroe Doctrine acquired a new significance. Purely defensive in the beginning, it was designed to safeguard the new world against European aggression. It denied the right of any old-world power to intervene in the political affairs of the western hemisphere or to extend territorial possessions in either North or South America. As originally promulgated there was no suggestion of American imperialism in the Monroe Doctrine. It was a solemn proclamation that the government of the United States would regard any intrusion of old-world imperialism on this side of the Atlantic as an unfriendly act. It was not a declaration of overlordship, but an assertion of the right of all American countries to freedom from external control. The fact that the Doctrine, which was not recognized in international law, was not flagrantly disregarded by the imperialistic nations of Europe was due, in the early period of our history, less to the ability of the United States to enforce it, than to the mutual fear and jealousy of the powers whose aggressions it was designed to check.

As capitalism developed in the United States, the Monroe Doctrine was given a distinctly imperialistic interpretation. This change of attitude on the part of the American government was clearly and unequivocally stated in 1895 with reference to the boundary dispute between British Guiana and Venezuela. Secretary Olney asserted that " the United States is practically sovereign on this continent, and its fiat is law upon the subjects to which it confines its interposition." He laid down the principle that the Monroe Doctrine is a part of international law, that it forbids a refusal by European nations to arbitrate territorial disputes with Latin-American countries, and that the United States would be justified in resorting to war to enforce such an interpretation. As this pronouncement was made three years before the Spanish-American War, it is evident that the latter event was less a cause than a consequence of the rapidly growing imperialism of the United States.

It would be difficult to find in modern diplomatic history a more aggressively imperialistic pronouncement than the interpretation which the American government thus gave to the Monroe Doctrine. Great Britain was clearly entitled to be regarded as an American power, inasmuch as her territorial possessions in North America were of greater extent than those of the United States, excluding Alaska. The assertion that the United States was " practically sovereign " in the western hemisphere was belligerently imperialistic. It indicated a profound change in the attitude of this country toward other American nations. The Monroe Doctrine, instead of serving as a means of protection against European aggression, as originally intended, had now become an instrument of American imperialism. Under the pretext of safeguarding the weaker American states against foreign aggression in accordance with the Monroe Doctrine, the government of the United States was seeking to ensure its own ascendancy throughout the western hemisphere.

Whatever moral influence the Monroe Doctrine may have had in the beginning, when advanced to justify self-determination on the part of American countries, was lost when it ceased to be a defense of democracy and became instead a cloak for the imperialism of the United States. If anything more was needed to destroy the moral effect of the Doctrine it was supplied in the annexation by the United States of Spain's colonies in the Far East. This was, of course, in direct violation of the policy of non-interference in old-world affairs, which had constituted the very foundation of the Monroe Doctrine. For the United States to claim the new world as a protectorate and at the same time to assert the right to acquire colonies in the old, reduced the Doctrine to an absurdity and left it without any support except that of sheer physical force.

CHAPTER XI

INTERNATIONAL RELATIONS AS A CHECK ON THE POWER OF THE STATE

Recognized limitations on the power of a state are needed for the protection of other states no less than for the protection of its own citizens. The idea of sovereignty, now generally accepted, which imputes unlimited power to the state is not only subversive of the rights and liberty of the individual, but it is also a standing menace to the peace and well-being of the world.

This conception of unlimited power was no part of the original doctrine of sovereignty, which merely implied independence of external control. As originally used, the term sovereignty represented an idea of governmental power which served in some measure to protect small and weak states against the strong. As a conception that every state is independent of external control regardless of its size or strength, the doctrine of sovereignty was calculated to impose a check on the tendency of strong states to encroach upon the weak. Thus interpreted it was designed to promote international peace by crystallizing a sentiment in all civilized nations that would condemn, and thus tend to prevent, acts of aggression. If the idea of sovereignty had continued to serve merely as a safeguard against aggression, it would have emphasized the independence rather than the unlimited power of the state.

Sovereignty, in this negative sense of freedom from external interference, may be regarded as an adaptation of the

237

principle of individual liberty to the relations between theoretically independent states; it is supposed to afford to a weak state the same kind of protection against other states that individual liberty in theory secures to the individual citizen against the government itself. Sovereignty as thus defined, if supported by the public opinion of the civilized world, must exert an appreciable influence in checking the rapacity of imperialistic states; just as the idea of individual liberty, in any country where it is prized by the people generally, may actually prevent governmental abridgment of individual rights.

In the light of such an interpretation, sovereignty is merely part of the general check and balance philosophy. According to this conception of sovereignty, the chief end of the state should be the establishment and safeguarding of liberty for individuals and associations of individuals, just as the primary concern of international organization should be the problem of protecting the rights and preserving the independence of the weaker states. But the right to independence was supposed to imply, both for the individual and for the state, the duty of recognizing the equal independence of others. This is the conception of individual liberty and sovereignty which found expression in the Declaration of Independence. The power of the state was assumed to be limited internally by the rights of individuals and externally by the rights of other states.

Coincident with the decline of faith in eighteenth century political philosophy, the conception of sovereignty was profoundly changed. Emphasis was shifted from the conception of independence to that of power. The distinctive feature of the earlier theory of sovereignty, which had been the limitations imposed on the power of the state, now became its absolute and unlimited authority. In theory, the state was no longer regarded as subject to either internal or external restraint, except such as was implied in the recognition of what is called international law. In the case of a strong state, its own will was practically the only law which it was bound to respect.

This new doctrine of governmental absolutism, which goes by the name of the sovereignty of the state, is irreconcilable either with individual liberty or with the rights and independence of the smaller nations. To emphasize the idea that the power of the state is absolute and unlimited is to lay a philosophical foundation for governmental encroachment on individual liberty and for the development of aggressive imperialism on the part of the more powerful states. By transforming the idea of sovereignty from a doctrine of the limitation of power to a theory that the authority of the state is unlimited, political writers have rendered society a very real disservice. To the prevalence of this concept is due, in no small degree, that pseudo-patriotism and national bumptiousness which are now a constant menace to the peace of the world.

It is not claimed by those who accept this new doctrine of sovereignty that it implies the right of a state to disregard those principles and usages which constitute what is generally called international law. Even the most powerful state professes to recognize the limitations on its authority which the existence of other independent political communities necessarily imposes. Sovereignty in the sense of unlimited power may be claimed by a state with respect to its own citizens, but no state to-day would dare to claim freedom to disregard international law. In practice, however, a powerful state may in large measure evade the limitations thus imposed, by interpreting them to suit its own purposes. On the assumption that there is no international authority set above the separate states of the world to interpret and enforce the principles supposed to govern international relations, each state may interpret these restraints to suit itself, subject only to the danger of incurring the ill-will, or exciting the hostility, of other states. Under these circumstances, it is inevitable that international law should be much less of a restraint on the strong states than upon the weak. Equality of rights for all countries, both great and small, is readily accepted by the weaker states as a means of restraining the strong, just as the doctrine of natural equality was originally defended with a view to bringing about the overthrow of political and economic privilege. But weak countries can not expect to achieve equality of treatment with the strong, so long as the latter are permitted to interpret their rights and obligations under international law from their own viewpoint and with reference to their own interests. Where law is interpreted by those whom it is supposed to restrain, it is likely to be ineffective when and where its protection is most needed.

International law is an expression of the need for an adequate check on the power of the state, in so far as its relations with other states are concerned. As representing a prevalent belief in the desirability of some external limitation on governmental authority, it has performed a highly useful function. But no satisfactory means has thus far been devised for ensuring a fair interpretation of its provisions and their enforcement against strong and weak countries alike. As a matter of fact, the powerful state is controlled by international law in much the same way, and in about the same degree, that the king's authority in relation to his own subjects was limited by the divine right theory of monarchy. The king was obligated to rule in accordance with natural or divine law, just as the state to-day is supposed to conform in all external matters to the requirements of international law. But the king himself was the final interpreter of natural or divine law, and was thus able to evade in large measure the restraints sought to be imposed on his authority. In like manner, the state, by placing its own interpretation on international law, may defeat the end which that law has in view. The only check on the power of the king to misinterpret or ignore natural or divine law was the possibility of revolution; just as the only check on the power of the state to disregard or violate the principles of international law is the fear of incurring the enmity of other states. In either case war has been the only means of making the limitation effective.

In the absence of any common and impartial agency to interpret international law and supervise international relations, every state is anxious not only to increase its own authority but to prevent, if possible, any increase in the authority of rival states. The instinct of self-preservation, in a world made up of independent nations, operates to make each desire power in order to secure itself against the danger of external aggression. The fact that no country alone is sufficiently strong to feel secure against any possible combination of opposing states makes necessary the formation of alliances and counter-alliances through which each state seeks to ensure the needed support in case its safety is menaced from without. This is usually referred to as the struggle to maintain the balance of power. It is merely an application of the check and balance theory of the state to international politics. It is assumed, and rightly so, that if any state should acquire a predominant position in international affairs, it would be a distinct menace to the interests and well-being of the rest of the world. Power, even though it may have been acquired as a means of protection, becomes a menace to international peace as soon as the country possessing it comes to feel stronger than any possible foe. It is no less necessary to maintain the balance of power in international politics, than it is to prevent some special interest from gaining the ascendancy in the state. But since this balance of power idea is based on the fear of attack and assumes that every nation should be prepared for war, it can not be regarded as in any real sense a guaranty of international peace.

The question naturally arises as to the possibility of supplanting these mutually antagonistic groups of nations by some permanent international organization which will serve as an agency for the regulation of those matters that fall within the field of international politics. Some form of permanent international organization is needed, not only to mediate between states in cases of disagreement, but to exercise such pressure — political and economic — as might be required to punish any state that attempted to wage an aggressive war. The desirability of such an agency is generally recognized. But whether it is practicable in the present state of political and social intelligence throughout the world may be doubted. It is not due to the failure to recognize the need for such an agency that the peoples of the world have continued to live in a state of international anarchy. It is due rather to the almost insuperable difficulties which must be overcome before any satisfactory international organization can be established. There is little to indicate that the world has reached the stage of intellectual and moral development that must constitute the only foundation on which enduring international coöperation can be based. Aggressive and selfish nationalism and ferocious religious and racial prejudice, everywhere so much in evidence, are incompatible with the maintenance of uninterrupted peaceful intercourse between nations.

The so-called League of Nations, set up at the close of the World War, was really nothing more than an association of the victorious powers for the purpose of dictating the terms of peace and enforcing them against the vanquished. It was designed to provide an international organization which should be dominated by the five leading powers amongst the victors. This was to be ensured by giving to these nations a permanent majority in the chief organ of the League, the council. This fact alone was sufficient to discredit the League in the eyes of all who were really desirous of making it representative of the interests of all nations. If anything more was needed to bring it into disrepute at the very start, there was the additional fact that to ensure its acceptance it was with deliberate intention intertwined with, and made part and parcel of, the most oppressive and vindictive peace settlement of modern times. Even if the plan of the League had itself been above criticism, it could not have been otherwise than disastrous to have thus tied it up with the terms of a peace which must of necessity be repudiated as soon as sanity and a sense of justice reasserted themselves in international politics.

The viewpoint from which the covenant of the League was framed, and the imperialistic outlook of the representatives of the five great powers, were clearly evidenced in the repudiation of the principle of international law which recognizes the equality of states regardless of their size or power. The so-called big five attempted to set up an international order in which their own governments would occupy for all time a privileged place — a position not freely accorded them by the nations of the world, but one assumed and held by virtue of their physical power as victors in the World War. Such special privileges in an international organization are no less incompatible with its professedly representative purpose, than class privileges within a state are irreconcilable with democracy. There is little in the international situation to justify the enthusiasm of that vast multitude of earnest but undiscerning people, who really thought that the War was being prosecuted against the Central Powers to " make the world safe for democracy." The disillusionment which has come to so many of those who accepted war propaganda at its face value has tended to create an atmosphere of suspicion, distrust, and cynicism, which constitutes an additional handicap to the success of the League.

Belief in the desirability of some form of world organization is not new. The need for safeguards against war has long been recognized. The means proposed for accomplishing this great end have varied from Dante's monarchical world state to Rousseau's plan for joining all important governments in a loose confederacy. So profoundly, indeed, are a great many people impressed by the constant menace of war, that they would grasp at any form of international organization, however defective it might be, which held out the promise of minimizing the danger. But though war is an evil to be averted if possible, it is not necessarily the greatest danger to which society is exposed. Nor has war always been wholly evil. It is the expression of one form of competition and has occasionally served as an agency of progress by breaking down barriers that have obstructed the normal growth and development of society. Granting so much, however, it must not be supposed that upon the whole its influence has been beneficial. When disputes between nations are finally decided by resort to force, they are no more likely to be settled justly than were those between individuals, when submitted in the past to the arbitrament of trial by battle.

We need, far more than we need an international state or a

league of nations, a spirit of international-mindedness — the sense of justice, spirit of tolerance, and capacity for coöperation — without which every attempt at world organization must fail. There is altogether too much readiness to ignore the fact that any successful international organization must rest upon an adequate intellectual and moral foundation. Doubtless, the tendency to regard it as something that can be forced is largely due to impatience with a system under which we are constantly exposed to the danger of war. A scheme of international control virtually imposed upon the world through the compulsion of a few strong militant countries would, however, be a poor substitute for international coöperation, and would be likely to occasion in the end more evil than it averted. Such an organization would inevitably be made to serve the interests of the dominant group of states, instead of functioning as a common and impartial agency of international coöperation, and as a means of protecting weak countries against the strong.

The dangers in a situation of this sort are exemplified in the history of the League of Nations from its inception down to date. Not only has the League failed thus far to bring about a decline in the spirit of militarism, but it has been accompanied by, if it has not been in some measure the cause of, that hysterical nationalism and intensification of political, economic, religious, and racial prejudice which have been so much in evidence since the close of the World War. It has been only too evident that the countries most active in organizing the League and planning to dominate it, have little faith in it as a peace-preserving agency. When members of the League, such as Poland and Greece, can disregard its authority for the purpose of waging wars of aggression, and France can ignore it in seizing the Ruhr, there is little ground for believing that it was designed by the victorious nations to be an effective check on their own power. Nor does membership in the League afford protection to a weak state against interference in its internal affairs by a strong state outside of the League, as the control of Haiti by American marines clearly shows. It is but reasonable to expect that the old struggle on the part of the strong nations for predominance, and on the part of the weaker countries for a balance of power, will continue even under such a league of nations.

That there is possibility of evil in any form of world organization should not be ignored. The growth of highly centralized industry, with its trusts and economic imperialism, has greatly increased the dangers of international control. The big business philosophy, which now so largely dominates the thinking of the Western World, should not be disregarded in estimating the probable consequences of such an innovation in world politics as the establishment of a league of nations. Centralization is a fundamental idea in the political and economic creed of present-day capitalism. A world made up of many small independent states is no more to the liking of the large-scale business man than active competition is approved in his own special industrial field. He wishes to have all his foreign investments and interests adequately protected by the militant imperialism of some strong capitalistic state or, perhaps better still, by a world organization which will be dominated by a small group of such states. The chief danger of such a league of governments is that, instead of protecting the weaker countries and the masses generally, it will serve the ends of present-day capitalism. It is altogether improbable that any league of governments instituted by the great present-day capitalistic states would abolish the evils of imperialism, except in so far as those evils were felt to be a burden by the capitalists themselves.

Were such a league of governments once firmly established and generally recognized as the regular agency for dealing with international affairs, it is reasonable to assume that the capitalistic class would favor the extension of its authority to many matters not previously recognized as properly subject to international control. This would be but a logical application of the belief in centralization, which has been so actively disseminated by both socialistic and capitalistic propaganda. The viewpoint thus inculcated, though designed to supply a justification for the suppression of competition and the growth of monopoly, lays the foundation for political as well as economic centralization. The main argument for increasing the functions and extending the authority of the general government at the expense of its subdivisions has been the alleged need of a regulating agency whose jurisdiction is coextensive with the interests to be regulated. The growth of large-scale business has thus been made to serve as a pretext for the development of the highly centralized modern state. But economic organization and private business interests are no longer confined within the boundaries of the national state. Industry in many lines is becoming, or has already become, international in the scope of its organization and the ramification of its interests. As a result, the argument heretofore used in defense of centralized government could be made to justify the extension of the powers of an international organ or agency. This would no doubt be done whenever capitalism felt that its interests demanded a higher degree of political centralization than would be possible under the national state.

The specious attempt to justify political centralization was, of course, intended for undiscriminating popular consumption. Capitalists quite naturally never have been, and never will be, in favor of an adequate regulative agency under popular control. If the policy of regulation is forced upon them, they will seek to make it ineffective by controlling the regulating authority.

Big business interests certainly would not favor a league of nations if they did not expect to control it; and that they would be able to dictate its policies seems likely. Inasmuch as they are now in practical control of the foreign offices of all capitalistic states, and inasmuch as such a league would probably be but an association of the various governments acting through their departments of foreign affairs — just as the present League is — the expectation of capitalistic control of the organization would seem to be justified. If the masses are unable to control the foreign affairs of a single state, it would be infinitely more difficult for the people of the world as a whole, hampered as they are by differences in race, culture, language, and religion, to exercise any effective control over the policies of such a league. If the several governments of the world, irrespective of their outward form, are practically uncontrolled in their conduct of foreign affairs, a league of such governments would be likely to represent a degree of irresponsibility exceeding anything hitherto known in modern political organization. In the present stage of intellectual and moral development, the difficulties that stand in the way of effective popular control of such an organization would seem to be insuperable.

It may be seriously doubted whether any form of international political organization is desirable if it is to fall under the control of the capitalist class. A league of nations or world government of this sort might tend to preserve peace, but it would probably be peace at the expense of progress. Political and economic innovations, under such an organization, would be frowned upon if not ruthlessly repressed, except in so far as they were conceived to be in line with the interests of organized wealth. A world in which countries were not free to try experiments in economic organization, even to the extent of abolishing private capital altogether, would certainly not be a free world. Yet there is little room for doubt that complete capitalistic domination would outlaw any change of this sort. No weak country would be permitted to experiment with a socialistic or communistic scheme of economic life; even a large and powerful country would find the whole capitalistic world arrayed against it. The attitude of the great capitalistic countries toward Russia since the Bolshevist Revolution is indicative of what might reasonably be expected from any international organization in which their influence was predominant. What capitalism desires is a form of political organization, national and international, which will tend to preserve the *status quo,* except where its own interests would be furthered by changes in the established order.[1] The one paramount purpose of plutocracy to-day being the preservation of all the essentials of private capitalism, its hostility to democratic innovation, either political or economic, is not difficult to understand. Capitalism is not necessarily opposed to the outward form of democracy, however, and may even favor it where the conditions are such that it would serve as a convenient disguise for capitalistic control.

---

[1] The slogans, " open diplomacy," " freedom of the seas," " removal of economic barriers," " reduction of armaments," " the destruction of arbitrary power," and " self-determination for large and small nations alike," may have served to arouse enthusiasm for the Allied cause, but it is beyond dispute that their influence upon the peace settlement and the subsequent course of international politics has been almost negligible. The war to " make the world safe for democracy " has not brought democracy, nor has it accomplished any of the objects above mentioned, largely because they were not part of the capitalistic plan of political and economic reorganization.

The tendency during recent decades has been increasingly toward the subjection of the weaker non-capitalistic countries whenever the interests of capital have been involved. Under the pretense of policing the world and maintaining law and order, capitalistic nations have attempted to justify innumerable encroachments on the freedom and independence of the weaker and less highly developed countries. A capitalistic league of nations would almost inevitably make this sort of interference a fixed policy, and thus strengthen the hold of capitalism on those regions not subject to local capitalistic control. The special privileges, political and economic, claimed and enforced by capitalism in such non-Christian and non-capitalistic countries as China and Turkey are likely to be discontinued, if at all, not because of the establishment of a league of nations, but only when and to the extent that non-Christian nations acquire the power to resist exploitation at the hands of Christian capitalism.

The world needs, far more than it does a league of nations or any form of a super-state, a new type of political philosophy — one which will combine the basic ideas of democracy with adequate provision for progress, political, economic, and social. Without a change in attitude toward institutional arrangements, little benefit and possibly much harm would come from the creation of an international agency of political control.

Every institutional arrangement which has in view the organization and exercise of political power needs, if it is to prove beneficial in the long run, a generally accepted viewpoint or background of political ideas which will tend to safeguard the people against the abuses to which those subject to political authority are always exposed. These dangers, as we have seen, are far greater in the case of a world agency than under the system of separate national states. For this reason any international organization of political power would make necessary, on the part of the people generally, a clear understanding of its possible evils as well as of its advantages. Until such time as the people in the leading nations of the world come to possess this degree of political intelligence, and are also sufficiently cosmopolitan in their outlook to make coöperation possible between nations widely different in language, race, and cultural inheritance, no international arrangement can rest upon a secure foundation, nor can there be any adequate guaranty that power entrusted to it will not be abused.

CHAPTER XII

THE JURY SYSTEM AS A CHECK
ON GOVERNMENTAL POWER [1]

The generally accepted view of the jury system is that it supplies a much needed check on governmental authority. An examination of its practical operation shows, however, that this popular conception is not based on fact. If the jury were what it is generally supposed to be — an effective democratic check on the courts in the administration of justice — it would be necessary to employ a method of selecting jurors that would leave nothing to official discretion, and to grant to their verdicts a greater degree of finality than they now have. If the selection of juries is to be practically under official control, and their findings subject to the power of the court to modify or set aside, the jury system is more likely to function as an organ of the government itself than as a popular safeguard against the abuse of official authority.

At the time of the American Revolution, the right of trial by jury was not only regarded as an essential feature of constitutional government, but was also the most highly prized constitutional check on governmental power. English experience under irresponsible government had shown that it was possible for courts to become instruments of oppression, unless they were constantly subject to some such popular

[1] The author acknowledges his indebtedness to Mr. Harry Marvin Kenin's thesis, *The Jury System* — submitted for the M. A. degree in Political Science, University of Washington, 1923 — for many facts which have been utilized in the preparation of this chapter.

restraint as the jury system was supposed to provide. Accepting the political theory of checks and balances and regarding government as a necessary evil, the people quite naturally felt that trial by jury was a necessary check on the power of the courts. Belief in the necessity for jury trial was as much a part of eighteenth century political philosophy as was the social contract theory, the doctrine of natural rights, or the theory of individual liberty.

As in the case of most of the so-called popular checks on official authority, the results obtained from jury trial have fallen far short of the advantages which have been claimed for it. This discrepancy between what was expected from, and what has actually been secured through, trial by jury is, however, not due primarily to any inherent defect in the institution itself, but rather to the opposition which it has encountered at the hands of legislatures, courts, and conservatives generally. Governments do not, of course, regard with favor any popular check of this sort; yet where jury trial is expressly provided for in a written constitution, or supported by an overwhelming and definitely crystallized public sentiment, it must be maintained at least in form. Unless public opinion is alert and highly intelligent, however, there are many ways in which the government may impair its effectiveness.

The efficacy of trial by jury may be lessened by prescribing qualifications which render large classes of citizens ineligible for jury service. If the qualifications of jurymen are not specified in the constitution, the legislature may fix them in such manner as to make even qualified voters ineligible. This has actually been done in a number of our states by the enactment of statutes requiring that all jurymen must be direct taxpayers. Where the right to serve on juries is thus limited, they cease to be representative of the people generally; and the section of the population excluded is virtually deprived of the benefit of this particular form of protection. Since the most serious problems in connection with the administration of justice arise out of inequality in the distribution of wealth, laws of this sort have the effect of withholding the protection afforded by a representative jury system from the very classes which most need it.

Free government to-day is based on the assumption that the people need to be represented not only in the legislative or policy moulding bodies, but also in that branch which applies the law to individual civil and criminal cases. The democratic theory of government is irreconcilably opposed to any restriction which would tend to make juries unrepresentative of the population generally. According to this view of the matter, trial by a representative jury is as much the right of the ordinary citizen as is the right to vote, and no less needed for his protection. A jury system in which all economic classes are adequately represented is no less essential for a fair and impartial administration of the law, than a widely extended suffrage is to ensure the choice of a representative lawmaking body.

Our present-day conservative political writers, however, do not accept this view of the jury system. They do not, it is true, expressly repudiate the idea that trial by jury is a right, especially in criminal cases, but they do attack it indirectly by defending restrictions on the eligibility of citizens for jury service and also by defending the complete subordination of the jury to the court.

The opposition to an effective jury system is not wholly conservative, however. It comes in part from those who believe in the right of the majority to control the state. The movement so much in evidence during recent decades to establish governmental absolutism is obviously incompatible with an effective jury system. All those who wish to break down the checks on governmental power become dissatisfied with trial by jury when it really functions as a means of protecting the individual citizen against the government. Radicals, no less than conservatives, are desirous of having their own way and are impatient of all restraints which interfere with the carrying out of their plans. Trial by a representative jury, under the unanimity rule, is a check on the government, whether that government be controlled by a minority or by a majority of the citizens. It is no less a check on the will of the majority in the one case than it is on the will of the ruling minority in the other. Tyranny of the majority no less than tyranny of the minority is likely to find expression in laws, or methods of administering them, which will deprive recalcitrant and supposedly dangerous classes of the right to trial by a jury on which they are represented.

Denial of effective jury trial may be accomplished by means of legislation which prescribes qualifications for jury service in such manner as to make the members of objectionable classes ineligible. It may also be accomplished without the virtual exclusion of this element from juries, by abolishing the rule requiring unanimity and allowing a verdict to be returned by some specified majority of the jury, such as three-fourths. This has been adopted in a few states for criminal cases not involving capital punishment. Whatever the considerations may be that have led to this innovation in the administration of criminal justice, it is apparent that its effect is to deprive any minority to which public opinion is hostile of that protection against governmental oppression which trial by jury ought to guarantee. It is, of course, this less fortunate element of the population, which regards itself as the victim of both economic injustice and political discrimination, that is most likely to hold political and economic opinions at variance with those accepted by the majority. The excluded class becomes almost inevitably receptive to the most radical propaganda; and the majority are more likely to use their political power to silence this refractory minority than to remove the cause of grievance. The so-called criminal syndicalism laws, which have been enacted in so many of our states in recent years, exemplify a form of governmental repression which it would be extremely difficult to invoke successfully, if all elements of our citizenry enjoyed the protection of a truly representative jury system.

Even where, as in most of our states, the unanimity rule still exists for criminal cases, and where no class is discriminated against in so far as the form of the law is concerned, the actual method of selecting juries is generally such as to permit the exclusion of minority representation in the kind of cases where such representation is most needed to ensure justice. If the purpose of the jury system is to give the people as distinguished from the government a means of restraining those clothed with official authority, it is not difficult to see that the government will seek to make this check ineffective by controlling the selection of jurymen. This has been done quite generally in the United States, as we have seen, by providing that only direct taxpayers may serve on juries — a requirement which tends, of course, to make juries representative of the viewpoint and interests of the property holding class. But the chief means of controlling the composition of juries is to vest large discretionary power in the judges, clerks, jury commissioners or other officials who have a part in their selection. In practically every state this method is employed in greater or less degree.

The general public assume that jurymen are drawn by lot and that everyone has an equal chance to be chosen. This may be true, in so far as those whose names happen to be on the jury list from which the selection is made are concerned. Choice by lot from an officially prepared list of citizens eligible for jury service is an altogether different thing, however, from choice by lot from the entire body of voters. Yet according to the method followed in all the states, the choice of jurymen by lot is made from such an officially approved list. The laws relating to this matter are so drawn as to give to the officials entrusted with the preparation of the lists a large measure of discretionary power. The persons whose names are included in the jury list are required, in addition to being citizens, qualified voters, and perhaps also taxpayers, to possess certain other qualifications of a mental or moral sort, which can be described only in a very indefinite and general way, and which, therefore, make it possible for the officials applying them to be governed very largely by personal views or prejudices. These qualifications are designated by such phrases as " suitable," " sound judgment," " well informed," " good character," " approved integrity," " sober and judicious," " good reputation," and " good moral character." It is thus made the duty of jury commissioners, or other officials to whom the preparation of these lists is entrusted, to exclude all who in their opinion do not possess the vague and ambiguous mental and moral qualifications required.

These officials may be depended upon to share the political, social, and economic prejudices of the dominant class in the community. We should, therefore, naturally expect jury lists to include only such as are known to have the viewpoint, and be amenable to the influence, of the interests politically dominant. Any unpopular element would almost certainly not be included. In a community where the ruling opinion is conservative, radicals will probably have no opportunity to serve on juries, as in one where the official class is under capitalistic control, the class conscious labor element will receive scant recognition in making up the jury list. Such terms as " suitable," " of sound judgment," or " of good moral character " are all that is needed to ensure the elimination of such elements in the population as may seem to be undesirable or doubtful to those who control the selection. The large discretionary power vested in the officials who interpret these terms in making up the jury lists explains the practical exclusion of the Negro from jury service in the southern states, the discrimination against the laboring class in many communities, and the total elimination of the more radical elements quite generally throughout the United States.

Juries, thus constituted, do not and can not function as a means of protecting the individual against the government. They are, in fact, much more likely merely to give the appearance of popular control to a method of deciding cases which really leaves this power in the hands of the government itself. Jury trial as we now have it tends to satisfy those who may believe in the need for a check of this sort, without in any way jeopardizing governmental control of the administration of justice.

Trial by a representative jury is especially needed for the protection of the public where judges are placed beyond the reach of direct popular control. When we consider the manner in which our federal judges are appointed and the ultra-conservative influences likely to play a determining part in their selection, the desirability of a jury system which would really serve as a check on them becomes obvious.

In the federal courts of the United States, however, the

jury system is even less of a check on the power of the judges than it is in the state courts. Under the federal law, the clerk of the court and a jury commissioner are required to make up a list of not fewer than three hundred persons eligible for jury service, from which the federal juries are drawn. Jurors in the federal courts are not subject to uniform requirements throughout the United States, but must conform to the qualifications imposed by law in the various states. Since the officials who prepare the jury list are appointed and may be removed by the court, the matter of determining the character of federal juries is virtually placed in the hands of the judges themselves. Federal judges are thus subject to less restraint at the hands of juries than are state judges, since they control in much larger degree the officials through whom jurymen are chosen.

It would be difficult to find any satisfactory justification for this situation. Conservatives attempt to defend the powers exercised by our federal judiciary, by appealing to the check and balance political theory, which has as its basic assumption the limitation of all political authority. To be consistent, however, they would have to admit the need of applying this principle to judges as well as to other public officials.

In conservative thought, the federal courts are designed to serve as a means of protecting the rights of individuals and minorities, not only against the majority but even against the government itself. This conception of the judicial branch was really inherited from England. But neither in England nor in the United States, originally, did it imply any special confidence in, or respect for, judges as such; it was the jury system rather than the judges which secured for the judicial branch the confidence of the people. The importance assigned in English political thought to the judiciary was not so much an indication of faith in judges as it was of a belief in the desirability of a system of administering justice which supplied an effective popular check on the courts. In England at the time of the American Revolution, the judicial branch was supposed to be checked through the right of trial by jury, and judges were subject to removal by a mere majority of the members in the two houses of Parliament. When the Constitution of the United States was adopted, however, federal judges were made practically irremovable by requiring a two-thirds majority in the Senate for conviction in impeachment proceedings, and although jury trial was guaranteed in criminal cases, its effectiveness was in large measure counteracted by the method employed in selecting jurors. The check on the federal courts, of trial by jury in criminal cases, was included in the Constitution as originally adopted; and the Sixth Amendment sought to make this right more secure against the government by providing that the accused " shall enjoy the right to a speedy and public trial by an impartial jury." The method of selecting juries followed in the federal courts tends, however, to defeat the very purpose of the Sixth Amendment. There is small assurance of " trial by an impartial jury " in these courts, where the preparation of the lists from which the jurors are drawn is so largely under the control of the judges themselves. To allow judges to have virtual control of the selection of the juries by which their authority is supposed to be limited, can not be regarded as calculated to guarantee trial by an impartial jury.

This method of selecting juries affords no guaranty whatever that the lists from which the jurors are drawn will be representative even of the majority. The persons composing these lists, though supposed to represent a community made up chiefly of wage earners, may in fact be capitalistic in viewpoint. This situation places labor at a very distinct dis-

advantage where laborers are charged with crimes in connection with the struggle between employers and employees.
Workers are likely to find themselves exposed to the danger
of trial by juries which are fairly representative of the very
class and interests which wish to use governmental force to
crush the resistance of organized labor.

Where, as in the case of our federal judiciary, the manner
of appointment and the tenure of office are such as to make
it reasonably certain that the judges will as a rule be conservative, it is obviously necessary that the people should
enjoy the protection of trial by juries that are fairly representative not of some particular group or class, but of the
citizens generally. Such juries, under the unanimity rule,
would afford protection not only for the majority, but also
for all important minorities. The kind of protection which
the jury system under the unanimity rule was designed to
provide is, of course, incompatible with a method of jury
selection which makes this body representative either of the
majority or of a minority alone. The jury is supposed to be
in a sense a miniature of the community as a whole. The
various interests which make up the body of citizens should
be represented on it proportionately, in so far as this
can be done in a body of twelve men. Thus constituted, it
would be a very effective safeguard against arbitrary interference with the administration of justice either by a selfish
minority, or by an overbearing majority.

It is, of course, in criminal cases that trial by jury is most
needed. But if the citizen needs to be protected against the
possible prejudice, bias, and intolerance of judges in the
trial of criminal cases, he also needs this protection, though
in lesser degree, in civil cases. Liberal American opinion
after the Revolution regarded the right of trial by jury as a
necessary precaution against governmental injustice, both

in criminal and civil cases. The Constitution of the United States, as adopted, however, contained no provision for trial by jury in civil cases in the federal courts. Moreover, the Constitution expressly gave to the Supreme Court of the United States a veto on the verdict of the jury in all jury cases over which it was given appellate jurisdiction, by providing that it should have this jurisdiction " both as to law and to fact." The Seventh Amendment, it is true, established the right of trial by jury in suits at common law; but it must not be supposed that the right to trial by jury applies, or ever has applied, to all civil cases. The federal Constitution guarantees it only for suits at common law. Admiralty and equity cases do not come within the scope of this constitutional guaranty. The wisdom of thus restricting the right of trial by jury in civil cases is by no means apparent. The particular kind of bias on the part of judges which makes jury trial a necessary safeguard in criminal cases may also influence the decisions of courts in equity and admiralty cases. The personal and property rights of the people may be greatly impaired by an official interpretation of the law which is out of touch with the general interests.

Any logical application of the check and balance theory of the state would attempt to safeguard society against this particular abuse of official authority. Such protection could be assured, however, only through the establishment of a popular check on judicial interpretation of the law — an extension of popular power to which conservative opinion is unalterably opposed. The people have yet to learn that they can not ensure the expression of their will by controlling merely those who make the laws; that it is even more important for them to control those who interpret the laws, if their will is to be a directing influence in the conduct of the state. If it is not consistent with the safety of the public to invest judges with the final power to decide questions of fact, it is difficult to see why it is not also dangerous to entrust independent and politically irresponsible judges with the power to place their own unchecked and uncontrolled interpretation on all law. Indeed, it would seem to one not versed in the intricacies of legal lore, that there is actually greater need for a popular check on judicial interpretation of the law than there is for protection against judicial error in deciding mere questions of fact.

To comprehend the reason for these limitations on the power of juries, one must bear in mind that trial by jury is a concession or compromise, wrung from the ruling classes in the struggle for constitutional government. As in the case of all other important steps in the movement to limit irresponsible power, the interests opposed to it sought to restrict its application and thwart its purpose wherever possible.

Of the influences which have helped to determine the present status of the jury system, the most important has been the viewpoint and attitude of the legal profession. It is perhaps inevitable that lawyers should as a rule look upon the administration of justice as a public function which should be entrusted only to those who have been specially trained for that purpose. They are naturally inclined to think that if laymen are to have any part in it — as under the jury system they would have — this part should be supervised and effectively controlled by judges, who will thus be able to make the administration of justice conform to the traditions and ideals of the legal profession. The exaltation of judges is regarded by lawyers as but a proper recognition of the surpassing importance of the profession to which they belong. Professional pride tends to make them supporters of judicial authority, and, though they may not openly oppose the jury system, they are usually unsympathetic with any plan to restrict the power of judges by making juries more representative or by giving them a more important part in the decision of cases.

That the legal profession has not been wholly sympathetic with trial by jury, even in criminal cases, is indicated by the rapidly increasing use of injunctions in labor disputes during the last two or three decades. The inherent conservatism of the legal profession, with its respect for precedent and its fear of democracy, tends to make it, and especially such of its members as are elevated to high judicial office, more concerned about the protection of property than the safeguarding of personal rights. It is this capitalistic bias of judges that has been responsible for the growth of government by injunction. If these officials had been in sympathy with labor and desirous of increasing instead of curbing the latter's economic power, we should have heard nothing of the injunction in labor disputes.

The reason why courts, with a capitalistic viewpoint, have felt it necessary to devise this method of dealing with certain so-called crimes of labor is obvious. The constitutional guaranty of jury trial in all criminal cases was regarded as an obstacle to the preservation of order and to the protection of capital in time of industrial troubles. Many acts which capitalists might regard as crimes and wish to have punished as such could not be satisfactorily dealt with under the regular criminal procedure. Either the acts themselves were not prohibited and punished by the criminal law, or, if they were thus prohibited, a jury trial, it was thought, did not ensure capital the protection to which it was entitled. Juries, though selected in the manner above described, could not always be depended upon to find the accused guilty in cases growing out of conflicts between labor and capital. Moreover, capitalists desired a more expeditious method of handling these labor cases, one which could be invoked even before the acts complained of had been committed, and which did not involve the inconvenience and uncertainty of trial by jury. What has been called in this country " government by injunction " is but the outgrowth of the efforts of judges to devise more effective means of limiting the power of organized labor to bring pressure to bear on employers in time of strikes. It is a conspicuous example of judge-made law and of the need for effective checks on judicial authority. The main significance of this new use of the injunction is that it nullifies the constitutional right of trial by jury in a type of criminal case where that right is urgently needed to prevent injustice.

The prevalent attitude of the legal profession and of the official class generally toward jury trial is clearly indicated in the control which courts are allowed to exercise over the verdicts of juries. The most striking feature of the jury's verdict is its lack of finality. The only exception to the rule that it is subject to judicial review and may be modified or set aside is where the jury in a criminal case finds the defendant not guilty. One reason why judges have not attempted to set aside verdicts of this sort is to be found in the fact that public interest in the struggle for constitutional government has been focused very largely on the establishment of trial by jury in criminal cases, as a safeguard against official tyranny. American written constitutions, however, have not left this matter to the caprice of judges or lawmaking bodies. The Fifth Amendment to the Constitution of the United States provides that no person shall " be subject for the same offense to be twice put in jeopardy of life or limb," and a similar provision is to be found almost without exception in state constitutions. Thus it would be futile for American judges, either federal or state, to attempt to set aside a verdict of acquittal, since under our constitutional system the defendant may not twice be brought to trial for the same offense.

Over every other finding of a jury, however, courts have practically unlimited control. They may set aside a verdict which declares a defendant guilty, or they may direct a verdict of acquittal. Moreover, even if the jury in criminal cases is allowed to determine the question of guilt, the degree of guilt is in fact very largely determined by the court, inasmuch as it may be permitted by the law to impose a penalty varying from the minimum of a nominal fine to the maximum of a long period of imprisonment. The tendency to confer on judges large discretionary power of this sort indicates quite clearly that our legislative bodies do not wish to make trial by jury an effective popular check on the courts, even in criminal cases.

It may seem strange that the public should attach so much importance to jury trial as we now have it. That there is no popular dissatisfaction with the method of selecting juries, or with the control which courts exercise over their verdicts, is probably to be accounted for by the failure of the people generally to understand the system in its practical operation. They do not possess sufficient power of discrimination to distinguish between a jury system which is really a check on the power of the courts and one which is such in name only.

The desirability of popular participation in the administration of justice through the jury system as it now exists may be questioned. One could consistently hold that trial by jury is a highly desirable check on the power of courts, and yet believe that it would be better to have no pretense of a popular check than to have the appearance of it without the reality. The present situation merely enables judges to shift responsibility without surrendering any real power.

Chapter XIII

PATRIOTISM AND GOVERNMENTAL POWER

The sentiment which we call patriotism has always been regarded by those in authority as the highest of all civic virtues. In every age and under every form of government, it has been sedulously inculcated as a means of lessening the friction between the governing and the governed and thereby of augmenting the power of the state.

There is, however, no unanimity of opinion as to what constitutes patriotism in any particular instance. When we attempt to translate it from a mere sentiment into civic conduct, we often find the widest possible disagreement. This conflict of opinion is due very largely to the influence which two diametrically opposed theories of the state have had upon present-day political thought.

Wherever the divine theory of the state was generally accepted by the people, those exercising temporal power were shielded against the annoyance and danger of popular criticism. According to this theory, all our institutions have received the stamp of divine approval. God established human society and supplied it with the governmental and other institutions suited to its needs. Moreover, He governed it through agents who were responsible to Him alone. And inasmuch as all our institutions emanated from God and were the expression of His will, they were entitled to the veneration of the people. To criticize them or those in authority was no mere temporal offense; it was blasphemy or defamation of the ruler of the universe.

The social contract theory of the state sought to modify this attitude toward institutions, by representing them as purely human devices which were entitled to popular support only in so far as they might serve a useful purpose. According to this newer view, there is a distinction to be made between things secular and things divine. The state and social institutions in general are of this world, partake of its imperfections, and may with entire propriety be modified from time to time as the need for change is recognized. The immunity from criticism claimed by rulers under the divine theory of the state may not, according to the social contract, justly be invoked to prevent advocacy of institutional reform or condemnation of official delinquency.

The persistence of the view that the state is divinely ordained has tended, however, to render abortive the attempt to develop a critical attitude toward political institutions. This older view is supposed to have been discarded long ago, and no doubt the great majority of the people in all enlightened countries would disclaim belief in it. But even though they may consciously reject a theory of this sort, which through long acceptance has gradually moulded their viewpoint toward institutional arrangements, they are likely to remain for an indefinite period subconsciously more or less under its influence.

It is not difficult to explain why the formal acceptance of the social contract doctrine, which supplied a totally new theoretical foundation for the state, has been productive of no greater practical results. The thoroughgoing acceptance of this view, with all that it logically implies, would have involved the complete subversion of the old political order. But such a complete transformation in viewpoint is of necessity a very slow process. No new idea that is revolutionary in its implications — as was the social contract conception of the state — can be assimilated by the people generally, except as the result of a long period of political and social readjustment. Mental inertia is a safeguard against any sudden change of this sort. The people generally may profess to accept the newer democratic viewpoint and still largely retain the old attitude toward the state with which it is wholly incompatible. Contradictions and inconsistencies of this sort are, and always have been, characteristic of the popular mind.

The persistence of the old theocratic viewpoint is not surprising when we consider that our modern conception of democracy has been superimposed upon the orthodox Christian idea of the universe as an absolute monarchy with God as ruler. To this highest authority, all who hold power in this world are conceived to be ultimately responsible. We may think of democracy as the most acceptable form of government for human society, but this belief must be interpreted in the light of the important fact that the place which we assign to it is a strictly subordinate one in a universe conceived to be monarchically organized. As a result of the effort to fit a scheme of this-world political democracy into the religious notion of a monarchically governed universe, we naturally carry over into the former much of the general viewpoint with which we approach questions recognized as purely religious. The tendency, therefore, is to view the institutions and problems of this world in much the same way that we regard those of the City of God. Imputing omniscience and infallibility to the supreme ruler, it is difficult to avoid a somewhat similar attitude toward those invested with temporal power.[1]

Thus under a democratic form of government the people

---

[1] Political ideas and religious beliefs are even now not clearly differentiated. So-called political opinion is not infrequently as much a matter of mere faith as are our religious beliefs.

often show the same inclination to deify institutions and exalt authority which was characteristic of those who believed that the state was divinely established. Even in the United States, which has throughout its history as a nation formally proclaimed its acceptance of the social contract theory of the state, survival of the older viewpoint is reflected in the exaltation of, and reverence for, judicial authority. The influence of this older conception of the state may also be seen in the tendency so often exhibited to regard the Constitution of the United States as sufficiently inspired to place it above the reach of profane criticism. Moreover, the general attitude which many people assume toward the government indicates a reverence strongly suggestive of divine right. They seem to think that the majority in a democracy have merely taken the place in the state formerly held by the king, succeeding to his rights and inheriting his powers. They have rejected monarchy without entirely rejecting the divine right doctrine which was its chief theoretical support. The divine right of the king has merely become the divine right of the majority to exercise supreme authority.

This viewpoint explains the tendency even in a professedly democratic society to regard criticism of public officials, or the majority they are supposed to represent, as something to be frowned upon and at times vigorously repressed. Even under normal conditions, society may insist upon an attitude toward those in authority which has the effect of shielding public officials against much-needed criticism. In times of social stress, when emotions are deeply aroused, the professed devotees of democracy readily shed their more modern political attire, and think and act as men did before there was any pretense of political democracy. A critical attitude toward the government in time of war is likely to be regarded by the politically orthodox as closely akin to treason. At such times even the more radical social groups are likely to come under the influence of the old uncritical attitude toward the state.

The newer and broader conceptions of civic duty which democracy is supposed to represent are promptly lost sight of in the pervading sense of national peril. To the protection of society as a whole every other consideration is subordinated. And inasmuch as coöperation for purposes of protection is more difficult where conflicting views are held in the matter of policies, governments are always disposed to yield to the temptation of making the supposed danger to society a pretext for silencing dissenters. What we call the rights of individuals naturally receive scant consideration at such times. Moreover, the point of view so easily and promptly assumed when the safety of society is supposed to be imperiled, is in ordinary times in the background of the popular mind and has an important subconscious influence upon the prevalent conception of patriotism.

The old theory that the state is divinely established would make patriotism mean, in its practical operation, loyalty to things as they are — an unquestioning submission to established authority. From the point of view of true democracy, however, citizens owe neither blind reverence to institutions nor implicit obedience to those invested with political power. An attitude such as this would be wholly incompatible with the fundamental purpose of democracy — popular control.

To make a fetish of laws or institutions may tend to preserve them for the time being, but it is almost certain to bring them into disrepute in the end, by arresting that normal growth and readjustment without which their social utility can not be kept unimpaired. Any conception of patriotism suited to the needs of a democratic society must avoid the error of making institutional arrangements ends in themselves. While seeking to preserve all that is good and serviceable in them, it should recognize the fact that they often fall far short of the ideal, and that the highest type of citizen is not one who conceives his duty to be to protect his country against change, but who is willing to make such personal sacrifices as may be required in order that its institutions may be brought to the highest possible degree of excellence.

It is obvious that this view of patriotism would not be regarded with favor in official circles. In present-day democratic governments, no less than was the case in the absolute monarchies of the past, those entrusted with political power are disposed to make patriotism synonymous with loyalty to the government as it now is. Moreover, they hold that in so far as patriotism connotes allegiance to a constitution, it is not as mere citizens may understand that instrument, but as it may be interpreted and applied by those who exercise authority under it. To inculcate this official view of patriotism strikes, of course, at the foundation of democratic control. Loyalty to the government as such, regardless of how it may misinterpret the fundamental law by which its authority is supposed to be limited, tends to prepare the way for governmental absolutism, by breaking down all those extra-governmental and popular checks on public officials, such as the right of criticism implied in freedom of speech, press, and assembly. This popular right can for all practical purposes be revoked wherever governmental and other special interests succeed in having their distorted notion of patriotism accepted by the people generally. That they have in large measure succeeded is indicated clearly enough by the ruthless disregard of individual rights which has been so much in evidence in recent years.

Where, as in the United States, public officials are supposed to be controlled by a fundamental law in the form of a constitution, it is obvious that such loyalty as the citizen owes to the government is subordinate to that which he owes to the supreme law of the state. If this were not the case, a constitution could not function as a popular check on governmental power, but would be a mere self-imposed limitation on official authority. The constitution as an agency through which the people are supposed to control the government must, if it is to accomplish its purpose, be generally recognized as having a higher claim on the loyalty of the citizen than those who exercise authority under it. The government is not entitled to the loyalty of the citizen except in so far as it acts in accordance with the constitution from which it derives its powers.

It is for the intelligence and conscience of the people generally, not for the government itself, to determine whether or not those in authority are entitled to popular support. In order that a constitution may actually serve to protect the people against the abuse of governmental power, its interpretation and enforcement must be under their control, either directly or through some branch of the government immediately responsible to them. If patriotism, as a popular regard for the basic features of a political system, is to have any significance as an assurance that the government will be controlled by the fundamental law, it must be something more than a blind homage to the constitution as that document may happen to be interpreted by public officials. It is necessary that there should be a more or less clearly defined popular interpretation of the constitutional system, which office holders could not afford to disregard, before loyalty to the constitution can really operate as a check on governmental power.

In the beginning of our history as a nation, the distinction between loyalty to the government and loyalty to the basic principles of our political organization was made both in our constitutional law and in popular thought. The recognition in the Declaration of Independence and in the early state constitutions of the popular right of revolution is evidence of this distinction. At that time the fundamental principles constituting the foundation of our political life were regarded as having the first claim on the loyalty of the citizen. Governments were to be respected and obeyed only in so far as they conformed to the limitations thus imposed on their authority. Indeed, the American Revolution was defended on the theory that citizens have the right, and are in duty bound, to protect their political institutions even against the government itself. The conception of patriotism with which we began our career as a nation was thus quite clearly designed to serve as a check on governmental power.

It is to be observed that eighteenth century political philosophy made the people themselves, and not the courts or even the government as a whole, the guardians and ultimate protectors of the Constitution, written and unwritten. This was necessarily implied in the social contract, the right of revolution, and the prevalent distrust of governmental power.

Democratic interpretation of the fundamental law, enforced through the right of revolution, was wholly incompatible with the purpose of the conservative class to make governmental power supreme. The main popular check on governmental power being the then widely accepted belief that the right of revolution was a necessary safeguard against tyranny, it was essential for the success of the conservative plan that this so-called right should be thoroughly discredited. To that end the idea was inculcated that popular sovereignty had been realized under our political system, and that revolution as a popular right had no legitimate place in the philosophy of a state organized on this principle.[2] The effect of discrediting the right of revolution was to make governmental interpretation of the constitutional system authoritative and final.

In order to lay a secure foundation for governmental supremacy, it was necessary to bring about a generally accepted philosophy which would identify patriotism with the belief that the Constitution was an expression of the popular will, that it constituted a fundamental law which the government could not disregard, and that in practical operation the American political system was a successful application of the doctrine of popular sovereignty. It would logically follow from the acceptance of this viewpoint that an ultimate popular check on governmental power, such as the right of revolution, was no longer needed to protect the people against the abuse of political authority.

At the beginning of our history, it was the state rather than the general government which was the object of patriotic solicitude. The citizen looked to the colonial charter and later to the state constitution for the protection and preservation of his rights. His allegiance was primarily to the local government of the commonwealth. This situation remained even after the adoption of the Constitution of the United States. In the mind of a large proportion of the people it was the state government that had first claim on the loyalty of the citizen. This local patriotism or states' rights sentiment was an almost insurmountable obstacle to the extension of central authority before the Civil War. To carry through successfully the nationalistic scheme of centralizing political power, it was necessary to develop a national patriotism that would effectually subordinate the

2 See ch. VIII.

sentiment of attachment to local institutions. Having accomplished this transfer of loyalty from the local to the general government, the growth of the powers of the latter at the expense of the states was assured. Patriotism, which in the early decades of our life as a nation was a check on governmental authority, both state and federal, has thus become in the course of our political development the mainstay of centralized governmental power.

CHAPTER XIV

INDIVIDUAL LIBERTY AND
GOVERNMENTAL AUTHORITY

American writers on political science, especially those with a conservative bias, take it for granted that the chief merit of our particular form of government is that it guarantees individual liberty through an effective limitation of political power. The rights of individuals, being expressly enumerated in our federal and state constitutions, are supposed to be thus placed " entirely beyond the power of the government to curtail." [1] This viewpoint, which is quite generally presented in American textbooks on political science, is merely an expression of the prevalent anthropomorphic conception of the Constitution of the United States as the guardian and protector of the rights of the people.

That the notion of the Constitution as self-enforcing was not accepted by the people in the early decades of American history, the emphasis on the right of revolution abundantly proves. Gradually, however, under the influence of skillful conservative propaganda, the fiction gained acceptance that the government was powerless to disregard rights enumerated in the fundamental law. The Constitution, having come to be regarded as an expression of the popular will, was relied upon to prevent the government from interfering with the liberty of the individual.

The growth of the new conception of sovereignty as unlimited political power, as well as the deification of the Con-

[1] Ogg and Ray, *Introduction to American Government*, p. 76 (1922).

stitution as the palladium of democracy, tended to modify the popular conception of constitutional law in its relation to individual liberty. The original idea of the Constitution, as a check on the power of the people no less than on that of the government itself, was difficult to reconcile with the new doctrine of popular sovereignty, which ascribed to the people untrammeled authority. The rights of individuals, as they were understood at the time of the American Revolution and in the period immediately following, constituted a recognized check on all political power, even that of the people themselves. This original conception of individual liberty has, however, been supplanted by the professedly more democratic one implied in the artificial distinction between state and government. The chief significance of the attempt on the part of recent American writers to make this distinction is to be found in the need for some means of harmonizing a check and balance constitution with the notion of popular sovereignty. According to the supporters of this distinction, the people politically organized constitute the state, make and amend the Constitution, through it control the government, and are the final repository of unlimited political power. Governmental authority is represented as being subject to the restraints imposed by a check and balance plan of organization, while the state, somewhat vaguely conceived as the people, is supposed to be subject to no limitation whatsoever.[2] Although individual liberty is represented as effectually safeguarded against governmental encroachment, the individual, we are told, " has no rights which the state is bound to recognize." [3]

To create belief in a human power that can legally override all restraints imposed for the protection of individuals

---

[2] For an extended discussion of this pseudo-distinction between state and government, see ch. VII.

[3] Ogg and Ray, *Introduction to American Government,* p. 75.

is to supplant the basic idea in the theory of individual liberty by one which serves as a foundation for governmental absolutism.

It is interesting to note that the conception of the ultimate unlimited power of the people had a distinctly conservative origin; that its object was not to establish popular supremacy, but to ensure the subordination of the popular will to governmental authority. Superficially viewed, this interpretation of our political system seems to concede to the people, acting as the state, a degree of political power which would satisfy even the advocates of the most extreme form of democracy. But only in appearance is it a concession to the demand for an extension of the power of the people. Under the pretense of subordinating governmental authority, it in fact makes that authority supreme. By reason of the fact that the government controls the interpretation and enforcement of the fundamental law, it has the power in no small degree to remove, evade, or ignore the restraints by which its authority is supposed to be limited. The people having no part in the interpretation of constitutional law, except through the public officials who exercise this power, are as a matter of course bound by the Constitution as thus interpreted. Instead of controlling the Constitution, they are controlled by it as interpreted and enforced by governmental agencies.

No one can understand clearly the status of individual liberty in this country without bearing in mind the place occupied by the judiciary under our constitutional system. The effectiveness of our constitutional guaranties of individual liberty was greatly impaired when the government, and especially the branch of it farthest removed from popular influence, the Supreme Court, acquired the recognized right to interpret them.

The attempt to promulgate the idea that back of the government and the Constitution are the people organized as an omnipotent state, subject to no legal or constitutional restraints, tends to destroy the philosophic foundation on which the conception of individual liberty rests. Although the rights of individuals are supposedly protected against the government, they are represented as at all times subject to abridgment or abolition by this so-called state. And when we realize that this supposed political entity, in so far as it has any real existence, is only another name for purely governmental agencies, we can see that the natural effect of this fiction is to clothe the government itself with that unlimited power imputed to the mythical state.

That liberty for the individual is desirable would be readily conceded by the great majority of the people in all enlightened countries. Their practice, however, seems to be but slightly influenced by what they profess to believe. They may accept individual liberty as a purely abstract principle, and yet, in applying it, they may defeat its purpose, by giving it a narrow and illiberal interpretation. Everyone believes in individual liberty for those whose economic interests and whose opinions on social, political, and religious questions are identical with his own. What is meant by individual liberty, however, is not the right to conform, which no one questions, but the right to act as one's own judgment dictates where his opinion is opposed to that generally held. There is no need for the advocacy of freedom for individual conduct that conforms to generally accepted standards. Liberty for the individual means nothing if it does not imply the right to pursue a course of conduct and to hold and advocate views which do not have the approval of the majority and which may even be strongly condemned by that majority.

Individual liberty is inseparably connected with the theory of progress. Individuals must be free to advance new ideas and try new methods if a higher type of civilization is to be attained. The only possible guaranty of progress is the freedom of individuals and groups to criticize any belief or doctrine — religious, social, political, or economic — and to advocate any change in institutional arrangements which to them may seem desirable. Our beliefs at any given time are at best only partially true. We approach the truth only by a slow, laborious process in which competition between opposing views gradually eliminates error.

That which is established needs no special protection against that which is merely proposed. The old and generally accepted is always difficult to discredit and supplant with the new. The very fact that it has the stamp of social approval gives it a prestige which the advocates of change can not easily overcome. In actual practice the burden of proof is always, and of course ought to be, on those who attack the old. The almost universal tendency to be skeptical concerning the merit of any new idea or proposed innovation is a sufficient guaranty that there is not likely to be any undue haste in discarding the old for the untried.

The chief danger is not that false ideas and doctrines will supplant established truth, but that established error will seek to protect itself against the truth by suppressing all dissenters. That this is not a purely imaginary danger is easily understood when we reflect that, while the general mental inertia of the people disinclines them to accept new ideas, there are almost always important vested interests whose material prosperity largely depends upon the retention of the old. Every important idea or belief that has been long accepted has the support of influential classes whose interest in protecting it against attack has a more selfish basis than a purely disinterested desire for the truth.

Liberty for the individual is necessary if we are to realize the Christian ideal of personal responsibility or the democratic ideal of self-government. Men can not be morally accountable for their conduct or politically self-governing unless they possess the degree of freedom from external control which individual liberty connotes. The theory of individual liberty recognizes that there is a field of human conduct within which the coercive power of the state or of the organized church should not be allowed to intrude except for the purpose of guaranteeing this freedom by punishing those who abuse it.

It would be wholly incorrect to say that majority rule necessarily implies individual liberty. Both are the outgrowth of the struggle against irresponsible power. But the conception of individual rights as a check on governmental authority is not closely related to the growth of modern democracy, except in so far as the former was one of the influences which paved the way for the latter by limiting the power of king and aristocracy. Since the majority have come to regard themselves as the final source of political power, their attitude toward the theory of individual liberty has profoundly changed. It was to the advantage of the majority in the eighteenth century to defend the rights of individuals against the state. Having accepted the idea of popular sovereignty, however, they now regard individual liberty as a check on their own power.

We may concede that democracy is more desirable than any other form of government, and yet realize that individual liberty is not necessarily secure where the majority are in control. The rights of individuals are supposed, it is true, to be most respected in a society organized as a political democracy. As a matter of fact, however, the majority may be fully as intolerant of dissenting opinion as kings and aristocracies have always been.

Indeed, there is some justification for the conservative view that in a democracy personal liberty is more likely to be abridged than under a government in which the people have less influence. The reason for this is obvious. A government which is supposed to represent the majority, and has its support, is more confident of ability to override all opposition than one which does not recognize the right of the majority to rule and which must avoid the danger of arousing too much popular opposition. Since democracy is less exposed to the danger of effective popular resistance, it may with impunity invade the sphere of individual liberty. A strong government — one that has no fear of effective opposition on the part of the people — is almost certain to disregard the rights of individuals whenever the recognition of such rights would seriously hamper it in carrying out its policies. But where the state rests upon a basis generally recognized as undemocratic, those who exercise authority are constantly reminded of the need for a cautious moderate policy — one which will in so far as possible conciliate all important elements in the population and thus safeguard the country against the danger of revolution. Respect on the part of the government for the rights of individuals is due in much larger measure to this balance of opposing interests within the state than it is to formal constitutional guaranties. De Tocqueville in his *Democracy in America,* published in 1835, recognizes this fact when he refers to the tyranny of the majority in the United States.

" I know no country," he tells us, " in which there is so little true independence of mind and freedom of discussion as in America. In any constitutional state in Europe every sort of religious and political theory may be advocated and propagated abroad; for there is no country in Europe so subdued by any single authority, as not to contain citizens who are ready to protect the man who raises his voice in the cause of truth, from the consequences of his hardihood. If he is unfortunate enough to live under an absolute government, the people is upon his side; if he inhabits a free country, he may find a shelter behind the authority of the throne, if he require one. The aristocratic part of society supports him in some countries, and the democracy in others. But in a nation where democratic institutions exist, organized like those of the United States, there is but one sole authority, one single element of strength and of success, with nothing beyond it." [4]

The old conflict between liberty and authority does not end with the emergence of democracy; it merely enters a new phase in which we must look to public opinion for the protection of individual rights. Political democracy is in no sense a substitute for individual liberty, which means the right of individual self-determination. Without individual liberty, political democracy is not likely to contribute much to the world's progress. If popular government is to free the world, it must exercise such self-restraint as may be required to keep it from encroaching on the rights of individuals. This, however, can not be ensured by formally proclaiming these rights in a written constitution. Such self-imposed checks are wholly ineffective, unless they are supported by a public opinion so clearly defined and so active that no government could afford to antagonize it.

Individual liberty in the United States to-day not only lacks the support of an active, intelligent public opinion, but often encounters a degree of popular hostility which renders

[4] Vol. I, p. 285. Tr. by Henry Reeve.

constitutional guaranties wholly ineffective. The rights most likely to be abridged or denied by the government, or by the irresponsible and misguided groups who are constantly interfering with the constitutional rights of others by resort to mob violence, are those most fundamental — the ones our American constitutions have sought to preserve by express guaranties of freedom of speech, press, and assembly.

Although the hostility to free discussion in present-day society is, of course, not entirely due to any one single cause, it may be regarded as mainly economic. Wherever there is a conflict of interests we may expect to see some opposition to the recognition of this fundamental right. Let any class feel that it is enjoying advantages or privileges, of which society, if fully informed, would disapprove, and it will inevitably regard with disfavor any attempt to bring them to the attention of the public. No doubt, so far as the masses are concerned, the hostility to free discussion is largely due to a blind instinctive fear that it will undermine opinions and beliefs which they associate with the well-being of society and not to any consciously selfish interest. This is not true, however, of the opposition to freedom of speech and discussion which comes from the more intelligent classes, who take a leading part in every attack on this right.

The formal acceptance of the democratic idea by the modern world has emphasized the importance of public opinion. To-day it is conceived to be highly desirable, if not necessary, to have the support of public opinion for any economic arrangement which we wish to preserve. Quite naturally, then, every important economic group seeks to control public opinion where its material interests are involved. And since opinion is largely determined by what one is permitted to see, to hear, and to read, it can be controlled only through some form of censorship and propaganda, such as was formerly exercised by church and state — as the history of religious and political persecution clearly shows.

Propaganda, in the sense of an organized effort either to popularize or to discredit some idea, viewpoint, institutional arrangement, or economic system, has a sinister significance when through a monopolistic control of news sources it is accompanied by the suppression of all competing propaganda. The power to establish a monopoly of this sort is one that society could not safely entrust to any agency, public or private. Monopoly in such a field is infinitely more dangerous than monopolistic control of industry. There can be nothing worthy of the name of intellectual freedom without free competition between ideas.

The control of opinion by purely private interests, which modern capitalism has made possible, has come to supply an effective substitute for the old form of avowed class control. From the point of view of the capitalist class, this new form of control has some distinct advantages over the old system. It is indirect and not obvious to those who lack political and social intelligence, and, therefore, not recognized by many as class control. Concealed, as it is, under the outward form of political democracy, it is less exposed to the danger of popular attack than was the old avowed and generally recognized class rule. Moreover, it gives to capitalists the benefits of actual control without requiring them to assume any of the responsibility which should accompany it.

The efficacy of capitalistic control of opinion depends upon the extent to which organized wealth owns or controls the various agencies through which public opinion is formed. Ownership of the press, news associations, theaters, moving pictures, and broadcasting stations, as well as some measure of direct control over public school education, is prerequisite to an effective scheme of propaganda. Complete monopoly of these is perhaps not attainable, though a capitalistic control, sufficiently extensive to afford some of the advantages of monopoly, has actually been brought about.

The influence which the capitalist class may exert directly through ownership is, however, much less of a menace than the indirect pressure it may bring to bear upon those supposedly independent. The economic and financial power of this class may be used quite effectively to control those who are outside of its organization and legally independent. There are many kinds of discrimination possible against those who refuse to recognize its unjust and illegal authority. An independent paper will soon discover that one penalty for independence is the loss of all advertising controlled by this class; and this loss is usually sufficient to mean the difference between success and failure. Had any newspaper in any conservative American community during the last few years frankly defended the constitutional right of free speech, it could hardly have failed to lose its most profitable advertisements. Of course, it might have defended freedom of speech, press, and assembly as a purely abstract principle with suitable qualifications, without incurring the active hostility of business — provided that it condoned the frequent interferences with the exercise of this right by mobs and by equally irresponsible public officials. But this purely formal acceptance of the principle of free speech is not to be confused with the defense of it as a practical policy. No one can be regarded as a real supporter of this fundamental right, who is not ready to condemn the violations of it that are so frequent in present-day society.

INDEX

Absolutism, movement to overthrow, 3

Adams, John, opposition to universal suffrage, 28; belief in government founded on property, 29

Alabama, suffrage requirements, 38n, 126

Alien and Sedition laws, 87, 88

Alliances, 241

Amendments. *See* Constitution of United States, amendments

American colonies, compulsory voting, 54

American Revolution, political result, 12; conception of the state during, 14; political thought, 15, 179; aim, 274

Apportionment of representation. *See* Representation

Aristocratic conception of state, 215

Armies, standing, a menace to individual liberty, 24; control of, 144; opposition to, 214. *See also* Preparedness

Articles of Confederation, state sovereignty under, 90, 91; framing and adoption of, 114; provisions for change in government, 119; disregard of provisions of, 120; defects, 122

Achley, R. L., quoted, 153

Australia, discrimination against cities, 76

Authority, limitation of, 3, 6, 162; after the Revolution, 12–26, 81, 85, 87, 148, 163; concentration of, in the business world, 203. *See also* Governmental authority; Political power

Balance of power, 241

Ballot, secrecy of, safeguarded, 47

Belgium, suffrage system, 49, 54

Berlin, representation restricted, 69

Bills of rights, 23, 25, 28

Bryce, James, 181

Buel, David, Jr., quoted, 32

Burgess, J. W., on distinction between government and state, 113, 154, 157, 160

Business, influence upon politics, 200; concentration of authority in, 203; competitive regulation of, 225; interests opposed to regulative agency, 248

Business men. *See* Capitalistic groups

Calder v. Bull, 103n

Calhoun, John C., constitutional interpretation, 92, 159

Capitalistic groups, political influence, 199, 223; economic influence, 202, 203, 221; influence upon foreign relations, 209; responsible for militarism, 212; governmental support of, 216; advocate cancellation of inter-Allied debts, 220; responsible for recent wars, 221; suppress competition, 226; opposed to regulative agency, 248

Censorship, 285

Census, state, provisions for, 68

Centralization of industry, 199, 228; danger of international control, 246; of political power, 90, 94, 186–201

Check and balance plan, in federal Constitution, 79, 81, 86, 88, 90, 93, 101, 147; in municipal government, 195

Check and balance theory, applied to economics, 202; to international politics, 241; political,

289